Understanding Nonviolence

Understanding Nonviolence:
Contours and Contexts

MAIA CARTER HALLWARD AND
JULIE M. NORMAN

polity

Copyright © Maia Carter Hallward and Julie Norman 2015

The right of Maia Carter Hallward and Julie Norman to be identified as Authors of this Work has been asserted in accordance with the UK Copyright, Designs and Patents Act 1988.

First published in 2015 by Polity Press
Reprinted 2017

Polity Press
65 Bridge Street
Cambridge CB2 1UR, UK

Polity Press
350 Main Street
Malden, MA 02148, USA

ISBN-13: 978-0-7456-8016-3
ISBN-13: 978-0-7456-8017-0 (pb)

A catalogue record for this book is available from the British Library.

Library of Congress Cataloging-in-Publication Data

Understanding nonviolence : contours and contexts / [edited by] Maia Carter Hallward, Julie Norman.
    pages cm
  Includes bibliographical references and index.
    ISBN 978-0-7456-8016-3 (hardback : alk. paper) – ISBN 978-0-7456-8017-0 (pbk. : alk. paper) 1. Nonviolence. 2. Social movements. I. Hallward, Maia Carter, 1976- II. Norman, Julie M.
    HM1281.U53 2014
    303.6'1–dc23
                                    2014017345

Typeset in 9.5/13 Swift light by
Servis Filmsetting Limited, Stockport, Cheshire
Printed and bound in the United States by LSC Communications

For further information on Polity, visit our website:
politybooks.com

Contents

Illustrations

Contributors

Mohammed Abu-Nimer is an Associate Professor of International Peace and Conflict Resolution at the School of International Service, American University. He is the director of the Center for Peacebuilding and Development. Dr Abu-Nimer has worked for over a decade on Arab–Israeli dialogue and peacebuilding efforts, the application of conflict resolution models in Muslim communities, inter-religious conflict resolution training, interfaith dialogue, and evaluation of conflict resolution programs. He has conducted numerous evaluations of peacebuilding projects, including, most recently, an assessment report on Islamic education in Niger and Chad. Dr Abu-Nimer is the co-founder and co-editor of the *Journal of Peacebuilding and Development*. He holds a PhD in conflict analysis and resolution from George Mason University.

Marcella Alvarez is Program Officer at the Centre for Applied Nonviolent Action and Strategies. She is the co-author of *Making Oppression Backfire* and helps to organize workshops with nonviolent resistance activists as well as working on CANVAS's academic program and publications. She lives in Belgrade, Serbia.

Maciej J. Bartkowski, PhD, is an Adjunct Professor at Johns Hopkins University, Krieger School, where he teaches strategic nonviolent resistance. He has taught seminars and spoken about strategic nonviolent conflict, movement mobilization, and civil resistance at various academic institutions and policy forums around the world. He has recently completed an edited volume, *Recovering Nonviolent History: Civil Resistance in Liberation Struggles* (www.recoveringnonviolenthistory.org), published by Lynne Rienner in 2013.

Amanda D. Clark is a PhD student at Kent State University studying transnational comparative politics and policy. Her research interests include foreign policy, intelligence, and security.

Howard Clark was the coordinator of War Resisters' International from 1985 to 1997 and the chairperson from 2008 until his death in 2013. His publications include, with Véronique Dudouet, *Nonviolent Civic Action in Support of Human Rights and Democratisation* (European Parliament Human Rights Sub-Committee, 2009); with Javier Gárate and Joanne Sheehan, *Handbook for Nonviolent Campaigns* (War Resisters' International, 2009), and with April Carter and Michael Randle, *Guide to Civil Resistance: People Power and Protest since 1945* (Merlin Press, 2013).

Patrick G. Coy is Professor and Director of the Center for Applied Conflict Management at Kent State University. He has edited or co-authored over a dozen books and thirty journal articles and book chapters. Recent publications have focused on international non-violent accompaniment, the development of the field of peace and conflict studies, and the US peace movement, among them *Contesting Patriotism: Culture, Power and Strategy in the Peace Movement* (Rowman & Littlefield, 2009).

Maia Carter Hallward is Associate Professor of Middle East Politics and jointly appointed with the PhD program in International Conflict Management at Kennesaw State University. She is the author of *Struggling for a Just Peace: Israeli and Palestinian Activism in the Second Intifada* (University Press of Florida, 2011) and *Transnational Activism and the Israeli–Palestinian Conflict* (Palgrave Macmillan, 2013). She also serves as associate editor of the *Journal of Peacebuilding and Development*.

Julie M. Norman is a Lecturer in Political Science at McGill University in Montreal, Canada. She is the author of *Civil Resistance: The Second Palestinian Intifada* (Routledge, 2010) and co-editor (with Maia Carter Hallward) of *Nonviolent Resistance in the Second Intifada: Activism and Advocacy* (Palgrave Macmillan, 2011). She has published on non-traditional forms of resistance, including media activism, legal advocacy, and prisoners' movements. She has a PhD in international relations from American University in Washington, DC.

Srdja Popovic is an experienced political party and nonviolent movement leader with excellent skills in leadership, targeted communications, motivation, and peer-to-peer mentoring. As a founding member of the Otpor! resistance movement credited with the downfall of Yugoslav President Slobodan Milošević and a proactive member of Serbia's Democratic Party, his expertise unites both partisan and NGO

sector skills and knowledge. Popovic has been active in Serbia's democratic movement since 1992 and has served as an environmental advi-
sor to both the prime minister and deputy prime minister of Serbia
(2000–3). Since 2003 he has been the executive director of the Centre
for Applied Nonviolent Action and Strategies (CANVAS), an international network of trainers and consultants from Serbia, Georgia,
South Africa, Ukraine, Lebanon and the Philippines engaged in the
transfer of knowledge concerning nonviolent democratic change
around the world. He lives in Belgrade, Serbia, with his wife Masha.

Peter (Jay) Smith, PhD, is Professor of Political Science at Athabasca
University, Alberta, Canada. He has published articles recently on new
communications technologies, globalization, trade politics, transnational networks, democracy, citizenship, and copyright in the *Journal
of World-Systems Theory*, the *Journal of Information Technology & Politics*,
Information, Communication and Society, and *Globalizations*. He is also
a contributor to *Handbook on World Social Forum Activism* (Paradigm,
2011), edited by Jackie Smith, Scott Byrd, Ellen Reese, and Elizabeth
Smythe.

Kurt Schock is Associate Professor of Sociology and Global Affairs and
Director of the International Institute for Peace at Rutgers University,
Newark. His book *Unarmed Insurrections: People Power Movements in
Nondemocracies* (University of Minnesota Press, 2005) received the Best
Book of the Year Award from the Comparative Democratization sec-
tion of the American Political Science Association. His books *Civil
Resistance Today* and *Comparative Perspectives on Civil Resistance* are forth-
coming, respectively, with Polity and the University of Minnesota
Press.

Stephen Zunes is Professor of Politics and International Studies at
the University of San Francisco, where he serves as coordinator of
the program in Middle Eastern Studies. He serves as a senior policy
analyst for the Foreign Policy in Focus project of the Institute for
Policy Studies and is an associate editor *of Peace Review*, a contributing
editor of *Tikkun*, and co-chair of the academic advisory committee for
the International Center on Nonviolent Conflict. Zunes is the author
of scores of articles for scholarly and general readership on Middle
Eastern politics, US foreign policy, international terrorism, nuclear
nonproliferation, strategic nonviolent action, and human rights. He
is the principal editor *of Nonviolent Social Movements* (Blackwell, 1999),
the author of *Tinderbox: US Middle East Policy and the Roots of Terrorism*

(Common Courage Press, 2003), and co-author (with Jacob Mundy) of *Western Sahara: War, Nationalism and Conflict Irresolution* (Syracuse University Press, 2010).

Acknowledgments

Thank you to all the authors who contributed chapters to this volume. Your expertise as scholars and practitioners provides the core of this book, and the project is a reflection of your experiences and insights. We especially wish to acknowledge Howard Clark, whose passing we mourn but whose lifelong contributions to the practice and study of nonviolence we celebrate.

Many other individuals also contributed to making this book possible. The authors are especially grateful to Amanda Guidero, Laura Johnston, and Amanda Woomer at Kennesaw State University for their invaluable assistance.

We are grateful to Louise Knight at Polity Press for her vision, enthusiasm, and guidance, to Pascal Porcheron for his assistance throughout the project, and to Clare Ansell, Caroline Richmond and Jane Robertson for their work during the publication process. We also thank the reviewers of the proposal and the manuscript who offered helpful comments, particularly Brian Martin, who provided extensive detailed feedback that was incredibly useful in the revision process.

We recognize that this book would not be possible without the contributions of the many activists around the world who are either subjects of the research or whose stories inspired us and others to pursue the study of nonviolent movements and unarmed resistance.

PART I

Foundations

CHAPTER 1

Introduction

Maia Carter Hallward and Julie M. Norman

Sometimes it only takes the initiative of one individual to start a mass movement that calls into question a government's actions and draws international attention. Erdem Gündüz, also known as the Standing Man, is one such individual. His silent protest of Turkish repression of media and civilian freedom during the Gezi Park protests in 2013 inspired countless others to join him. On the evening of June 17, 2013, after the Turkish government issued a ban on demonstrating, Gündüz stood motionless for six hours in Istanbul's Taksim Square, looking toward the Ataturk Cultural Center. He did not move, despite harassment from police and passersby. Throughout the night, hundreds of others joined Gündüz, first in Istanbul, then throughout Turkey and beyond, in his silent protest against the Turkish government. As Mert Uzun Mehmet, one of the protesters in Taksim Square, said, "If they attack when we are united and throwing slogans, then we're going to try to do nothing" (as cited in Birnbaum 2013).

Early in the morning the following day, in Taksim Square, Turkish police arrived and arrested the silent protesters without the earlier tactics of tear gas and water cannons, but under the spotlight of international media. What began as a local issue – to protect development of green spaces in Istanbul – erupted into an international spectacle. The United Nations, the European Union, groups such as Human Rights Watch and Amnesty International, and countries such as Germany (which awarded Gündüz with its M100 Media Award for making his mark on Europe and working for democracy and human rights (Gaydazhleva 2013)), condemned the harsh tactics of police against protesters and demanded de-escalation and dialogue (McElroy 2013).

Interest in nonviolence, both scholarly and popular, has surged in recent years, sparked largely by the protests and demonstrations that characterized the early revolutions of the "Arab Spring," the global mobilization of urban activists in the Occupy Wall Street movement, and the increasing use of social media, new technology, and transnational networks to amplify the visibility of nonviolent campaigns. At the same time as large-scale employment of nonviolent action is more evident in the Western media, new research is revealing important historical trends regarding the outcomes of civil resistance movements on processes of political change (Bartkowski 2013b; Chenoweth and Stephan 2011; Schock 2014; Global Nonviolent Action Database). The concept of nonviolence that forms the theoretical foundation for these manifestations of "people power" is thus emerging as an area of primary importance for students, scholars, practitioners, and policymakers. No longer relegated as a sub-field of peace studies, nonviolence is now a core concept for those engaged in the fields of political science, international relations, public policy, and social change.

Yet, how do we understand, define, and study nonviolence? What are its philosophical and historical origins? What tactics and strategies are involved in nonviolent movements, and how do they function differently in diverse contexts? What limitations are there to nonviolent approaches, and how are the dynamics of nonviolent campaigns shifting? To date, there has been no comprehensive text that addresses these questions. *Understanding Nonviolence: Contours and Contexts* is designed as a core textbook to provide a nuanced overview of the field of nonviolence studies, drawing from the expertise of key scholars working on these issues. By providing an overview of the history and basic concepts of nonviolence, as well as highlighting key challenges facing scholars and practitioners, this book strives to engage students in critical debates surrounding the study and execution of nonviolent campaigns.

Challenges in defining nonviolence

Although the study of nonviolence has expanded considerably in recent years, the challenge of defining nonviolence and nonviolent movements is inherently contentious. As evidenced in the language used in this chapter and throughout the book, even the terminology used to discuss nonviolence – nonviolent action, civil resistance, unarmed insurrections, popular resistance, nonviolent revolutions – varies across the field. This challenge stems in part from the fact that the term "nonviolence" frames the concept in opposition to violence, giving it a negative orientation that says what it is *not* rather than what it *is*. The term also contributes to misconceptions surrounding what constitutes nonviolence, given that, although activists engaging in nonviolent action refrain from the use of physical violence, their opponents (such as the police or army) often *do* use physical violence to contain or quell the activists. Consequently, the media often frames *biased media*

such encounters as "violent confrontations between protesters and police" despite the fact that only one side (i.e., the police) employed violence. Furthermore, the fact that scholars and activists come to the study and practice of nonviolence from a wide range of disciplines and experiences contributes to the challenge of identifying concrete terms or definitions. The (false) assumption by many in the general public that one must be ethically committed to nonviolence and completely reject violence in order to engage in nonviolent action also gives rise to confusion over the scope of nonviolence, since activists engage in nonviolent action for a mix of "principled" and "pragmatic" reasons. As we aim to show in this book, however, rather than being a limitation, the diversity of approaches to nonviolence allows for it to be implemented and examined in various contours and contexts. Each chapter offers a slightly different interpretation and application of nonviolence, and we challenge students to think critically about how and when the term "nonviolence" is best employed.

Diverse definitions notwithstanding, the following definitions best reflect our understandings of nonviolence in undertaking this book. First, our approach is articulated by Kurt Schock in *Unarmed Insurrections* (2005, p. 6):

> Nonviolent action is nonviolent – it does not involve physical violence or the threat of physical violence against human beings – and it is active – it involves activity in the collective pursuit of social or political objectives. More specifically, nonviolent action involves an active process of bringing political, economic, social, emotional, or moral pressure to bear in the wielding of power in contentious interactions between collective actors. Nonviolent action is noninstitutional, that is, it operates outside the bounds of institutionalized political channels, and it is indeterminate, that is, the procedures for determining the outcome of the conflict are not specified in advance.

nonviolent action = using other forms of power for pressure

Similarly, Nepstad (2011b, p. xvii) defines nonviolence as "a civilian-based form of struggle that employs social, economic, and political forms of power without resorting to violence or the threat of violence." Adam Roberts (2009, p. 2) defines the concept in the language of "civil resistance" – a term used instead of, or in addition to, "nonviolence" in several chapters in this book:

> Civil resistance is a type of political action that relies on the use of non-violent methods . . . It involves a range of widespread and sustained activities that challenge a particular power, force, policy, or regime – hence the term "resistance". The adjective "civil" in this context denotes that which pertains to a citizen or society, implying that movements' goals are "civil" in the sense of being widely

Table 1.1 The boundaries of nonviolent action and conventional politics

Nonviolent action	Conventional politics	Violence	Borderline cases
Burning a draft card	Requesting service as a conscientious objector	Physically attacking or harassing members of the military	Self-immolation in protest of war
Serving jail time rather than enlisting	Serving in the military when drafted		
Rallies in locale where gatherings are forbidden	Rallies in areas where they are routine	Rallies in which violence is employed	Rallies in which violence is threatened and/or property is damaged
Landowners driving very slowly on county roads to block the Keystone Pipeline trucks	Letter-writing campaign against oil pipeline; anti-pipeline candidates running for local office	Taking oil company workers hostage	Sabotage of the oil pipeline
Forcing a change of government through the outpouring of millions of citizens in Egypt in 2011	Launching a political campaign to vote a disliked leader out of office	Staging a military coup to oust a leader	Burning the office building of an authoritarian leader's political party after hours

shared in a society; and it denotes that the action concerned is non-military or non-violent in character.

The definitions above resonate with us because they emphasize the *constructive* nature of nonviolence, which seeks to create a new social structure or new patterns of relationships rather than simply destroying the existing ones (Mattaini 2003). For example, Zunes and Kurtz (1999, p. 314) note that "the creation of alternative structures provides both a moral and a practical underpinning for efforts at bringing about fundamental social change."

Occasionally one hears the out-of-date "passive resistance" used to characterize nonviolent movements. This inaccurate portrayal was dismissed by Gandhi almost a century ago, for "nonviolence implies much more than an 'act of abstaining' and encompasses a positive, action component that is directed toward the reduction of social injustice and the building of cultures of peace" (Mayton 2001, p. 143). The (mis)representation of nonviolent action as "passive" or as "pacifist" contributes to several of the most common critiques of nonviolent action. Some, for example, argue that appeals for nonviolence, when equated with pacifism, call on aggrieved parties to relinquish their right to (armed) resistance while making no such demand of those in power (Bartkowski 2013b; Gelderloos 2007). At the same time, others dismiss nonviolent action if there is not a clear and overt ethical rejection of arms on the part of all involved activists. However, practitioners of nonviolent action are not necessarily, or even usually, pacifists. In fact, George Lakey, founder of the Global Nonviolent Action Database housed at Swarthmore College,[1] has said: "most pacifists do not practice nonviolent resistance, and most people who do practice nonviolent resistance are not pacifists" (cited in Schock 2005, p. 11).

Hannah Arendt also noted the irony of calling nonviolence "passive resistance" given that "it is one of the most active and efficient ways of action ever devised, because it cannot be countered by fighting" (cited in Bharadwaj 1998, p. 79). In fact, the strength of nonviolent opposition may be so powerful that opponents feel *as if* violence had been done to them. As Deming (1971, p. 205) notes, nonviolent activists also use a form of force, not only moral appeal. She says, "if nonviolent action is as bold as it must be in any real battle for change, some at least of those resisting the change are bound to *feel* that injury has been done to them. For they feel it is injury to be shaken out of the accustomed pattern of their lives."

In using unarmed tactics in this way, nonviolence is distinct from forgiveness, reconciliation, dialogue, or normalization. Likewise, nonviolent action refers to nonconventional politics outside the normal realm of political activity (Martin 2009a) and is distinct from electoral processes and normal democratic procedures. As Schock notes, "nonviolent action is a means for prosecuting conflict and should be distinguished from means of conflict resolution" (Schock 2005, p. 8). Furthermore, nonviolent action is distinct from the "unviolent" techniques of conflict management, third-party mediation, or negotiation. Likewise, although voting and lobbying do not involve physical violence, they occur through institutionalized channels and thus are not considered nonviolent actions per se (Schock 2005; McCarthy and Kruegler 1993).

The chapters in the "Contours" section of this book explore the diversity of strategies and tactics employed by nonviolent movements. While specific actions differ, the active, contentious nature of nonviolent activism is evident in the various approaches and case studies.

Why nonviolence?

Why do movements opt for unarmed methods of struggle? What do they hope to achieve? Again, while the goals and objectives of movements vary by context, nonviolence is rooted largely in redistributing power, with most nonviolent strategies aiming to "depriv[e] the power-holders of the deepest sources of their power, outflanking their more visible coercive instruments" (Ash 2009, p. 375). Conceptualizing power as "diffuse or heterogeneous, rather than monolithic or homogeneous ... [and as] relational rather than self-generated," nonviolent movements seek to question the obedience and consent of ordinary people as a way of initiating socio-political and economic change (Atack 2006, p. 89).

Once that power is leveraged, however, scholars distinguish between "revolutionary" nonviolence, which seeks to fundamentally change social structures and patterns of relations that cause and sustain conflict, and "reformist" nonviolence, which seeks to change leaders or policies (Schock 2005; Spence and McLeod 2002). Still others focus on the role of nonviolence in seeking to eliminate broader structures of violence rather than simply to end particular wars, promoting justice in combination with peace and functioning as an "enduring and constant" form of social movement (Wehr 1995, p. 83). As Gandhi noted, "a nonviolent revolution is not just a program of seizure of power. It is a program of transformation of relationships, ending in a peaceful transfer of power" (cited in Merton 1965, p. 28).

One of the arguments in favor of strategic nonviolence is that, for parties who are traditionally weak in terms of access to conventional symbols of hard power, it provides a mechanism for achieving greater parity in the struggle for freedom from oppression. It also allows for more broad-based participation, with individuals from all backgrounds able to engage in nonviolent movements by removing their consent from the regime (Bharadwaj 1998, p. 79).

In addition to its mobilizing capacity, nonviolent resistance has been demonstrably more effective than armed struggle at achieving goals related to regime change or secession, or against foreign occupation (Chenoweth and Stephan 2011). Even though most scholars and practitioners recognize the likelihood of suffering at the hands of opponents who do not share the commitment to nonviolent methods, they note that causing suffering often backfires against repressive regimes over time (Nepstad 2011b; Chenoweth and Stephan 2011). Furthermore, armed struggles – in part on account of the hierarchical style of military campaigns – are more likely to turn into authoritarian regimes as compared to nonviolent campaigns, which are more horizontal, grassroots, and cross-sectoral in nature (Bartkowski 2013a, p. 351). Indeed, because nonviolent action is generally participatory in nature, it is hard to use the techniques of nonviolence to build systems of oppression (Martin 2009a). In sum, democratic, nonviolent means are more likely to result in more democratic ends (Summy 1993; Martin 2009a).

On a more individual level, many choose nonviolent resistance because it is consistent with their worldview and ideology (Smithey 2013, p. 43). While not all may adhere to a Gandhian level of nonviolent discipline and commitment – and Gandhi himself approved of some use of arms in certain circumstances (Losurdo 2010, p. 96) – there are many who choose nonviolent struggle because it is in accord with their beliefs regarding the sanctity of life. Members of the historic peace churches, such as Quakers, Mennonites, and Brethren, as well as activists engaged in both secular and religiously affiliated work, exercise their beliefs when they stand against militarism or seek to confront injustices through nonviolent means. A commitment to unarmed resistance is usually easier to obtain from social groups demanding enhanced rights, as the means are consistent with their desired ends. For example, students campaigning for increased rights, or minorities seeking recognition, may see armed struggle as inconsistent with their arguments for why they deserve those rights. Similarly, the tenets of nonviolence are often more compatible with the self-defined identities of groups engaged in social justice campaigns than are those of armed struggle. The Martin Luther King, Jr. Center for Nonviolent Social Change, for example, cites six principles of nonviolence, among them a call to "attack forces of evil, not persons doing evil," to "accept suffering without retaliation for the sake of the cause to achieve the goal," and a belief that "the universe is on the side of justice."[2]

Nevertheless, the decision to practice nonviolence may be controversial. Critics suggest that nonviolence is encouraged by those benefiting from the continued state monopoly on violence, and that the relative success of nonviolent movements is due at least in part to the established power structures preference for dealing with nonviolent leaders, such as Martin Luther King, Jr., over more militant ones. Frantz Fanon, for example, argued that nonviolence serves the interests of imperial powers and that violence was a legitimate tactic in revolutionary struggles (Coy 2013; Gelderloos 2007). Furthermore, since there is no screening for who can use nonviolent methods, there may be cases in which the state adopts unarmed means to support systems of violence. However, precisely because of the broader structural dimensions of power and violence, not all "unarmed" actions may qualify as "nonviolence." Nonviolent action also may not be the best method in a given situation; at times dialogue is called for as a preliminary step, or perhaps community organizing is needed to lay the groundwork for social change before engaging in nonviolent action (Martin 2009a).

The case studies included in this textbook provide a number of reasons as to why individuals and groups opt for nonviolent resistance and illustrate how they make use of nonviolent resistance in the course of their struggles. As the chapters in the "Contexts" section of this book illustrate, nonviolent movements embrace a variety of goals and objectives and achieve different outcomes; however, all engage in some way in the transformation of existing power relations.

Outline of the book

This book is divided into three parts, with the first aimed at introductory and core background material for the study of nonviolence (chapters 1 and 2), the second aimed at fundamental frameworks and cross-cutting themes in the study of nonviolence (chapters 3–6), and the third focusing on different contexts for the study of nonviolence (chapters 7–10). We hope that this will provide a general understanding of the theory and practice of nonviolence before exploring how nonviolent struggles emerge and play out in different socio-political and geographic contexts. We intend this book to demonstrate the interplay between theory and practice as well as the multifaceted and diverse approaches to the study and exercise of nonviolence.

After the overview and history offered in the first part of the book, the second part looks at the "contours" of nonviolence, general themes and approaches that guide and shape nonviolent struggles of all types. Chapter 3, "Spiritual and Religious Approaches to Nonviolence," by Mohammed Abu-Nimer, examines the influence of morality, philosophy, and spirituality, looking at arguments that nonviolence does not separate the ends from the means, and therefore provides activists with the moral high ground and a deeper sense of commitment to the cause and willingness to suffer in the face of repressive countermeasures, even as he argues that religious leaders often refrain from using moral arguments in their nonviolent campaigns, partly from strategic considerations. Using the case study of the Arab uprising in Egypt, Abu-Nimer challenges common assumptions not only about principled nonviolence but also about the possibility of nonviolence in the Arab world. Chapter 4, "Tactical and Strategic Approaches to Nonviolence," by Howard Clark, explores the strategic, logical rationale for pursuing nonviolence, without necessarily any ethical or moral justification. The chapter focuses on the cases of Kosovo and Chile to illustrate the dynamics and challenges of a pragmatically oriented nonviolent struggle and raises questions regarding situations in which nonviolent campaigns may be more or less successful, such as where the oppressive regime does not rely on the people for support or legitimacy, as well as exploring the importance of local context in devising an appropriate strategy.

Chapter 5, "Questions of Strategy," by Stephen Zunes, examines how those involved in two anti-colonial struggles – the movement for independence in Western Sahara and the anti-apartheid movement in South Africa – shifted to primarily nonviolent strategies after initially relying on tactics of guerrilla warfare. It discusses the strategic reasons for a movement to engage in nonviolent resistance even if it never relinquishes the right to armed resistance, as well as general strategies and tactics that activists have used successfully. The chapter looks at challenges facing nonviolent activists, including the tendency of industrialized countries in the Global North to provide arms and other support to authoritarian regimes. The final chapter in Part II, "New Media and Advocacy," by Srdja Popovic and Marcella Alvarez, engages in a critical discussion of how social media and technological tools such as Facebook, Twitter, and other digital platforms contribute to nonviolent campaigns. In addition to the role of new media and technology in organizing campaigns and spreading the word afield, the chapter discusses the limits of technology, notably how states and other targets of nonviolence can shut down servers or use technology to gather intelligence on activists.

Part III explores four different contexts in which nonviolent action has been used to enact various levels of socio-political and economic change. Chapter 7, "Civil Rights and Domestic Policy," by Patrick Coy and Amanda Clark, provides an in-depth case study of the student-led sit-in movement in Nashville, Tennessee, during the American civil rights struggle, using the framework of Adam Curle's conflict progression matrix. Applying the pillars of support model to the movement itself, they illustrate how disadvantaged communities within a state practice nonviolence to improve their civil and social rights within their local or national context. Chapter 8, "Revolutions and Democratic Transitions," by Maciej J. Bartkowski, focuses on nonviolent movements aimed at overthrowing rather than reforming political systems. Drawing on research by Chenoweth and Stephan that challenges the commonly held assumption that violence is a more effective way of challenging a ruthless state adversary, and disproving the notion that nonviolent resistance can work only in democratic contexts, this chapter discusses the role of nonviolent strategies in struggles against non-democratic regimes, for independence, and in challenging political oppression. It explores the role of the two-level game in spreading the nonviolent battlefield and increasing support for activists' goals, and argues that nonviolent methods are more likely to contribute to successful democratic transitions than strategies of armed resistance.

Chapters 9 and 10 shift away from the traditional emphasis on "pro-democracy movements" to more of an economic focus, exploring movements working for social justice and against structural violence. Chapter 9, "Rural Movements and Economic Policy," by Kurt Schock, compares three cases in which rural peasants or workers have mobilized nonviolently to address land issues, labor rights, and economic policies that adversely affect them. Exploring the Landless Rural Workers Movement in Brazil, the United Farm Workers in California, and the Assembly of the Poor in Thailand, the chapter gives voice to the rural peasants and farmers whose struggles are often neglected in the urban bias of much of the media and social science scholarship on nonviolent movements. Chapter 10, "Transnational Movements and Global Civil Society," by Peter (Jay) Smith, analyzes the transnational dimensions of nonviolent campaigns as activism increasingly spans international borders. Using the case studies of the World Social

Forum and La Via Campesina, one of the world's largest transnational networks, the chapter points out that, while the global justice movement advocates for nonviolence, it does not clearly define it, nor can it enforce it across a diverse range of countries, issues, and actors. Using the concept of prefigurative politics to examine the connection between the practices of groups involved in the global justice movement and the aims they seek to achieve, the chapter discusses the challenges of maintaining cohesion across a loose network of horizontally organized activist groups with various degrees of commitment to nonviolence.

The concluding chapter of the book, "Future Directions," highlights common themes across the case studies, including the relationship between structure and agency and the continuums of violence–nonviolence and principled–pragmatic approaches. The conclusion also reflects on current challenges in the field and explores new areas of study, among them the role of new media and the use of humor and small acts of resistance. In closing, it raises questions and poses suggestions for concerned citizens, students, and researchers seeking to engage in the field as either scholars or activists committed to social change.

Suggestions for further reading and research

Centre for Applied Nonviolent Action and Strategies (CANVAS), www.canvas-opedia.org.

International Center on Nonviolent Conflict, *Movements and Campaigns*, http://nonviolent-conflict.org/index.php/movements-and-campaigns/movements-and-campaigns-summaries.

The King Center, *The King Philosophy*, www.thekingcenter.org/king-philosophy#sub2.

Global Nonviolent Action Database, http://nvdatabase.swarthmore.edu/.

Waging Nonviolence, http://wagingnonviolence.org.

CHAPTER 2

Understanding Nonviolence

Maia Carter Hallward and Julie M. Norman

Individuals and groups have practiced nonviolent resistance through-out history by engaging in acts of omission or commission against oppressive authorities, and documentation of civil resistance goes back as far as the early Roman Republic (Howes 2014). In this chapter, however, we focus our discussion on the historical development of nonviolence as both a field of study and a form of resistance from the early twentieth century to the present. While many contemporary practitioners of nonviolent resistance have drawn from older philoso-phies and texts, both religious and secular, we are concerned most with how recent theories and applications have informed each other over the past century, leading to the emergence of nonviolence as a distinct area of inquiry.

History of nonviolence

Much of the twentieth-century interest in nonviolence was inspired by Gandhi's campaign to resist British rule over India and to build a nonviolent society. Gandhi was influenced by secular writers such as Henry David Thoreau ("On Civil Disobedience") and Leo Tolstoy ("Notes for Soldiers") (Carter 2009; Cortwright 2006, p. 14), as well as by his study of the Hungarian nonviolent struggle of the 1850s and 1860s and the 1905 Russian Revolution (Bartkowski 2013a, p. 347). After studying in London and engaging in nonviolent resistance in South Africa, Gandhi returned to India in 1915 and became the leader of the Indian National Congress in 1921. Designating his method of nonviolent resistance *satyagraha*, often translated as "truth force,"[1] he called for his followers to pursue *ahimsa*, a form of deep univer-sal love (Cortwright 2006, p. 16). Gandhi's nonviolence was rooted in a belief of the primacy of means, which necessitated the exercise of nonviolence. While he considered civil resistance to be a form of nonviolent warfare, he held firm that activists should seek truth and remember that "the goal is not defeating the adversary but achieving understanding and political accommodation" (ibid., p. 19). Gandhi

14

encouraged the masses that he mobilized to stop their use of British goods, and he advocated civil disobedience, recognizing that the British imprisonment of thousands of protesters actually posed a challenge to the regime while increasing publicity for the movement. In the famous Salt March of 1930, Gandhi mobilized tens of thousands of Indians to march to the sea in defiance of the British monopoly and tax (although he has been criticized by some for calling off protests too early in exchange for meager promises from the British) (ibid., p. 25; Roberts 2009, p. 7; Weber 2000).

The scholarly study of nonviolence began during the same time as Gandhi's early campaigns, coinciding with the demonstrations, protests, and strikes of the American labor movement. Clarence Case's *Non-Violent Coercion: A Study in the Methods of Social Pressure* (1923) provided one of the first systematic analyses of the sociological dynamics of civil resistance (Carter 2009), while Richard Gregg's *The Power of Nonviolence* (1934) brought further scholarly attention to nonviolence as employed by Gandhi. In the field of theology, Reinhold Niebuhr, whose views on nonviolence and politics would later influence Martin Luther King, Jr., was one of the first theologians to take serious note of Gandhi's work.

By the mid-twentieth century, the American civil rights movement helped further spread awareness about the power of nonviolent action while also illustrating some of the key debates regarding its efficacy for effecting social change. According to Cortwright (2006, p. 55), Martin Luther King, Jr., "was the person who more than any other brought to life Gandhi's ideas and methods and developed nonviolent action as an effective instrument of political change."[2] At the same time, grassroots organizing by student groups, churches, and civic associations reflected the importance of local mobilizing efforts in sustained nonviolent movements. From the Montgomery bus boycott in 1955 to the March on Washington in 1963, and from the Freedom Rides to the demonstrations in Birmingham, the civil rights movement reflected both moral-religious and strategic approaches to nonviolence, serving as an inspiration and model for other rights campaigns while also informing a new wave of scholarship on civil resistance and nonviolence in both principled and pragmatic contexts. Although some popular accounts of the start of civil rights movement suggest it began "spontaneously" when Rosa Parks refused to give up her seat on the bus, Parks's action was strategically calculated and the result of much careful planning on the part of civil rights leaders. In contrast, many of the large-scale protests that characterized the 2011 Arab uprisings were more characteristic of spontaneous nonviolent action.[3]

Also in the 1960s, Cesar Chavez drew on the work of Gandhi and King in his struggle against the conditions facing Mexican and Filipino farmworkers in the US (Cortwright 2006), as discussed further in chapter 9. Outside the US, popular movements in Ghana, Malawi, and Zambia drew primarily on nonviolent methods in their struggle for independence from colonial powers, while others in Mozambique used methods of nonviolent resistance alongside armed struggles (Carter 2009; Momba and Gadsden 2013). Likewise, the African National Congress (ANC) in South Africa relied primarily on nonviolent tactics in its decades-long struggle against the apartheid regime, although the movement also employed some violent actions (Schock 2005), as discussed in chapter 5. The citizens of many Latin American countries, including Guatemala and El Salvador in 1944, used nonviolent resistance to topple dictators in the first half of the twentieth century (Parkman 1990). Elsewhere, citizens in Czechoslovakia engaged in nonviolent resistance against the invasion of the Soviet Union and other Warsaw Pact countries during the 1968 Prague Spring, while strikes in Poland in 1970–1 forced a change of government policy to increase food prices and also served as a source of inspiration for mass strikes in the 1980s (Carter 2009, pp. 30–1), as discussed in chapter 8.

The utilization of nonviolent methods in the 1960s inspired further interest in the analysis and theory of civil resistance, with Gene Sharp's seminal trilogy *The Politics of Nonviolent Action* (1973) remaining a key resource for nonviolent activists and researchers. Recognizing that power is central to the analysis and conduct of nonviolent resistance, Sharp based his analysis on the consent theory of power,[4] which assumes that power is dispersed (also sometimes called "pluralistic"), rather than monolithic, and distributed throughout society. It assumes that rulers depend on the governed for their power and that, when the governed withdraw their consent (either their active consent or their passive acceptance of the regime's legitimacy through following laws and complying with expectations), the regime loses its power and ability to rule, particularly when the military, police, and other functionaries of the state likewise withdraw their loyalty (Sharp 1973; Atack 2006). Sharp reframed Richard Gregg's concept of "moral jiu-jitsu" into "political jiu-jitsu," indicating how repression can backfire when nonviolent movements use regime crackdowns to their advantage in garnering broader support (Carter 2009, p. 31). Focusing on the strategy of nonviolent action, Sharp's work examines the politics, methods, and dynamics of nonviolent action and describes almost 200 methods, which he classifies into the categories

Sharp → 200+ methods of nonviolence

of symbolic protest and persuasion, non-cooperation, and nonviolent intervention (Sharp 1973). The first category includes largely symbolic acts, such as public speeches, petitions, leafleting, picketing, displays of symbols, prayer services, vigils, marches, teach-ins, and walk-outs, all tactics used broadly by social movements. The second category, non-cooperation, may be legal or illegal and requires deliberately withdrawing cooperation from normal social, economic, or political activities that contribute to structures of social, political, or economic violence. Among these tactics are engaging in a wide range of social, economic, or political boycotts, striking, staying at home, participating in a rent strike, refusing to pay fees, refusing to accept appointed officials, and civil disobedience of "illegitimate" laws (Sharp 2005, p. 61). The third category, nonviolent intervention, is more disruptive and can be used offensively or defensively; in either case, these tactics are harder to sustain and likely to bring a harsher response from authorities. Intervention tactics include fasting, sit-ins, nonviolent raids, nonviolent interjection of one's body between a person and his or her objective, guerrilla theater, establishing alternative social institutions, civil disobedience of "neutral" laws, defiance of blockades, and nonviolent land seizure (Sharp 2005, pp. 62–4).

① symbolic
② non-cooperation
③ non-violent intervention

Sharp's idea of pluralistic power was reflected in the nonviolent movements of the 1980s and 1990s, which, because of the popular, consent-oriented nature of the uprisings, commentators called "people power" revolutions.[5] Popular resistance in the Philippines, joined by religious groups and the military, helped overthrow the Marcos regime in 1986, and in 1987 Palestinians used nonviolent methods during the first *intifada* to try to "shake off" the Israeli occupation. The Solidarity strikes in Poland, the "Velvet Revolution" in Czechoslovakia, and the fall of the Berlin Wall in East Germany resulted from citizen-based resistance (Carter 2009; Nepstad 2011b). Nonviolent organizing in Chile by labor unions, universities, and churches forced military dictator General Augusto Pinochet to step down from the presidency in 1988 (Kurtz 2009).

The dawn of the twenty-first century brought a new wave of nonviolent revolutions in the former Soviet Union – the so-called color revolutions – including the Orange Revolution in Ukraine and the Rose Revolution in Georgia, which were inspired in part by the nonviolent overthrow of Slobodan Milošević in Serbia in 2000, organized by the Serbian student group Otpor!. Nonviolent movements were not always successful in bringing about democracy or transforming unequal societies even when they were able to oust authoritarian rulers, as evident in the 2005 Cedar Revolution in Lebanon or in the 2006 civil

Table 2.1 Examples and types of nonviolent action and conventional politics

Example of nonviolent action	Type of NV activity (Sharp 1973)
American Studies Association (ASA) statement aligning itself with the cultural boycott of Israeli academic institutions as a result of Israel's ongoing occupation of the Palestinian territories	Signed public statement (protest and persuasion)
Setting up stuffed animals and other toys with signs protesting governmental leaders in Russia	Humorous skits and pranks (protest and persuasion)
American Friends Service Committee (AFSC's) Eyes Wide Open exhibit of boots commemorating and visually documenting US war deaths in Iraq	Demonstrative funerals (protest and persuasion)
US consumer boycott of grapes as a result of the harsh treatment of California grape companies toward migrant workers	Consumer boycott (economic non-cooperation)
Members of the Nigerian National Union of Electricity Employees (NUEE) strikes over the flagrant abuse of human and trade union rights in the power sector	Industry strike (economic non-cooperation)
In Albania in 1996 the socialist party boycotted elections as a result of allegations of electoral fraud; new elections were later held under international supervision	Boycott of elections (political non-cooperation)
Teams of black and white students sit in at segregated lunch counters throughout the Southern United States during the civil rights movement to challenge such discriminatory policies	Sit-in (nonviolent physical intervention)
Landless workers in Brazil organize as part of the Landless Workers Movement (MST) to occupy tracts of land that are otherwise lying fallow in the face of severe socio-economic inequality	Nonviolent land seizure (nonviolent economic intervention)
The Free Gaza movement and the Freedom Flotilla sail to the Gaza Strip with ships loaded with humanitarian aid in defiance of Israel's blockade	Defiance of blockades (nonviolent intervention)

resistance movement in Nepal (Carter 2009). In December 2010 a wave of uprisings spread throughout much of the Middle East when a young street vendor in Tunisia set himself on fire in protest to worsening socio-economic conditions and government corruption. The initial demonstrations that followed in Tunisia and Egypt were largely nonviolent and succeeded in ousting authoritarian rulers, even if the transition to democracy remains as yet elusive. Unarmed demonstrations elsewhere in the region, including Yemen, Syria, and Bahrain, began nonviolently, although some were brutally suppressed; the civil war in Syria continues at the time of writing.

The scholarly study of nonviolence has continued to develop in recent years, with texts such as *Strategic Nonviolent Conflict* (1994), by Peter Ackerman and Christopher Kruegler; *Nonviolent Social Movements* (1999), edited by Stephen Zunes, Lester Kurtz, and Sarah Beth Asher; *Unarmed Insurrections* (2005), by Kurt Schock; *Civil Resistance and Power Politics* (2009), edited by Adam Roberts and Timothy Garton Ash; and *Nonviolent Revolutions* (2011), by Sharon Erickson Nepstad, helping establish a distinct field for nonviolence studies. Erica Chenoweth and Maria Stephan's groundbreaking 2011 study of 323 resistance campaigns between 1900 and 2006, *Why Civil Resistance Works*, which demonstrated quantitatively that nonviolent campaigns are more than twice as likely as violent campaigns to achieve some or all of their objectives, further helped position the study of nonviolence increasingly in the academic mainstream.[6]

Debates in the field

As with all fields of research, there are a number of debates among those studying (and practicing) nonviolence. These debates are perhaps further amplified by the fairly recent emergence of nonviolence as an area of study, as well as the interdisciplinary nature of the field, which includes aspects of sociology (especially social movement studies), political science, psychology, and anthropology.

"Principled" vs. "pragmatic" nonviolence

One of the major areas of debate in nonviolence studies is in how scholars identify actors' orientation toward "principle" or "pragmatism." While the motivations of each are neither entirely principled nor entirely pragmatic, the scholarship has tended to treat these two approaches to nonviolent action as distinct categories. For example, Schock (2005, p. xvii) argues that "a distinction can be made between nonviolent action as a method of struggle and nonviolent action as a lifestyle," and Stiehm (1968, p. 24) suggests that the two approaches "are different in their motivations, their assumptions, and their implications. As a result, they are in some ways incompatible," even though both traditions "are similar in their disavowal of violence, in many of their choices of action techniques, in their capacity to inspire martyrdom, in their goals chosen for action, and in their rhetoric."

Those who take a pragmatic approach employ nonviolent methods for strategic purposes. Roberts (2009, p. 3) affirms that the selection of nonviolent methods is often "related to the context rather than to any absolute ethical principle: [the methods] may spring from a society's traditions of political action, from its experience of war and violence, from legal considerations, from a desire to expose the adversary's violence as unprovoked, or from calculations that civil resistance would be more likely than violent means to achieve success." In this way, nonviolence is a strategy rather than a lifestyle or a religious belief. Galtung (1965, p. 230), for example, specifies that nonviolence is a "style of action" rather than a mindset, and should be limited to "patterns of behavior observable by others." Likewise, Sharp differentiated the techniques of nonviolence from any set belief system, suggesting that the action and strategy were what made a movement nonviolent, and not the beliefs or values of those engaging in the action (Weber 2003, p. 255). Schock (2003, p. 709) contends that, "while some major proponents of nonviolent action have been morally committed to nonviolence, nonviolent action *per se* does not require proponents or activists to be morally committed to nonviolence, or hold any sort of ideological, religious, or metaphysical beliefs."

Those who take a principled approach to nonviolence tend to see it as "more than a method of social action. It is a philosophy of life, a radically different way of being and doing" (Cortwright 2006, p. 2). Oppenheimer (1965, pp. 124–5), for example, emphasizes that nonviolence involves not only one's outlook on life but also communication and understanding, a willingness to suffer when one withdraws from a coercive system, respect for each individual, and expressing love and understanding. Those who affirm that "nonviolence is a holistic rather than dualistic philosophy . . . regard means as important as ends, arguing that violent means dehumanize and set up an unresolvable discord of inconsistency between objectives and methods" (Branagan 2003, p. 51).

Some advocates of principled nonviolence have argued that, "as long as nonviolence is embraced on pragmatic grounds and, not truth or morality, but success and power . . . are made the criteria of its efficacy, it prepares itself for self-defeat" (Bharadwaj 1998, p. 79). However, many scholars have noted that most contemporary nonviolent resistance campaigns have been conducted strategically and pragmatically, and that "the claim that a general belief in nonviolence is a necessary foundation of campaigns of civil resistance has sometimes morphed into the narrow conclusion that any setbacks are due to a lack of principled commitment rather than to other causes" (Roberts 2009, p. 8).

Indeed, many proponents of nonviolence, including both King and

Gandhi, used both strategy and principle in adopting nonviolence (Raab 2006), and Satha-Anand (2002) argues that what Bharadwaj (1998, p. 79) calls the "irreconcilable differences" between principled and pragmatic nonviolence are actually not so irreconcilable. Satha-Anand (2002, p. 9) asserts that, "while ethical imperatives are not present for the pragmatic strategists, the theoretical, pragmatic imperative requires that he or she must be committed to nonviolence or risk becoming just another ordinary pragmatic strategist and not a nonviolent one." Although the pragmatic approach to nonviolence may emphasize strategy and effectiveness over values and principles, those deemed "principled" nonviolent activists are often falsely equated with pacifists or religious believers, when many of them simply see their nonviolent activism as stemming from a certain values orientation or believe that social change will be more effective and lasting if the means and ends are consistent (Coy 2013, p. 258). For example, Smith (1976, p. 120) suggests that "the use of ethical means may have social contagion effects and may result in outcomes of greater reward and may have definite cognitive changes of a dissonance reducing nature."

Indeed, while the distinction between pragmatic and principled approaches may be analytically useful in some circumstances, in practice, the dividing line between "principled" and "pragmatic" is not always so clear. Faith traditions have provided language and moral justification for nonviolence; according to Cortwright (2006, p. 13), nonviolence is a core tenet of nearly all major religions – Buddhism, Taoism, Hinduism, Islam, Judaism, and Christianity – complementing calls for peacebuilding and social justice.[7] Religious leaders have also been strategic in their use of religious spaces – which often remain available for organizing and protest when other public spaces are closed by authoritarian regimes, as in the cases of East Germany under communism and Kenya under Moi (Nepstad 2011b). Zunes and Kurtz (1999, p. 304) argue that

> even the most exclusively nonviolent of these movements do not necessarily subscribe to the Gandhian ethic, which implies the goal of converting an opponent through moral appeal; nonviolence can also assume a coercive component. In many cases the core of the movement is a handful of people acting on moral or religious principles who initiate the struggle or sustain it between mass mobilizations that necessarily involve people who are using nonviolence for its efficacy more than its ethics.

Deming (1971, p. 207) notes that the power of nonviolence comes through the combination of "two pressures – the pressure of our defiance of him and the pressure of our respect for his life – and it happens that in combination these two pressures are uniquely effective." In other words, the moral acknowledgement of the value of the life of one's opponent strengthens the otherwise pragmatic strategy of non-cooperation.

Coercion vs. conversion

A related difference of opinion in the scholarship on nonviolent action deals with the place of coercion in nonviolent resistance. While some affirm that nonviolence is "a complex and well-defined philosophy of social change, which emphasizes conversion, rather than coercive or confrontational action" (Branagan 2003, p. 51), others underscore the inherent contention of civil resistance, noting that "not everything that is not violent is considered nonviolent action. Nonviolent action refers to specific actions that involve risk and invoke nonviolent pressure or nonviolent coercion in contentious interactions between opposing groups" (Schock 2005, p. 7). Some others fall in the middle, recognizing that, "while there is often a need to be oppositional, activists ideally balance this with the creation of positive practices or 'parallel institutions'" (Powers and Vogele 1997, p. 434; Branagan 2003).

In a study of the US civil rights movement, Wirmark (1974, p. 128) argues that, although it at times seeks change through the mechanism of conversion, nonviolence more frequently involves the mechanism of coercion, differentiating it from what peace scholar and economist Kenneth Boulding considers "unviolent" behavior (Ash 2009, p. 371). Deming (1971, pp. 211–12) suggests that, while nonviolent action is forceful, in contrast to violence, which she says makes people "dizzy," nonviolence should reach the mind (not the heart) of opponents to prevent the mindless, reflexive action that occurs out of fear. Although certain coercive tactics of nonviolent action may cause harm – strikes and boycotts, for example, can cause economic harm[8] – such tactics are intended to avoid direct physical harm.

Most scholars and activists emphasize the need to engage in careful planning, to specify clear goals, and to analyze systems of power relations (Coy 2013; Satha-Anand 2002). Most also highlight the need for nonviolent discipline and for maintaining unity in the movement as critical factors for conversion, noting that even small acts of violence not only alter the tenor of the movement but also impact chances for success (Nepstad 2011b). Nevertheless, some see nonviolence as just "one of many means of action attempting to use power effectively in struggles to prevail over an adversary" (McCarthy and Kruegler 1993, p. 4).

Nonviolence vs. violence

There is some debate among scholars and practitioners as to how to define nonviolent movements given the historical pattern of relationships between armed and unarmed struggle in liberation movements – for example, between Sinn Fein and the Irish Republican Army (IRA), between nonviolent activists and the armed wing of the ANC in South Africa, or between the nonviolent League for a Democratic Kosovo and the Kosovo Liberation Army (Ash 2009, p. 374; Schock 2005, p. 159). A similar debate occurs over what constitutes nonviolence: Does property damage to oppressive structures count as nonviolence? Is limited (unarmed) violence or violence in cases of self-defense permissible?[9]

Cortwright (2006, p. 27) observes that "an action is nonviolent if it avoids imposing physical harm and if it does not deprive people of necessities or lower standards below subsistence." Yet, the line between "violent" and "nonviolent" can be indeterminate, such as when a movement has multiple wings, when a leading figure experiences a transformation, or when both violent and nonviolent campaigns are waged simultaneously. The relationship is further complicated by the range of definitions of "violence," since, as Losurdo (2010, p. 85) argues, "great historical crises oblige us to choose not between violence and nonviolence, but between two different forms of violence. Nonviolent movements are no exception to this rule." Losurdo's critique, which contrasts the (false) choice between the violence of joining the Union army or the violence of slavery, raises questions similar to those of theologian Reinhold Niebuhr, who believed that nonviolence alone would not be enough to bring about economic justice (Chernus n.d.). However, both scholars ignore the fact that nonviolent action often seeks to challenge both direct and structural forms of violence; during the US civil war, for example, many individuals involved in the Underground Railroad engaged in nonviolent action against both slavery and military service. Schock (2005, p. 6) suggests that, "rather than being viewed as half of a rigid violent–nonviolent dichotomy, nonviolent action may be better understood as a set of methods with special features that are different from those of both violent resistance and institutional politics."

Few nonviolent struggles are purely nonviolent, since riots, acts of arson, or murders of collaborators may occur, making the continuum concept useful for helping to classify movements. Nelson Mandela refused to denounce the armed struggle when a prisoner in South Africa, and even Gandhi noted that it was better to use violence than "to put on the cloak of non-violence to cover impotence" (Schock 2005;

Ash 2009; Zunes and Kurtz 1999; Merton 1965, p. 37). Some movements generally classified as "nonviolent" have been successful in part as a result of armed resistance by compatriots. Armed resistance by the ANC outside of South Africa, for example, "symbolized a will to resist apartheid" (Carter 2009, p. 36), although "the anti-apartheid struggle could not have succeeded without broad-based campaigns of nonviolent action" (Schock 2005, p. 159). The existence of a radical or an armed flank is not always positive, however. While at times a "positive radical flank effect" may boost the leverage of "moderates" due to the regime's fear of a more extreme or violent group also pressing for change, radical flanks can also have a detrimental effect by undermining the credibility of the movement or threatening their ability to attract external support (ibid., p. 157).

One of the major questions regarding the relationship between violence and nonviolence stems from the influence of colonialism and imperialism. For example, Frantz Fanon's 1963 *The Wretched of the Earth* portrays nonviolence as a doctrine that served imperial interests, deeming armed struggle legitimate in the face of colonialism (Coy 2013). Mao Zedong also asserted that "a revolution is an insurrection, an act of violence whereby one class overthrows another ... Proper limits have to be exceeded in order to right a wrong, or else the wrong cannot be righted" (cited in Nepstad 2011b, p. xviii). Others question calls for oppressed populations to make use of nonviolence, since they often ignore severe power asymmetries, structural violence, and/or colonial policies that have systematically targeted the population in question (Losurdo 2010; Gelderloos 2007). Such arguments emphasize that, in such cases, nonviolent resistance can mask or encourage systems of patriarchy and state power.

Some have argued that nonviolence has been transformed from a tool in the anti-colonial struggle to a force for imperialism, as the United States and others discredit enemies and challengers as "violent" and call on them to be "nonviolent," all the while defining what constitutes "nonviolent" action (Losurdo 2010, p. 85). The call for nonviolence might, in such circumstances, "be misinterpreted as denial of a population's right to choose its own means of struggle" (Bartkowski 2013b, p. 10) or be seen as what Michael Walzer calls "a disguised form of surrender" (cited ibid., p. 20). Likewise, some have viewed American efforts to train nonviolent activists in various countries around the world as a form of external intervention and neo-imperialism, criticizing the role of nonviolent trainers for colluding with the perceived imperialist agenda of the US government, while others debate whether "opponents" should be trained in nonviolent

Box 2.1 Defining success in the Egyptian revolution

The case of Egypt in the Arab Awakening illustrates some of the challenges in defining "success." On January 25, 2011, thousands of protesters took to the streets in Egypt, inspired by events in Tunisia, to protest against the Mubarak regime. At first, President Mubarak responded by violently repressing the protests, killing hundreds in the process. However, by February 11, the protesters were seemingly victorious – President Mubarak resigned, after nearly thirty years of autocratic rule – and the parliament was dissolved by the military (Kanalley 2011). Under the interim government appointed by the Supreme Council of the Armed Forces, Egyptians began the long road toward democracy, starting with a vote for constitutional reforms (Associated Press 2013).

However, the same protesters who were so successful at mobilizing large crowds were unable to organize a viable political movement, resulting in a presidential run-off between Muhammad Morsi, the Muslim Brotherhood candidate, and Ahmed Shafiq, the last Mubarak-appointed prime minister (Associated Press 2013) and, finally, the election of Morsi. While the elections themselves were uncontested, the realization of substantive democracy proved elusive, as Morsi sought to consolidate power through a November 22 declaration that rendered all of his decisions indisputable, protected the Constituent Assembly, charged with overseeing drafting of the new constitution, from legal challenges in the Supreme Constitutional Court, and removed the prosecutor general from office (PBS 2013). Morsi also attempted to remove the remaining vestiges of the Mubarak regime from the military by forcing top military leaders to retire and appointing General Abdul Fattah el-Sisi as his defense minister (ibid.). Meanwhile, opponents withdrew from participating in drafting a new constitution in protest of Islamist domination of the process (Associated Press 2013).

On January 25, 2013, hundreds of thousands of Egyptians again protested throughout Egypt, this time against Morsi and the lack of economic development, democratic change, and social inclusion of minorities. By June 30 the crowds had swelled to the millions, and on July 3 the Egyptian military removed Morsi from office and placed him under arrest (Associated Press 2013), leading to increasing political and sectarian violence in August. By the start of 2014, the military had regained its prominent place in the affairs of the Egyptian state, usurping the democratic transition (BBC 2013).

methods, with some suggesting that opportunity can be transformative for all involved and others citing it as problematic (Martin 2009a; Gelderloos 2007).

From a pragmatic viewpoint, research suggests that, the more nonviolent discipline is exerted within a nonviolent movement, the more likely activists are to cultivate sympathy in response to repression of their movement, and the more likely they are to convince security forces to defect (Zunes and Kurtz 1999; Nepstad 2011b). Schock (2005, p. 161) contends that, while armed resistance may provide symbolic encouragement to those engaging in nonviolent resistance, unarmed revolutions in both South Africa and Palestine emerged rather independently, carried out by those who directly experienced oppression (rather than via leadership in exile). In these cases, nonviolent movement success relied not on "the amount of violence that accompanie[d] it, but rather the ability to remain resilient in a repressive context and to increase its leverage relative to the state, either by directly severing the state's sources of support or by mobilizing the crucial support of third parties that have leverage against the target state." Pearlman notes that, particularly in movements for self-determination, nonviolent action depends on a degree of group cohesion, and that groups lacking a coherent and resilient organizational structure may not be able to employ nonviolent methods consistently (Pearlman 2012, 2011). The need for collective purpose and for nonviolent discipline is affirmed by other studies as well. Nepstad (2011a, p. 488) observes that, "in nonviolent struggles, when military defectors take up armed struggle against the state, the nonviolent aspect of the struggle will dissipate and the nation will likely slide into civil war." The consequences of such defections are evident in the downslide to civil war that occurred in Libya and Syria in the wake of the initial nonviolent protests in 2011.

Universal approaches vs. cultural relativism

Although some argue that "nonviolent action is independent of cultures and belief systems" (McCarthy and Kruegler 1993, p. 4), others have suggested that "there may be specific cultural and psychological factors residing in an individual, a subculture, or a total culture that may predispose him or it to an acceptance of this philosophy" (Oppenheimer 1965, p. 125). For example, some scholars have noted that nonviolent action is not as effective for minority groups who are culturally very different, especially in situations of widespread prejudice that prevent them from winning majority support against government repression (Zunes and Kurtz 1999, p. 317; Oppenheimer 1965). However, people coming from a range of different cultures have waged successful nonviolent resistance campaigns all over the world. Although Schock (2005, p. 3) asserts that scholarship has traditionally focused on more "politically developed" as opposed to "underdeveloped and nondemocratic countries," nonviolent resistance has been demonstrated to be an effective tool – given the right combination of structural and strategic factors – in authoritarian regimes as well as in democracies and "underdeveloped" countries (Nepstad 2011b; Zunes et al., 1999).

Nonetheless, culture is an important variable in nonviolent resistance campaigns. Activists have long faced the challenge of countering the false assumption that Gandhi's relative success was due to unique facets of Hindu culture, or that nonviolence was somehow a "Western" phenomenon that could not work in troubled regions such as the Middle East (Carter 2009; King 2007). Successful nonviolent campaigns "draw on existing cultures of resistance" (Schock 2003, p. 710), and different situations and societies call for different approaches to nonviolent struggle. As Adam Roberts cautions, "any approach that sees one form of action, or one political destination, as universally applicable risks suffering from what might be termed the 'Comintern fallacy' – the mistake of appearing to know best what is good for all other societies" (Roberts 2009, p. 21). A wide variety of cultural resources contribute to nonviolent action campaigns, from music, art, slogans, and chosen clothing styles that seek to appeal to broader audiences (Branagan 2003) to the national, ethnic, or religious "glue" that holds the movement together in the nonviolent pursuit of their objectives (Ash 2009, p. 379). To be successful, nonviolent campaigns must be rooted in the local community structure, and this organized structure will determine what methods and strategies will be most effective in a given context (Wirmark 1974).

Culture not only affects tactical choices in nonviolent action campaigns, some of which may be more available on account of local values, customs, and identities, but the process of nonviolent resistance itself can catalyze and transform collective identities, "awakening [nonviolent activists] to their shared values, common history, collective understanding, and unifying vision of their cultural, linguistic, social, and political roots as well as a communal life and destiny in a defined public space" (Bartkowski 2013b, p. 5; Smithey 2013). Through nonviolent action, activists develop a common identity, and this generation of a common identity can be an essential factor in mobilizing individuals to take action (Wirmark 1974). Culture can be used to highlight similarities between protesters and security forces to encourage defection and undermine regime legitimacy; at the same time, regimes can use cultural differences to undermine such actions, as evidenced by the Chinese government's decision in 1989 to bring in troops from peripheral regions of the country who did not share language or identity with the Tiananmen Square protesters (Smithey 2013; Nepstad 2011b).

Some consider that psychological differences may cause some societies to react differently to nonviolent resistance than others (Oppenheimer 1965). Rabbi Michael Lerner, for example, suggests that the collective post-traumatic stress disorder (PTSD) of Israeli and Palestinian societies makes certain tactics, such as a broad-based boycott, counterproductive because of the "circle the wagons" reaction it produces (Lerner 2012). Souad Dajani has also noted that often ethnic and religious identities intersect with social class and hierarchies of power, making people's decision to "obey" rulers less a matter of free individual choice (cited in Zunes and Kurtz 1999, p. 307). However, "in some cases symbolically rich nonviolent movements have been used ... as vehicles for identity deployment by which marginalized collective identities are openly expressed in order to encourage public debate or to make use of culturally resonant identities to enhance legitimacy" (Smithey 2013, p. 35). It is important to remember that, although cultural forms can be relatively stable, culture is also dynamic, and new identities and tactics can and do emerge in response to new circumstances and interactions. In the Algerian campaign against French rule, for example, Muslim women sometimes wore the veil to symbolize their resistance to colonial influence, while at other times they dressed in Western attire to carry out covert missions more easily (Smithey 2013).

Measuring "success"

Perhaps one of the most challenging areas of the study of nonviolence is how one measures success. Not only is the timescale for nonviolent struggle long, but the goals of nonviolent campaigns can be systemic in nature: protesters often seek not only the downfall of a particular leader but a broader change in the regime. Many have questioned the extent to which Gandhi was successful in India, for example, given that India and Pakistan were partitioned despite his opposition and consequently went to war, resulting in thousands of refugees and enduring animosity between the countries (Ash 2009). Furthermore, some have argued it was not only Gandhi's nonviolent campaign that led to India's independence but also colonial fatigue on the part of the British after fighting two world wars, and concern that the armed struggle used by Arabs and Jews in the Palestinian Mandate might spread to India (Gelderloos 2007).

Likewise, scholars and activists have raised questions regarding the causal impact of nonviolence in the American civil rights movement. While the majority of the movement was nonviolent, a radical flank boosted the appeal of the moderates, and the US government intervened to protect the activists against white extremist attacks (Martin 2009a). In addition, black activists did not gain full political and economic equality as a result of their struggle – this battle continues to be waged – and those seeking liberation from white imperialism did not achieve their goals (Gelderloos 2007, p. 8). Spence and McLeod (2002, pp. 63–4) argue for a "protracted international struggle to build a peaceful, just, and sustainable world" given the entrenched nature of structural violence in the international system. The success of this kind of long-term, future-oriented approach is difficult to measure, although nonviolence "when carried out systematically can achieve tangible results in policy and structural areas" (Summy 1993, p. 16). A more "principled" versus more "pragmatic" orientation to nonviolent action may affect how success is defined; Weber (2003, p. 256), for example, suggests Gene Sharp "secularized" Gandhi by focusing more on achieving goals than transforming conflict.

A number of scholars have conducted studies demonstrating the success of nonviolent movements by examining campaign goal achievement or regime change; in the case outlined in box 2.1, the initial Egyptian campaign was a success given its ability to depose Mubarak, although many argue the broader "regime" was left in place. Another hallmark of success is "the transfer of allegiance from one source of authority and legitimacy to another" (Zunes and Kurtz 1999, p. 315). Nepstad (2011b) defines success as having managed to overthrow a regime but distinguishes the process of defeating a political ruler from the process of building a new, democratic system, which, as Schock (2005, p. xxvi) cautions, "is not the promised land of political development." Nepstad argues that political revolutions have diferent dynamics than social revolutions, and that the dynamics leading to comprehensive social, cultural, and economic transformation should be explored separately. Omitting situations of foreign occupations and looking solely at case studies involving the overthrow of oppressive rulers, Nepstad finds that the key factor for success is protesters' ability to remove the sanctioning power of states by undermining troop loyalty. In addition, successful nonviolent movements have an effective ideology of rebellion, free spaces in which mobilizing organizations can direct and coordinate the movement, and a credible, unified leadership system that can respond intelligently and with authority to changing circumstances (Nepstad 2011b, p. 6).

At times, even when movements have been "successful" in overthrowing a regime, new dictators and new problems may arise (Zunes and Kurtz 1999), as has been evident in Egypt in the wake of the 2011 removal of Hosni Mubarak from power. However, Chenoweth and Stephan (2011) found that nonviolent campaigns were successful 53 percent of the time, compared to only 26 percent of the time for violent campaigns, with success measured as a correlation between stated objectives and policy outcomes. Movements are encouraged to define goals clearly so that all parties to the conflict can understand what is being sought; not only does this help focus the energy of a movement, it also helps to gauge the extent to which it is successful (Schock 2005, p. 164).

Even if one measures the success of nonviolence by goal achievement, outcomes can be ambiguous, and the success of a movement may be evaluated *ex post facto* by standards that were not as critical to those engaged in the movement at the time (Ash 2009, p. 390). Furthermore, campaigns often have multiple goals and overlapping impacts that may lead to "success" in some but not all aspects. For example, "widespread participation in nonviolent resistance can broaden and amplify the impact of collective action on national identity," as occurred in the movement to defend the Bangla language (Smithey 2013, p. 41), and nonviolent campaigns can shift public opinion, such as when minority groups are able to obtain the support of a neutral public (Oppenheimer 1965). For example, the largely unarmed resistance of Palestinians in the first *intifada* helped shift international opinion away from the perception of Palestinians as terrorists. The importance of the "battle of ideas" and struggles over popular legitimacy in nonviolent resistance campaigns further contributes to the challenge of measuring success (Bartkowski 2013b, p. 5). Civil resistance can not only lay the foundation for an engaged and politicized citizenry but also set the stage for the "nationwide institutions of economic, civic, and political governance necessary for running a country after its independence, even if democratic changes in these newly independent states [leave] much to be desired" (ibid., p. 24).

Nonviolent campaigns often involve multiple tactics and are most successful when protesters do not rely on a single method of action. Boycotts, for example, may be more effective when combined with demonstrations and civil disobedience and when organized for specific local initiatives (Cortwright 2006, p. 88). Often tactics such as boycott are best for applying pressure to gain leverage in negotiations (ibid., pp. 90–1); some suggest success can be measured by bringing the opponent to the negotiating table, so that a "win–win" solution can be found rather than "hound[ing] him into submission" (Summy 1993, p. 19), whereas others see dialogue as a possible capitulation to one's opponent.

Schock (2005, p. 12) notes that there are often extreme standards for measuring the success of nonviolent struggles relative to those that engage in violence, such as guerrilla struggles, which are not presumed to be a futile strategy across the board after one failed effort. People assessing nonviolent movements tend to think in terms of "isolated moments" rather than the long term and may consider that the existence of any casualties at all reflects a failed nonviolent movement (Deming 1971). Those nonviolent movements that are most successful in promoting political change in non-democracies are those that "remain resilient in the face of repression, undermine state power, and in many cases attract the support of third parties" (Schock 2005, p. xxii). Schock also points to the importance of decentralized leadership, which, he argues, promotes democracy but also prevents opposition from completely disrupting the movement when a leader is captured.

Even if decentralized, movement leadership requires "a sufficient degree of coordination and aggregation" (Schock 2005, p. 144), which is in keeping with the findings of Bartkowski (2013a) and Nepstad (2011b) regarding the need for a unified and legitimate leadership for successful nonviolent revolutions. In a study of historical cases of nonviolent liberation movements, Barkowski (2013a, p. 350) adds discipline, self-sustaining collective organizing, and coalition build-ing to unity and resilience as key factors for success. Nepstad (2011b, p. 132) also underscores the importance of training, observing that, in all three of the failed nonviolent revolutions she studied, "there were moments when demonstrators became aggressive and sometimes rioted," suggesting that movements were more likely to encourage troop defection when they acted nonviolently, since external threats are likely to generate in-group cohesion among soldiers.

The role of third parties in contributing to nonviolent movement success is an area of debate within the field. Nepstad and Chenoweth and Stephan all suggest that international support and sanctions do not necessarily help nonviolent insurrections. Not only might outside financial support delegitimize a movement, but reliance on external support may diminish local efforts to build a mass movement (Nepstad 2011b, pp. 13–14). Schock (2005, p. 154) notes that the impact of exter-nal influence may depend on several factors, including the extent of a regime's integration in the international system, the degree of dependence on another country, and the nature of economic relations with other countries. Indeed, some have argued that the "durable and friendly international relations between authoritarian regimes and democratic Western states constitute the main explanatory variable for the initial success of nonviolent revolutions in Iran, Tunisia, and Egypt" (Coy 2013, p. 262). Some movements, however, particularly those functioning under a foreign occupation, seek the support of third parties in the international community, such as the Palestinian call for boycott, divestment, and sanctions to end Israel's occupation, to help offset asymmetric power relations as well to address the fact that the ruling regime does not necessarily view those seeking change as legitimate or as part of the body politic. Consequently, external support can either provide necessary assistance and resources or undermine the legitimacy of civil resistance campaigns. In Iran, for example, nonviolent protesters are seen as potential agents of the United States, which has vocally "advocated regime change and financed activities aimed at achieving it," and has consequently placed civil resistance "in a situation of political and moral vulnerability" (Roberts 2009, p. 23).

New frontiers in studying nonviolence

There are a number of ongoing challenges in the field of nonviolence studies, including the relationship between scholarly oriented and practitioner-oriented studies. One challenge is for scholars to make their work accessible to the policy and practitioner community, and to ensure that their scholarship is not "uninteresting and unintelligible to activists and policy makers" so as to improve foreign and domestic policies. At the same time, however, some scholars and practitioners worry about the extent to which they want policymakers to consider their research, since it could also be used to co-opt nonviolent strategy and goals (Martin 2005, p. 248).

Some scholars question whether nonviolent options are likely to be adopted on a broad scale, even if the literature increasingly points to their effectiveness. As one asserts, "reliance on violence, threat, and coercion runs very deeply in contemporary cultures" (Mattaini 2003, p. 162). Violence is normalized as "appropriate human behavior" by the media and existing interpersonal and international discourse (Satha-Anand 2002, p. 9). Martin (2002, p. 7), for example, suggests that "perhaps the attraction of violence has less to do with proven or likely effectiveness and more to do with symbolic expression of masculine virility or attachment to secrecy, hierarchy and exclusionary politics."

Even when movements choose nonviolent methods, those methods are "not free of ambiguity" due to the fact that blunt instruments such as boycotts and sanctions or other nonviolent but coercive measures can cause harm to the innocent as well as to the adversary (Cortwright 2006, p. 27). Galtung (1965, p. 229) argues that an economic boycott that covers matters of subsistence should be considered violent. A strike by hospital workers, for example, could have harmful consequences if no arrangement was made for patient care (Roberts 2009). At times, even when movements have been "successful" in overthrowing a regime, new dictators and new problems may arise, as was evident in the wake of the 1978–9 Iranian revolution that replaced the shah with Ayatollah Khomeini (Zunes and Kurtz 1999). In short, "nonviolent action is not a panacea, nor is it always effective in promoting political change" (Schock 2005, p. 23).

Terminology, as alluded to earlier, remains a challenge for scholars and activists. Calling anti-regime nonviolent movements "revolutions" suggests a subtext of violence; similarly, there is a question of the relationship between nonviolence, which is often defined as action outside the normal institutional channels of politics, with elections and negotiations (Ash 2009, p. 376). At times, broad-based boycotts of elections can have an impact on undermining the perceived legitimacy of a regime; likewise, negotiations may provide a way of obtaining movement goals.

A challenge related to the earlier question of third-party support deals with when external non-military intervention is and is not legitimate. Just as the field of humanitarianism has engaged in the debate over when humanitarian intervention is legitimate and justified, more should be done to explore how and when cross-border influences from transnational advocacy to fundraising, to training, and other knowledge transfers are both appropriate and effective (Ash 2009, p. 387). These questions have significant moral weight given the unequal status of activists in various parts of the international system, regardless of whether one is dealing with movements related to democracy, economic justice, human rights, the environment, or gender. As Gottlieb (2011, p. 42) advocates, "those who enjoy economic, spiritual, and political privilege in a network of relationships cannot create a solution on their own. They must rely on the vision and efforts of those who suffer the pangs of systemic injustice to articulate the way forward." At the same time, on account of the supremacy of transnational institutions in a globalized world, even when parties are successful in achieving their goals at the state level, international actors may have the power to reverse the state's action, as was the case in 1997 when the United States and the International Monetary Fund (IMF) forced Nicaragua to implement a massively resisted austerity plan, or when donors endorsed an unfair Kenyan election because Moi consented to their minimal demands (Zunes and Kurtz 1999, p. 320; Nepstad 2011b).

The increasing use of social media within both local and global networks represents another area in need of further research. While the effectiveness of Facebook, Twitter, and YouTube in recent uprisings has been widely acknowledged, more work remains to be done on how these tools are utilized at different stages in nonviolent struggles. As noted in chapter 6, social media can be hijacked by oppressive regimes, and social media tools are only useful when used strategically by activists. Additionally, some activists have noted that having many Facebook fans or Twitter followers does not necessarily mean all of those people will mobilize for action; it is easier to click a button on a screen or a phone than it is to engage in a public protest or stand in front of a bulldozer.

Another pressing challenge involves how the international community can best support nonviolent movements for change in their own societies. Although there were a number of nonviolent efforts against the Bashar al-Assad regime in the early stages of the 2011 protests in Syria, international media coverage focused on those groups that engaged in armed struggle against the regime (Bartkowski and Kahf 2013; Deasy 2012; Khalek 2013; Zouhour 2013). International coverage of and support for nonviolent efforts may at times be counterproductive, however, particularly when activists are likely to be targeted by the regime or, as in Iran, might be seen as foreign agents involved in externally supported regime change. In the situation of ongoing civil war in Syria, where as of August 2014 over 160,000 were reported to have been killed and hundreds of thousands more have become refugees in neighboring countries, many question whether nonviolent resistance is naïve and impractical (Hashemi 2013; Zouhour 2013). Such debates have long surrounded studies of nonviolence, as evident in the argument that there "may be situations of pure conflict where violence is necessary to end exploitative colonialism, tyrannical regimes, or justified revolutionary movements" (Smith 1976, p. 124). Others continue to advocate for nonviolent measures, arguing that they provide the best chance of success as well as post-conflict stability. As discussed earlier in this chapter, the initial "success" of the protests in Tunisia and Egypt has been followed by difficulties in transitioning to democratic governance, with political assassinations in Tunisia and a military coup of the elected president in Egypt. As discussed by Bartkowski in chapter 8, there are many challenges facing activists engaged in nonviolent resistance to authoritarian rulers; nevertheless, nonviolence often remains a more effective means of engaging in political struggle, particularly in asymmetric situations.

The chapters that follow investigate the general contours and range of contexts of nonviolent movements, exploring both principled and pragmatic reasons for engaging in nonviolent struggle. The aftermath of the Arab uprisings continues to unfold, and, as it does, our understanding of the trajectory of nonviolent revolutions continues to evolve also. The authors in this volume seek to explain some of the challenges and opportunities facing those engaged in nonviolent action while also raising questions for further study.

Questions for discussion

1 What historical factors have shaped the emergence of nonviolence as an area of study?
2 What has been the relationship between violence and nonviolence in the quest for socio-political change?
3 Does nonviolence work only in certain cultural contexts?
4 What are some of the key debates in the field of nonviolence studies?

Suggestions for further reading and research

King, Martin Luther, Jr. (2000) *Why We Can't Wait*. New York: Signet Classics.
Sharp, Gene (1979) *Gandhi as a Political Strategist*. Boston: Porter Sargent.

PART II

Contours

CHAPTER 3

Spiritual and Religious Approaches to Nonviolence

Mohammed Abu-Nimer[1]

Nonviolent strategies and movements have been increasingly visible in the last two decades as modes of resistance and as frameworks to advocate for justice. In the early 1990s, a number of Eastern European societies, such as Georgia and Poland, implemented nonviolent strategies to replace authoritarian political regimes and install new leadership. More recently, several Arab societies followed this example and revolted against their dictatorial regimes. In addition, the use of nonviolent methods has been seen in peace movements, environmental movements, and labor movements. Many religious leaders stood in the forefront of these movements and argued for nonviolent revolutions. Their voices endorsing nonviolent strategies were often highlighted by media and analysts as well.

Despite the increasing prevalence of nonviolent campaigns in the last two decades, there continue to be many debates regarding their motives, objectives, strategies, and criteria of success. Although the distinction between principled and pragmatic nonviolence may be somewhat arbitrary, this chapter focuses on what is often called the "principled" school of nonviolent struggle, rooted in philosophical, moral, and spiritual traditions that emphasize the sacredness of life. Activists adhering to this approach rely on nonviolent modes of struggle less for strategic or instrumental reasons and more from a belief that it is the "right" approach (King 1998). Drawing on the texts of major faith traditions (Buddhism, Taoism, Hinduism, Bahai, Judaism, Christianity, and Islam) as well as real-world examples of nonviolent action carried out by religiously or morally grounded actors (spiritual leaders, NGOs, etc.), the chapter traces the rationales, strategies, and tactics used in the "principled" approach to nonviolence and discusses the similarities and differences found within this broad category (Abu-Nimer 2003; Magid 2005; Zaru 2008).

In discussing this approach, the chapter draws on the experience and wisdom of noted leaders such as Thich Nhat Hanh, Gandhi, and Martin Luther King, Jr., to illustrate the difference between those committed philosophically to nonviolence for moral reasons and those choosing nonviolence for strategic purposes. The primary questions guiding this discussion include: What is the role of religious traditions in nonviolent resistance movements? What differentiates principled from pragmatic approaches to nonviolence? Are there cases in which even those committed spiritually to the practice of nonviolence are willing to use force? How do scholar-practitioners respond to criticisms that nonviolence is naïve and would not work in extreme contexts?

Common assumptions regarding principled nonviolence

In the course of exploring the topic of principled nonviolence and addressing the questions outlined above, a number of assumptions should be addressed. First, nonviolence is often perceived as morally superior to violence. Not only have scholars and activists tended to attribute a higher degree of morality to nonviolence, but many historical civilizations and cultural traditions have associated the capacity to refrain from using violence as a virtuous and morally higher standard. Regardless of the nature of the violence being deployed, people feel pressure to explain and justify their use of it (both internally to self and externally to others).

Second, nonviolence is a learned attribute. Every human being has the capacity to respond to a situation violently or nonviolently regardless of his or her individual or collective background. The choice of how to respond to triggers (such as discrimination or violence) is a perceptional and cognitive decision shaped in part by environmental factors. Thus, cultural and religious socialization agents play a crucial role in regulating and legitimizing violent and nonviolent responses to external and internal triggers (Fry and Björkqvist 1997).

Third, nonviolence exists on a continuum. Nonviolent and violent behaviors and attitudes are responses that exist on a continuum rather than presenting a clear dichotomy. The scale starts from absolute pacifism on one end and ends with the absolute endorsement of all forms of violent responses on the other. Various beliefs and attitudes regarding political resistance fall along this continuum.

Fourth, collective actions do not reflect all individual beliefs. Human civilization has yet to bridge the gap between individual moral values and behaviors and their collective manifestations. Such gaps exist in all public and private spheres in which individuals adopt certain values and behaviors, while their society or collective group fails to adopt such values and act upon them. Thus individuals can believe in nonviolence, and some might even practice it in their own individual and private lives; however, these practices remain limited to small groups and are not broadly expressed as social or cultural norms.

Religion and nonviolence

Nonviolent values and practices are often grounded in and inspired by religious and spiritual beliefs and rituals. Many scholars contend that religions are foundational sources for the conceptualization and implementation of nonviolence. As Barash and Webel assert, "Nonviolence is intimately associated with certain ethical and religious traditions, notably Buddhism, Hinduism, and Christian pacifism" (2009, p. 458). It is not only these three traditions that have a history of nonviolence, however. There are many episodes in Islamic history that illustrate the use of nonviolent methods, including the thirteen years of nonviolent struggle and resistance of the Prophet (PBUH) in the Meccan context, and Muslim pioneers of nonviolence such as Khalis Jalabi, a Syrian doctor who has emphasized the connection between Islam and nonviolence, have coined the term "civic jihad" (Abu-Nimer 2004). In Judaism, Rabbi Lynn Gottlieb has written on Jewish approaches to nonviolence (2011), and groups such as Shomer Shalom use Jewish principles to support nonviolent engagement.

Religious values and beliefs, rituals, institutions, leaders, and followers impact perceptions of legitimacy and credibility as well as the dissemination of the principles and practices of many nonviolent political movements. The importance of religious justification for nonviolent action is reflected, for example, in questions such as: Are there Islamic theological resources that inspire, justify, and support the call for principled nonviolent movements in Muslim societies? What are the current and historical obstacles to the spread of Christian nonviolent values and norms in Western societies despite their political stability and economic wealth? What is the potential influence of the Buddhist faith in the spread of nonviolence in contemporary Asian cultures? What are the religious and spiritual sources of Hinduism that can reduce the structures of violence in the Indian subcontinent? These are meta-questions that scholars of religion and peace studies can explore in systematic and rigorous ways. The remainder of this chapter will focus primarily on the role of religion in spreading cultures of political nonviolence, looking particularly at the role of Muslim and Christian religious leaders in recent examples of nonviolent resistance in the Middle East.

Before beginning the discussion, however, it is important to define terms clearly. Nonviolence is a set of attitudes, actions, or behaviors intended to persuade the other to change their opinions, perceptions, and actions. Nonviolent methods use peaceful means to achieve peaceful outcomes. This means that actors do not use any form of violence (physical nor psychological) to retaliate against the actions of their opponents. Instead, they absorb anger and damage while sending a steadfast message of patience and insistence on overcoming injustice. The major features of nonviolent action famously articulated by Martin Luther King, Jr., are:

1 "It is nonaggressive physically but dynamically aggressive spiritually."
2 "It does not seek to humiliate the opponent," but to persuade the opponent to change through new understanding and awareness of moral shame so as to reconstruct the "beloved communities."
3 "It is directed against forces of evil rather than against persons who are caught in these forces."
4 Nonviolence seeks to avoid not only "external physical violence but also internal violence of spirit."
5 Nonviolence is "based on the conviction that the universe is on the side of justice." (King 1957, pp. 166–7)[2]

Mohandas Gandhi, Martin Luther King, Abdul Ghaffar Khan, Thich Nhat Hanh, and the Dalai Lama are all globally recognized spiritual leaders who have articulated various definitions of nonviolence and who have set many detailed conditions as to how their followers should best practice nonviolence on the individual and collective levels. These religious and political leaders share a number of common attributes regarding the belief and practice of nonviolence.

First, the deeper the spiritual beliefs and practices of individuals, the more committed they will be to the principles of nonviolence. The depth of an individual's commitment is an indicator of that individual's spiritual strength. Thus, on many occasions when these leaders have encountered injustice and hostilities from oppressive enemies and institutions, they often returned to their faith to derive further strength and inspiration to continue their journey (such as Desmond Tutu, the Dalai Lama, and others who consistently rooted their resistance in their faith tradition).

Second, the beliefs and values of nonviolence are not exclusive to one faith group, religious institution, or set of scriptures.[3] Each of the above leaders was effective in authentically articulating religious values and beliefs from his own tradition, placing these specific values in religious or primary faith language[4] that allowed people of that faith both to understand and to internalize the meaning of nonviolence: Gandhi's concepts of *satyagraha* (soul force or truth force) and *ahimsa* (nonviolent love); Abdul Ghaffar Khan's concept of *sabr* (patience); the Dalai Lama's and Thich Nhat Hanh's concept of "compassion"; and King's concept of "witnessing." These values are all deeply rooted in their respective traditions in a way that allowed such leaders to communicate effectively with their followers through the language of faith and spirituality. For example, King preached that "Darkness cannot drive out darkness; only light can do that. Hate cannot drive out hate; only love can do that" (1967, p. 62). Similarly Gandhi left no doubt that, although he could be angry, his non-cooperation was rooted in love and not hatred.

Third, in their spiritual framing of nonviolence, each of these religious leaders operated from a minority theological position rather than from the dominant and mainstream theological framework of their specific faith tradition. Even when religious figures and authorities have agreed with such interpretations of scripture, many opposed their deployment in the political realm or for political ends. For example, many Christian leaders in the late 1950s and the 1960s did not disagree with the theological basis of King's nonviolent framework. Nevertheless, they debated or opposed his call to deploy these teachings for the purpose of changing the American governance system. Similarly, some Muslim theologians who do not disagree with and may even subscribe to religious sources of nonviolence oppose the deployment of these principles and practices in the fight against certain dictators or enemies (Abu-Nimer 2012). And Jewish religious leaders who have agreed that there is a nonviolent tradition in Judaism do not necessarily endorse the application of these traditions in political terms (for example, only a small number of rabbis have endorsed the nonviolent actions against the Israeli occupation of Palestinian territories).

Fourth, religiously motivated nonviolent resistance has for the most part relied on the strong and exceptional charisma of those leaders who managed to set a role model for their followers and provide a strong spiritual and theological foundation of their framework of resistance. Thus, among many other factors, the death of such exceptional leaders has been important in the decline of these religiously motivated resistance movements. This point is underscored when we consider the targeted assassination of leaders such as Gandhi and King as acts themselves intended to weaken their movements.

Fifth, parallel to these religious leaders' calls for nonviolent resistance, there are always other factions and groups within their religious communities who call for and practice violent resistance or adopt militant strategies.[5] Indian Muslims opposed Abdul Ghaffar Khan, and

Gandhi faced fierce resistance from other Hindu priests and the religious establishment. However, this challenge does not always emerge from within the same religious tradition. Thus, while the doctrines of all major religions emphasize peacefulness and oppose killing, there are numerous violations of these doctrines in practice. An additional complication stems from different interpretations of texts and articulations of beliefs, with some religious figures challenging violence and others accommodating it. An example of this contradiction between belief and action is the Judeo-Christian commandment "Thou shalt not kill" contrasted with the acceptance of killing by soldiers and, in some countries, capital punishment. Horrific acts by believers – including the Crusades, the Rwandan genocide, the Holocaust, the 1965–6 genocide in Indonesia, and the 1971 genocide in Bangladesh – illustrate that religious beliefs do not always inhibit violence, and that religious adherents of principled nonviolence coexist with religious tolerance or advocacy of violence. This indicates a perennial struggle within religious communities over beliefs and actions concerning violence, making principled nonviolence a difficult choice, especially in the face of nationalism and militarism.

Principled and pragmatic approaches

The above spiritual leaders represent the call for a principled approach to nonviolent resistance, deeply rooted in religious morals and values, as opposed to a nonviolent resistance approach based on mechanical, pragmatic, or strategic calculations of what may be the most effective methods in fighting unjust systems. The Metta Center for Nonviolence provides a succinct contrast of the two approaches. It describes pragmatic or strategic nonviolence as a course of action that leaves the door open for violence if nonviolence does not "work," whereas

> principled nonviolence is not only more effective in the short term but can move humanity toward a new paradigm as it involves another order of belief regarding human nature and human relationships. Strategic nonviolence, for example, still presupposes that the means can justify the ends, whereas for Gandhi, "Means are ends in the making." (Metta Center for Nonviolence n.d.)

The strategic, or pragmatic, approach to nonviolence can be defined as a framework that focuses on identifying effective techniques and strategies to confront a system of oppression with the objective of minimizing human casualties and infrastructure destruction. By delegitimizing the authority and power bases of the rulers, strategic nonviolence activists work for the collapse of the existing system of laws and strive to put in their place a new system based on their political values and morals. Replacing the old system of governance with a new system is the objective of many strategic nonviolence movements.[6] (See chapter 4 for more on strategic nonviolence.)

Strategic nonviolent resistance becomes successful only where there is sufficient preparation for it. The group has to be ready to engage in such resistance, particularly in actively establishing the conditions necessary for effective mass nonviolent resistance. Since the end of World War II there has been a dramatic increase in the interest in nonviolent methods of resistance, which has allowed scholars to systematically explore conditions for effective resistance. For example, Sibley (1944) identified four major conditions for successful strategic nonviolent defense, which, when "invaders" is replaced with "regime/opponent," have broader relevance: (1) no service or supplies to be furnished to invaders; (2) no orders to be obeyed except those of the constitutional civil authorities; (3) no insult or injury to be offered the invader; and (4) all public officials pledge to die rather than surrender. However, one also might argue that these conditions apply to both principled and strategic nonviolent approaches.

Supporters of strategic nonviolence have identified several critiques of a principled approach, including

- absolute selflessness is not possible for every individual;
- the need for social change is too critical to allow the time to wait and insist on a principled approach;
- not all people embrace spirituality;
- for nonviolent approaches to be relevant to international affairs, they cannot be based on mystics, religious figures, clergy, martyrdom, or other politically marginalized figures (which belies a certain sensibility over where the "political" is to be found – i.e., in the "secular" as opposed to the "religious");
- and, related to this last point, international state powers are not going to dismantle their military systems and follow religious and spiritual values and norms as a shield against violence and aggression.

Obviously the same argument can be used against strategic nonviolent approaches. However, the demand of spiritual commitment adds another layer of resistance among politicians, who are often trained to separate religion from politics. Principled nonviolence avoids viewing the changing of unjust political systems as an end in itself, but rather views human moral transformation as the primary objective of the call for nonviolence. Thus the struggle to change the apartheid system in South Africa from a principled nonviolent approach would have focused on the transformation of individual whites and blacks regardless of their class or political affiliation. The principled nonviolence approach aims to transform the individual from within based on specific moral values and utilizes this internal transformation to change systems of oppression. In the case of religious leaders, these values are derived from their faith tradition.[7] Thus, King called for fellowship among all Americans and all people – drawing from a Christian understanding of reconciliation and right relationships constitutive of the "beloved community" – while the Dalai Lama presses for human compassion to be a main measure for human interaction.

Despite the contrast between these two nonviolent frameworks, they have a number of commonalities. For example, both share the objective of changing a regime or an oppressive system of governance, and both use similar tactics for change (such as strikes, protest, boycotts, etc., as outlined in chapter 2). The failure or success of both also often depends on similar factors, relating to level of preparedness, systematic planning, sustainability of resources, use of media and public outreach, leadership structure, discipline among followers, and cultural environment of the movement.

Dynamics of principled nonviolence

Adherents of principled nonviolence see it as morally right and effective, based in part on the ethics of responsibility (Childress 1982). This is premised on the sanctity of human life: the nonviolent resister puts his life in the hands of his opponent and entrusts him with it. Childress highlights three features of principled nonviolent resistance: recognition of sacred boundaries of action, voluntary assumption of risk, and a sense of equality. The nonviolent resister makes him- or herself vulnerable to physical assault, injury, and death, not to mention imprisonment, taking a greater risk through a reliance (but not full confidence) on the opponent's sense of moral responsibility and making the assumption that the latter can control his or her actions and refrain from killing or injuring the resister.

Such an approach is in alignment with Gandhi's distinction between "nonviolence of the weak" and "nonviolence of the strong"[8] as an effective force for transformation. This is similar to the distinction between the notion of "unviolence," where violence is not possible, and nonviolence, which involves a voluntary decision or commitment. These distinctions impact the opponent in different ways. Childress (1982, p. 20) argues that it is more powerful, and ultimately more effective, to allow an opponent to feel secure from knowing the resister will not harm them physically than for the resister to derive a sense of security from defending themselves with weapons.

This speaks to another element of the principled approach to non-violent resistance, namely that suffering is generally accepted as an inescapable component for success.[9] In fact, Gandhi declared that "Suffering is the law of human beings; war is the law of the jungle. But suffering is infinitely more powerful than the law of the jungle for converting the opponent and opening his ears, which are other-wise shut, to the voice of reason ... suffering, not the sword, is the badge of the human race" (see Bose 1957; cited in Barash and Webel 2009, p. 460). This type of suffering is not based on passivity or self-victimization, but rather it is active and even confrontational. "Not to be confused with passive suffering or nonresistance, nonviolent action involves suffering in resistance, in noncooperation, or disobedience" (Childress 1982, p. 21). It is the suffering generated by nonviolent campaigns which often stimulates a sense of injustice in third par-ties, and not from the opponent, as would be expected. Most religious traditions embrace the value and experience of suffering as part of the individual and collective spiritual journey. Such belief systems allow for a distinct link between principled nonviolence and religion.[10]

Separating the person from the problem, or separating the evildoer from the evil deeds, is a third important feature of principled nonvio-lent campaigns. If the nonviolent resister targets the deeds and not the people who perform them, the conflict becomes depersonalized, allowing a sense of trust to emerge in the opponent while keeping attention relentlessly focused on the sources of injustice. Principled nonviolent methods provide a great deal of space for activists to separate the problem from the wrongdoing or system of oppression because of the belief in human connectedness and the assumption of divine existence in every human. Thus, a Buddhist priest who was jailed for thirty-four years in a Chinese prison was able to forgive the guards and embrace them with compassion for their humanity. For all his years in prison the monk did not cooperate or confess to any wrongdoing, yet he was able to maintain his human dignity on account of his religious convictions.[11]

Religion and nonviolent resistance in the 2011 Arab uprisings

The 2011 political movements – secular and religious – in the Middle East were striking, with four post-colonial Arab regimes (Tunisia,

Egypt, Yemen, and Libya) tumbling, other regimes confronting mass movements (Bahrain, Syria, Lebanon), and others enacting reforms to calm protesters (Morocco, Jordan, Saudi Arabia). An important feature of several of these nonviolent movements has been the utilization of religious identity to garner support. While there remains much uncertainty over the political future in countries such as Egypt, it is clear that the power of nonviolent mass mobilization (by youth movements and veteran religious and secular political parties and leaders) has proved a significant strategy to shake loose from the post-colonial regimes that devastated the political, economic, and social fabrics of these societies. For many observers of the region, in contrast to veteran activists, the downfall of authoritarian regimes in the so-called Arab Spring might seem surprising or sudden. However, as Dr Emad Siyam from the Egyptian group Kefaya ("Enough") said, "I spent 35 years of my life waiting for this moment; therefore I will not leave the Square before the regime collapses" (Abu-Nimer 2011).[12]

There are many examples of strategic nonviolence in Middle Eastern history (Crow et al. 1990; Stephan 2009). The deployment of such methods is not new, either culturally or religiously. Among many examples, one might cite Iranian mass civil disobedience, strikes, and non-cooperation to confront and bring down the Iranian dictatorship between 1977 and 1979; Syrian Druze resistance to Israeli occupation, most notably their campaign to reject Israeli identification cards and their nonviolent confrontation of Israeli soldiers, disarming them, negotiating the release of their prisoners, and offering cookies to Israeli soldiers when they stormed their villages; the 2005 Cedar Revolution's use of social media to mobilize hundreds of thousands to liberate Lebanon from Syrian security and military forces; and several Egyptian movements, from struggles against British colonial forces in 1919 to the more recent Kefaya movement, which began in 2003 in protest against the US invasion of Iraq and later joined other groups in challenging the Mubarak regime.

While the region's history is rich in examples of nonviolent resistance, a key feature of contemporary movements is their utilization of religious symbols, beliefs, and references to convey their messages. The study of religion and nonviolence in the Middle Eastern context is exceptionally important today because of political transitions in Islamic parties and campaigns that have been major political forces in the protest against Egyptian, Tunisian, Libyan, Syrian, Bahraini, Jordanian, and Yemini regimes. While there are stark differences between the Islamic political movements in each of these countries, their use of nonviolent strategy and action to convey their views and demands and to increase their political influence has been remarkable.

The nonviolent revolutions that have swept the Arab world, especially in the Tunisian, Egyptian, and Yemeni cases, challenge a number of myths and misperceptions about both Arab societies and religious nonviolent political movements held by American, European, and certain Arab analysts since the early post-colonial era, which gave birth to these authoritarian regimes. These myths include:

Myth 1 Arab society is essentially "authoritarian." Many analysts and scholars have argued that the average Arab citizen, on account of the authoritarian characteristics of many Arab societies, is incapable of overthrowing his or her leader. Yet in Egypt and Tunisia, as we saw, activists effectively organized in highly egalitarian groups, with horizontal organizational structures (or networks), that defied the myth of the need for one "father figure" to step in and lead the nation toward peaceful or militant revolution.[13] Numerous examples demonstrate that Islamic youth movement leaders have been effective in mobilizing large nonviolent masses in these societies (Democracy Now 2011), although these movements are not necessarily rooted in principled nonviolence. Instead, they are often a combination of mass movements following a strategic approach with a few principled leaders who attempt to maintain the mobilization of diverse forces.

Myth 2 The fabric of Arab Muslim tribal society acts as a constraint. The tribal nature of Arab societies is often characterized as a major obstacle that prevents social and political movements from peacefully overthrowing a dictatorship, because analysts suggest dictators and their security apparatus will manipulate tribal networks and coalitions to successfully maintain control over the entire society (Barakat 1993). Indeed, the Libyan, Tunisian, Egyptian, and Yemeni leaders unsuccessfully deployed this strategy to divide the protesters: although some tribal groups stood with their respective regimes, the majority of the public in these countries continued to support the peaceful process of political change, and tribal leaders in both Libya and Yemen defied the ruling dictatorships. For example, in Yemen, thousands of protesters from a wide range of tribal affiliations managed to organize peaceful marches and demonstrations to challenge the regime despite the efforts of various politicians to split the movement based on tribal, sectarian, and regional affiliations. Thus, contrary to the assumptions of Western analysts, tribal divisions did not always pose an obstacle, since protesters emphasized their religious unity and solidarity across religious sectarian and ethnic divides.

Myth 3 Nonviolent resistance is contrary to Islam. Since the 9/11 attacks and the US government's declaration of war on "Islamic" terrorism, many policymakers and private individuals hold an essentialist view of Islam or Muslims that links members of the faith with violence. Nonviolent resistance movements were therefore not considered to be a viable path to political change in Muslim and Arab societies. However, through their peaceful campaigns against authoritarian regimes, Tunisian, Jordanian, and Egyptian Islamic movements have illustrated how effective political religious leadership committed to a strategic non-violent movement can be. The Tunisian Islamic leader Rashed Ghannouchi, and others in Egypt such as Abul Ela Madi, declared on many occasions before, during, and after the revolution that *nidal al silmi* (peaceful struggle) or *nidal al madani* (civil strug-gle) is the only way to confront the rulers of Tunisia. Islamist groups in Egypt were very creative in mobilizing protesters through mosques. In their Friday *khotba,* imams called for non-violent resistance and urged their followers to occupy the streets and public squares, leading to the mobilization of millions after Friday prayers. In addition, the Egyptian Islamists, like all other Egyptian groups, adopted the protest slogan *silmiyya* – "peaceful" – as their main message throughout the entire con-frontation with the regime. The term has since been adopted by Lebanese, Yemeni, Bahraini, and other protest groups in the Arab world.

Myth 4 The myth that young adults in the Arab world are politically apathetic, politically ignorant, and potential recruits for suicide bombing was disproved when the world watched millions of youth marching peacefully and chanting unifying and univer-salist slogans such as "freedom, equality, and dignity for all" and "Christian and Muslims are united against oppression." The powerful and well-organized Islamic youth leaders who used the media and the internet to send their messages nationally, region-ally, and globally illustrated to all that they are capable of politi-cal strategy and of carefully negotiating their demands without compromising their constituencies. Youth leaders in Yemen utilized their Islamic religious values and norms to ensure discipline and order in their marches. For example, organizers decided to separate the marches by gender, accommodated the prayer times and coordinated their marches based on the Friday prayer, in a number of cases declared fasting, and, when attacked by the security forces, sought shelter in the mosques.[14]

Myth 5 The formula of nonviolence cannot be indigenous. Neither Egyptian nor Tunisian protesters followed a Western formula of nonviolent resistance campaigns, as some have argued in the wake of their revolutions.[15] Indeed, throughout the last decade there have been training workshops in nonviolence and tools for democratic change in both societies. However, the spontaneous organizing and the creative strategies and actions deployed in dealing with the ruling elite and regime illustrate that Arab and Muslim societies are rich in indigenous cultural and religious sources (rituals, values, and symbols) that can be woven into the making and sustaining of principled nonviolent movements. This insight into the local expressions of nonviolence, particularly its principled and religious features (the integration of Islamic symbols and rituals in the nonviolent protest campaigns – slogans, pictures, days of strikes) is instructive, especially for Western civil societies and government departments that have supported local Arab and Muslim civil society groups and projects with the aim of exporting models of social and political change through their funding of certain approaches or individuals.[16]

Arab nonviolent movements are not based on a "principled approach"

The various Arab revolutions or movements have varied in their level and degree of adopting nonviolent strategies. Nevertheless, in each of the revolts since 2010 there have been groups and voices that managed to systematically insist on using nonviolent means. In the Tunisian case, such groups were in the majority and managed to bring the regime down with the least blood and violence, while the Syrian experience of nonviolent revolt was overwhelmed by the brutal reaction of the regime as well as by the armed militant groups fighting against it. In between these two extremes, the leaders of the masses in Egypt, Bahrain, and Yemen managed to exhibit a significant degree of discipline and strategic planning in carrying out their peaceful protests.

The question and assumption of whether leaders and activists are fully convinced and adhere to the "principled nonviolent approach" seems an irrelevant and unrealistic measure to utilize when reflecting on the success of these revolutions. In fact, it might be problematic to expect millions of people in Egypt, Yemen, or Tunisia to adhere totally to a unified and spiritually guided principled nonviolent framework, considering the nature and scope of their regimes' oppression, the nature of the leadership, and the historical experiences and context. When all leaders and followers are fully devoted to principled nonviolence, then discipline is easier to maintain and violence by rulers is more likely to backfire. However, such expectations are not realistic and should not be used to judge or evaluate the success or failure of the movement. The sole measurement for success should be the ability of these groups to strategically plan and equip their followers with the capacity to withstand the pressure from outside to pick up arms and abandon the nonviolent approach. Is it possible to achieve such an outcome without the principled approach? Without a doubt, yes, and many examples demonstrate the possibility of regime change through strategic nonviolent approaches.

In the context of the Arab revolutions, principled nonviolent voices were certainly visible among leaders and followers (for example, Jawdat Said in Syria, Egyptian imams and priests who sat in Tahrir Square in Egypt, the Nobel Prize Laureate Tawakkol Karman from Yemen); however, they did not constitute the dominant voices. The discourse and narrative of the protesters' leaders does not indicate a particularly principled approach, especially an Islamic principled nonviolent approach. In fact, one can argue that the masses in the Arab world gradually "rediscovered" their power to replace their dictatorial regimes. However, this rediscovery was not based on a deep conviction in an Islamic or non-Islamic "principled nonviolence approach" but, rather, was rooted in at least three realizations: the regime will not change by itself (reform); the masses have no other means to confront the regime except by thousands pouring into the street to disable the current system; and it is possible to do this.

Unfortunately, the leaders and masses in all the cases did not have plans for the day after the collapse of the regime. Thus, we are witnessing a great deal of post-revolution aftershock, confusion, and even descent into violent confrontation between various forces who are competing to shape the future of these societies. This reality is a product of many factors that affected and shaped the revolutions in these societies. The lack of a comprehensive nonviolent strategy is only one of the factors that contributed to the backlash dynamics.

Conclusion

It is impossible to unlink Arab nonviolent movements from Islamic and Christian religious identity, as reflected in the discourse, symbols,

Box 3.1 The Syrian Gandhi

Jawdat Said was one of the most renowned principled nonviolent religious leaders in the Arab and Muslim world. After a six-month speaking tour in 2012 in the United States and Canada, the 81-year-old returned to his homeland of Syria to resume his fight against the Syrian regime. Sheikh Said has written many books and articles about the Islamic spiritual and religious foundations that support nonviolent resistance. His book *Be Like the Son of Adam* is one of the best-recognized publications in Arabic that outlines the theological principles of Islamic nonviolence. Sheikh Said not only preached for over fifty years (since 1966, when he published his book *The Problem of Violence in Islamic Action*), but he has practiced his preaching by opposing the Assad family regime since the early 1980s, having been jailed many times. In 2000, when he voted "No" in the referendum for Bashar al-Assad, an official retrieved his "No" vote and replaced it with a "Yes." When Sheik Said protested, he was again arrested.

Sheikh Said's influence on the Syrian nonviolent opposition was clear in the early phase of the revolt, when many of his followers organized marches and protest campaigns in the town of Dara'a. Several of his followers were killed by the Syrian regime in the initial months of the revolution, including Ghiyath Matar, a 26-year-old who was arrested September 26, 2011, and, according to Human Rights Watch, tortured to death.

Jawdat Said opposed the use of arms by both the Free Syrian Army and government forces and called for the elimination of all weapons. In March 2012 he appealed to Islamic religious principles and beliefs when he opposed the claim that the Syrian opposition has the moral right to use arms in fighting against the regime, stating, "Those who refuse to see still believe in the power of arms. These people believe in the power of arms and not in the power of truth." Such a principled stand in the midst of a war that saw many atrocities carried out by the Syrian regime against civilians reflects the power of conviction in principled nonviolence by which Sheik Said lived until his death in 2012.

and organizing methods of the activists. Organizers of these movements and campaigns managed to integrate their call for peaceful marches and resistance with local religious and cultural identities. In fact, without the religious symbols and discourse, neither secular nor religious leaders could mobilize their constituencies to march behind them against the oppressive regimes. In the case of Islamic contexts, the question is not whether religious symbols and discourse can be utilized in mobilizing and sustaining the masses, but rather to what extent religious discourse is utilized to promote a principled or strategic nonviolent framework. By using religious frameworks to mobilize nonviolent resistance, organizers in some cases (if not aware) might contribute to the formation and cementation of sectarian and religious identities that already exist in such societies. In addition, over-utilization of religious symbols and identities in such campaigns often excludes the non-religious or secular voices in the society. Thus, in principled or strategic nonviolent movements, the scope, nature, and intensity of religious references should be measured carefully and deployed wisely for the service of the campaigns.

Recent evidence from Middle Eastern cases (Egypt, Tunisia, Yemen, Syria, and Jordan) indicates that activists in each of these contexts have opted to use strategic forms of nonviolent resistance instead of promoting principled nonviolent frameworks. Examples of such strategic decisions can be seen in the heavy reliance on military and security forces in dealing with the secular opposition groups who became a minority after the regimes collapsed. In addition, several members of the Egyptian Muslim Brotherhood have resorted to violent strategies in the wake of President Morsi's removal by the military. Also, a significant part of the Muslim Brotherhood discourses in these societies has been focused on justice and punitive measures against previous regimes' security forces. The discourse rarely relates to values of compassion, forgiveness, or reconciliation. On the contrary, Brotherhood sympathizers utilize fear and punishment in their speeches against the police and soldiers who opposed them. Such strategies of resistance push followers away from a principled nonviolent approach toward a temporary and less committed or disciplined strategic of nonviolence.

The clear choice of strategic nonviolence by many Muslim Brotherhood followers and leaders as well as secular opposition groups should not lead us to underestimate the historical breakthrough of having millions of Muslims and Christians in the Arab world marching peacefully beside each other to overthrow a dictatorship. It is also important to emphasize the creativity in generating nonviolent strategies and methods by religiously motivated protesters who improvised new ways to express their dissent, anger, and victimhood against their own security forces and political dictatorship with incredible energy and spontaneity. In addition, there are many individuals who joined and operated in these various movements in Egypt, Tunisia, Yemen, and Syria who are disciplined and committed to principled nonviolence (leaders such as Khalis Jalabi and Jawdat Said in Syria, Tawakul Karman in Yemen, and others).

The above achievements are indicators of the need to demythologize perceptions of the nature of Arab and Muslim societies by both Muslims and non-Muslims. Peaceful and nonviolent religious believes marching by the thousands is a new image that should be crucial to revising government policies in the Arab world, Europe, and the

United States on how to respond to religiously motivated protest movements and political opposition. The greatest challenge that faces Egyptians, Tunisians, Libyans, and Yemenis is that of maintaining the gains of their revolutions and sustaining the national energy and solidarity generated by their powerful and transforming nonviolent resistance campaigns. Nonetheless, from the perspective of a non-violent paradigm, the Egyptian, Tunisian, and other ongoing social and political campaigns for peaceful change in the Arab world have provided another powerful historical example to counter the realist paradigm in international relations.[17] The global culture of nonvio-lence has certainly gained at least a few more successful examples to prove that people power mustered for change is more humane, and far less costly, than bombs.

A number of conclusions can be drawn from this discussion of the Arab Spring and principled nonviolence resistance. First, regardless of the nature of the nonviolent movement (principled or strategic), there is a crucial need for peace and nonviolent activists to develop compre-hensive planning and capacity-building skills to guide the transition from one political reality to the other. Second, in a context such as the Arab Spring, the utilization of religious identities (symbols, rituals, and beliefs) is necessary to mobilize a majority of the public to endorse nonviolent methods. Generic, universalist, and humanist appeals or discourses speak to only part of the public; a majority still need a religious and cultural contextualization for nonviolence resistance. Third, the use of principled nonviolence approaches is certainly more effective in maintaining the nonviolent discipline that discredits dictatorial regimes when they resort to violence; however, it is unre-alistic to expect that the majority of people will abide by, believe in, and internalize such an approach. The strategic nonviolence approach tends to be the primary framework of operation among the masses or even a majority of the leaders. Fourth, further research is needed to explore the conditions and structures that bring the masses and a majority of elite leaders to adopt principled rather than strategic approaches to nonviolence.

Questions for discussion

1 What is the relationship between religion and nonviolence?
2 How might a principled nonviolent approach have changed the dynamics or outcomes of some of the Arab uprisings?
3 What myths exist in the West regarding the possibility of nonvio-lence in the Middle East, and what are their limitations?

4 What are the strengths and weaknesses of the principled approach to nonviolence?

Suggestions for further reading and research

Appleby, Scott (2000) *The Ambivalence of the Sacred: Religion, Violence, and Reconciliation.* Lanham, MD: Rowman & Littlefield.

Cavanaugh, William T. (2009) *The Myth of Religious Violence: Secular Ideology and the Roots of Modern Conflict.* Oxford: Oxford University Press.

Deats, Richard (2009) *Active Nonviolence across the World.* www.peaceworkersus.org/ media/documents/active_nonviolence_across_the_world.pdf [updated version of "The Global Spread of Active Nonviolence," *Fellowship* (July–August 1996)].

Nojeim, Michael (2004) *Gandhi and King: The Power of Nonviolent Resistance.* Westport, CT: Praeger.

CHAPTER 4

Tactical and Strategic Approaches to Nonviolence

Howard Clark[1]

"Violence," writes Jonathan Schell, "is a method by which the ruthless few can subdue the passive many. Nonviolence is a means by which the active many can overcome the ruthless few" (Schell 2003, p. 23). Schell expresses well one of the central claims of advocates of nonviolence. Yet it is only part of the story. My overall argument, writing not only as a scholar of nonviolent action but also as an activist and advocate, is that pragmatic nonviolence is not just about "the masses" or about following leaders and the strategies they ordain. Rather it is about highly motivated people taking up concrete initiatives on their own account, making their own meanings from their context. In addition, whatever power non-cooperation has to restrain or undermine an adversary, there needs to be an equal emphasis on the process of popular empowerment – that is, of acting together and generating "cooperative power." This involves the power of communication in its many forms, including the power of counter-information to official "truths"; the power to organize, reach out, and make alliances with people and other groups; the power to disrupt and defy; and the power simply to do things differently, showing an alternative to an existing oppressive system and developing new centers of power in society.

This chapter focuses on the role of nonviolent action in situations where "success" seemed remote but pragmatic activists asked, "What can we do now?" Beginning with the kind of repression exercised under military dictatorships, it will pay particular attention to the emergence of pockets of resistance under the Chilean military dictatorship. The second case discussed, Kosovo in the 1990s, is a situation that culminated in war and international military intervention. Its key interest for the study of nonviolent action is that the conditions for nonviolent struggle were not at all promising. In particular, the oppressive regime did not depend on the oppressed population, and therefore the most powerful weapon in the nonviolent armory – the mass withdrawal of cooperation – had little leverage, a situation that currently obtains in Palestine, Papua, Tibet, and the Western Sahara (see chapter 5 for more on the Western Saharan case).

The term "pragmatism" in discussions of nonviolence is usually taken to indicate the use of nonviolent methods on grounds of effectiveness rather than out of a philosophy of nonviolence. This chapter, however, also applies "pragmatism" to the style of activism. When American community organizer Saul Alinsky urged pragmatism, the point was that "you do what you can with what you've got" (Alinsky 1971, p. 138).

Pragmatism and principle

Most examples of nonviolent action in social struggles before Gandhi – such as strikes in the labor movement, boycotts, or the kind of disruptive disobedience seen in the cause of women's suffrage – were "pragmatic" in origin. Each in its context was considered to be an effective way to challenge those in power and collectively advance a cause, generally without resorting to violence, although this was rarely a matter of principle.

Relatively few movements have adopted a strategy of nonviolence from a pacifist position of rejecting the use of arms in all circumstances. Usually their view is either that there is not really an armed option or that nonviolence is worth trying. This might grow into a *strategic* commitment, and it may become part of the ethos of the movement. Gandhi and Martin Luther King, Jr., the two personalities most associated with *principled* nonviolence, both seem to have turned to nonviolent action for pragmatic reasons, Gandhi campaigning against discrimination in South Africa, and King when thrust to the forefront in the 1956 Montgomery bus boycott. Their philosophical commitment and principled understanding of how to wage nonviolent conflict grew out of their practice and reflection.

Common pragmatic reasons why movements adopt a policy of nonviolence include the following.

- Other methods have reached an impasse, whether legal processes have revealed the grievance group's institutional powerlessness or armed struggle has proved ineffective.
- Violence is more likely to provoke brutal reprisals.
- Nonviolent methods are more accessible and encourage mass participation, unlike conventional channels, which favor privileged groups, or armed struggle, which is confined to those with weapons or physical means.
- Nonviolence overcomes the threshold of fear by offering an array of methods, from "heroic" (high-risk) to "non-heroic" (low-risk).

- Nonviolent methods are seen as more democratic and legitimate, therefore more likely to appeal to potential allies within the society and internationally.
- Nonviolent action has succeeded elsewhere.
- The nonviolence of the *means* is more in line with desired *ends* such as democratization or respect for human rights.
- Nonviolence resonates with an ethos in the cultural context, such as the concept of *sumud* (steadfastness) in Palestinian culture.

Gandhi came to see nonviolence as a philosophy of life, demanding high standards of principled practitioners. However, aware that most members of the Indian National Congress were less principled, he convinced this mass movement to adopt a less exacting, more pragmatic version – nonviolence as a policy or expedient. He argued that "Nonviolence being a policy means that it can upon due notice be given up when it proves unsuccessful or ineffective. But . . . whilst a particular policy is pursued, it must be pursued with all one's heart" (Gandhi 1999, Vol. 26, p. 248). It must be "of the truthful" (ibid., p. 293), and those engaged should follow a code of discipline (a sample code is included in Bondurant 1965, pp. 38–9).

Subsequently a school of advocacy for "pragmatic" nonviolence has grown up, building on the work of Gene Sharp and also exemplified by Ackerman and Kruegler (1994) and Helvey (2004). Sharp sometimes refers to nonviolent action as "a means of combat" (Sharp 1990b, p. 37). With skill and consistent adherence, the "nonviolent weapons system" can, he argues, "turn the opponent's violence and repression against his own power position" (Sharp 1973, p. 112). Sharp's most important book is the three-volume *The Politics of Nonviolent Action* (1973). The first volume revolves around the argument that tyrannical power can be defeated by popular non-cooperation. The second volume describes 198 methods illustrating nonviolent action and grouped under the headings "Protest and Persuasion," "Non-cooperation" (social, economic and political), and "Nonviolent Intervention," meaning acts of disruption to challenge the status quo or acts of construction to present alternatives. The third and longest volume, *The Dynamics of Nonviolent Action*, addresses a range of strategic questions. Sharp explicitly limits this discussion to contexts of mass action, usually involving non-cooperation, where developed movements have a recognizable leadership structure. Ackerman and Kruegler (1994) build on this by proposing twelve principles of strategic nonviolent conflict, which Ackerman has subsequently simplified to three essential characteristics for effectiveness – planning, unity, and nonviolent discipline

– while former US army colonel Helvey brings a military perspective on combat decision-making and guidance on making a detailed strategic assessment of the potential strengths and weak points of those in conflict.

Unfortunately, these insights offer little to groups where there is not yet a movement, or who are outside the mainstream of a movement, or where the movement has been suppressed or is stagnating, having lost hope and direction. In repressive contexts, practical organizing is likely to begin by devising means of communication and meeting and to be based in the wellspring of a movement – its motivation, its values, its collective identity – and build from there.

Marshall Ganz presents motivation as the most important component of what he calls "strategic capacity." Arguing that strategic capacity itself is the most vital component in the effectiveness of a movement (see chapter 8), Ganz identifies this capacity as deriving from motivation, combined with a movement's ability to learn as it goes and its access to "salient knowledge" – including understanding of its own support base and potential and possible points for leverage. Referring back to the activist "pragmatism" of Alinsky, whose starting point was "you do what you can with what you have," Ganz presents strategy as "how we turn what we have into what we need to get what we want" (Ganz 2009, p. 8). In contrast to the rather linear strategic approach of Sharp, Ackerman, and Helvey, Ganz argues that "strategy is a verb – something you do, not something you have. An ongoing interactive process of experimentation, learning and adaptation. Because the unknown is almost by definition such a big factor in social movements, we often can't get the information we need to make good strategic choices until we begin to act" (ibid., p. 10).

Box 4.1 Context specificity

The Polish ginger groups that emerged in the mid-1980s during the period when Solidarność had lost direction – such as the Orange Alternative (see chapter 8) and Freedom and Peace – often used the term *konkretny*, which translates as concrete or practical (or even pragmatic, were it not for the connotations of "lack of principle" in colloquial uses of "pragmatism"). Padraic Kenney (2002) argues that they revitalized a stagnant struggle, demonstrating that pragmatic activism in nonviolent struggle is not following a template determined by a central committee but rather being motivated to experiment in one's own context.

Pragmatism: Beneath the radar

Before the emergence of any public movement, there is – especially in repressive societies – a period of rather disorganised disquiet. Scott (1990) has written of "hidden transcripts" through which subordinated groups "negate" the hegemonic official narratives, referring on various occasions to the thinking of Václav Havel, who, as a dissident in communist Czechoslovakia, had stressed the importance of a "hidden sphere," of "parallel structures" where people would not live the lie required by authoritarian communism. Clearly such an approach has much to offer the study of pragmatic nonviolence about the conditions under which overt resistance can emerge, an area which Sharp observed in 1973 was under-researched but could be especially important "for political situations which make it difficult to organize nonviolent action on a large scale" (1973, p. 462).

Some of the forms of everyday resistance listed by Scott tend to be individualistic – for example, poaching – and can be seen less as challenging the patterns of domination than coping with them. However, there is clearly scope for everyday activities to consciously build up a sense of common purpose and mutual support. This can be seen in the work of social movement scholar Hank Johnston, who has tried to model the evolution of resistance under authoritarian regimes, in cases largely drawn from the Baltic states of the Soviet Union and Franco's Spain (Johnston 2011, pp. 97–135). Johnston suggests there is a progression of protest forms: submerged opposition under a totalitarian regime might be expressed in jokes and grumbling with people you trust; these trusted contacts later extend into hidden networks capable of further expansion; it becomes possible to set up or take over apparently innocuous and apolitical associations (literary or cultural circles, hobby clubs, church groups, Scouts) and convert them into spaces where opposition can grow; these might be "duplicitous" associations (formally serving one purpose while in reality pursuing others), or they might be spaces which enjoy a certain institutional protection, such as churches in some societies.

From these associations and networks emerges defiance: perhaps at a low level, such as graffiti or flag-flying, or in using official events as opportunities to express public feelings. (For instance, during the Uruguayan dictatorship, the crowd at international football matches would be rather subdued in singing the national anthem until they approached the chorus, when they would roar the phrase "tyrants tremble" (Crawshaw and Jackson 2010, pp. 8–9.) Open defiance emerges, sometimes with what Johnston calls "hit and run

Box 4.2 Laying the foundations: Gandhi's campaigns of "constructive work"

Perhaps Gandhi's most painful experience was the "Himalayan miscalculation," which convinced him to prioritize constructive work. In 1919 Gandhi called an all-India campaign against British repressive legislation, the Rowlatt Acts. This descended into protester violence – spontaneous and organized – and British reprisals. Despite Gandhi's previous local successes and his painstaking preparations, there was neither the organizational infrastructure nor the nonviolent discipline necessary for India-wide civil disobedience. As Bob Overy argues, "Gandhi's principal response to the Rowlatt débâcle was to devise an additional method of mobilizing civilians on a mass scale which fell far short of civil disobedience and other methods of civil resistance. This was to initiate a coordinated program of constructive work" (2002, p. 133).

This constructive work initially had three themes – *swadeshi* (home production), promoting communal harmony (Hindu–Muslim), and removing "untouchability" and other social evils. It expanded throughout Gandhi's life, and indeed beyond. Some commentators present this as an expression of "right living," and its ambition was certainly to begin "building a new social order within the shell of the old." Yet for Gandhi it also fulfilled a range of immediate strategic functions.

Constructive work would instill patience and discipline for the struggle ahead. It would nurture unity across religious, caste, and class distinctions, linking the urban elite with the great majority of the population living in villages. And, in building the movement and its organizational strength, it would specifically address the issue of scale: "if it was impossible to rely on inexperienced *satyagraha* leaders to launch civil resistance campaigns across the continent, what [Gandhi] could do with much less risk was to invite them to introduce the nation to campaigns of constructive work" (Overy 2002, p. 134).

actions" – graffiti are again the most universal low-risk example, while the provocations of the feminist punk band Pussy Riot in Russia are a recent high-risk example. This pattern of gradual escalation, building on foundational "constructive work," low-risk actions, and submerged networks, is evident in the cases of Chile and Kosovo.

Chile

The gestation of protest in Pinochet's Chile is now well documented, although not in the literature on nonviolence. Pinochet's rule began with a reign of terror in which the military regime attempted to eradicate opposition, ultimately killing more than 3,000 opponents. Some died publicly and became symbols, such as singer Victor Jara; many simply disappeared. Other opponents tried to help each other survive, while a few began documenting human rights violations and connecting with international human rights networks. Church-sponsored "humanitarian programs" afforded some cover – and later funding – for activists to develop projects promoting mutual support and solidarity. Such programs began with material needs, especially for families of the disappeared or people dismissed from their work, and ranged from kitchens, community gardens, and food cooperatives to income-generating projects, such as cooperative laundries (Fruhling 1992).

The first sewing circle began as early as 1974, bringing together fourteen women who had had loved ones detained or disappeared. They began transforming recycled rags into *arpilleras* (tapestries), expressing their experience of life under dictatorship, their (suppressed rather than "hidden") transcripts.[2] Church contacts then smuggled these out of the country for sale to the international solidarity movement, as a source of income for the *arpilleristas* and political education internationally. More groups formed in Santiago and further afield, a powerful yet covert network of mutual support under the auspices of the Catholic Church's Vicaría de Solidaridad but with their own structures of coordination. These *arpilleristas* founded the Association of Relatives of the Detained Disappeared and organized the first public protests – such as fasts or chain-ins demanding information about the disappeared – and many were arrested on multiple occasions for their persistence. From the pain of the *arpilleristas* grew a powerful form of communication, and quite naturally from one form of creativity grew others – music, song, and dance.

Several years passed before there were mass nonviolent protests – the *jornadas de protesta* (protest days) that aimed to show that mass "non-heroic" protest was possible (Martinez 1992). The first was an intense experience in a society that had not seen mass protest for a decade, including "nonviolent activities such as banging on pots and pans at a specified hour, honking car horns, boycotting stores and markets, and keeping children home from school. Political and social leaders held unauthorized public meetings in public plazas as symbolic acts of dissent, and industrial workers staged work slowdowns" (Arriagada 1988, p. 56). The *jornadas* were repeated four more times in 1983, but, as regime repression again hardened, the protests themselves began to lose discipline and by 1984 had degenerated into a routinized violence. They nevertheless had succeeded in showing what was possible, producing some loss of fear, while also beginning the process of increasing press freedom. Two elements of the success of the *jornadas* stemmed directly from the networks built up by social programs. First, the *jornadas* spread from their initially middle-class base to poor neighborhoods as a result of these networks (Huneeus 2009), and, second, they were particularly creative in some poor neighborhoods, where groups blocked off roads to declare "liberated zones" for street theater, music, and other performances (Aliaga Rojas, 2012, p. 23).

During this period of the *jornadas de protestas*, there emerged a new disciplined form of "lightning" nonviolent actions, involving *arpilleristas*. The Movement Against Torture was initiated by a network of radical Christians in September 1983, and later that year incorporated the name of Sebastian Acevedo (MCTSA) to honor a worker who died by public self-immolation, demanding to know the whereabouts of his son and daughter. MCTSA was a coalition drawing on former detainees, *arpilleristas*, and other family members of the detained and disappeared, radical Christians, and others. Although it was open to all, its purpose was "to test the potential of nonviolence" in a campaign against torture (Vidal 2002, p. 89). Therefore it adopted some simple guidelines for the actions: no aggression by action or word against the police; not to resist detention but to try to accompany those detained; not to flee from the police but to stay in place until the action is ended.

Most actions lasted a few minutes, taking place at sites implicated with torture – the first, and most frequent, was the headquarters of the intelligence agency, the CNI (Central Nacional de Informaciones). Activists would arrive at an agreed time – about seventy people for the first action, often more than 100 in later actions, and more than 500 on one occasion. They would unfurl a big banner with that day's slogan and stop the traffic. Other standard elements of the "liturgy" were the Song – "Yo te nombro libertad" – and the Denunciation – a call-and-response declamation about that day's protest site. When police arrived to disperse the protesters, often two activists would deliberately wait to be detained, thereby establishing in the police record (and for official news media) that the action had actually happened. Each action was accompanied by an open letter to the head of the target institution and a press release.

In the six and a half years of its existence, the MCTSA organized 178 actions in Santiago de Chile, while in other cities parallel groups adopted the same basic format for similar actions. The gradual escalation from the hidden transcripts of the *arpilleristas* to the small-scale demonstrations and then days of protest reflects the trajectory from submerged opposition to open defiance described above, and illustrates how low-risk, less visible "constructive work" laid the foundation that made later mobilization possible.

Kosovo[3]

Kosovo, with a population of roughly 2 million, about 90 percent Albanian, had for fifteen years participated as an equal in Yugoslav federal institutions when, in 1989, Serbia unconstitutionally annulled this autonomy and adopted programs to "re-Serbianize" Kosovo. This was not yet military "ethnic cleansing" – that came with the war, especially in 1999 – but Kosovars faced brutal police harassment, mass dismissals from work, and a legislative program reverting to the days of systematic anti-Albanian discrimination and Serbian privilege.

When I first visited Kosovo in the winter of 1991–2, Kosovo Albanians were already proud of their nonviolent movement. They had a new identity as a people who refused to retaliate as Serb forces tried to provoke violence; instead of the socially backward stereotypes mocked in Serbian media, they were modern Europeans, practicing religious tolerance and committed to eradicate traits of their society such as the blood feud and women's illiteracy. Even while the numbers fired from work rose, they were showing they could organize their own market economy and were worthy of self-determination.

Kosovars were in the process of building unity and demonstrating popular will. A massive new party, the Democratic League for Kosova (LDK), cooperated with other recently formed parties in a Coordinating Committee of Political Parties to decide by consensus on next steps in the struggle. Most adults had signed a petition "For Democracy, Against Violence," which had been presented to the United Nations in 1990, and in September 1991 they had organized an illegal referendum on self-determination in which 87 percent of the electorate had voted. For most of the year, teachers had been working without pay, using the curriculum adopted under autonomy but now banned. In September, however, they and Albanian pupils were shut out of the schools, and every day police were at the school gates to violently disperse protesting parents.

Nobody could explain how the nonviolence had begun. The LDK, formed in December 1989, was initially skeptical about nonviolence: its founders' thinking was more in terms of an armed uprising. Nevertheless, arguments for nonviolence could be found in the recent success of "velvet revolutions" in communist countries, the calls for nonviolence from long-term political prisoners released after serving lengthy sentences, and perhaps above all in the growing perception that Milošević aimed to provoke war. The Kosovo Albanian intellectual Shkëlzen Maliqi observed that "nonviolence imposed itself" and then became a mark of identity (Maliqi 1998, p. 101).

From January 1992 onwards, Kosovo Albanians managed their own parallel school system, from primary school through to university, with around 300,000 students and 20,000 teachers. This was the flagship of the self-declared "Republic of Kosova" and the main recipient of the funds collected by the 1,000 volunteer "tax collectors" (dismissed state tax collectors). The LDK also established a "government-in-exile" collecting further "taxes" in the diaspora and engaging in propaganda. A humanitarian network, the Mother Teresa Association (MTA), had opened its first health clinic, offering free treatment to people of all ethnic groups, staffed by physicians dismissed by the Serbian authorities. By the end of 1997 they had a network of ninety-one clinics, including a gynecological unit, and 7,000 volunteers distributing humanitarian support. Such constructive activities were vital in maintaining the Albanian community and way of life in Kosovo, especially as the number of Albanians in employment plummeted. Of the 164,210 Albanians in employment in 1990, 146,025 (or 83 percent) would lose their jobs; all this was assiduously documented by the independent federation of trade unions formed during 1990. In May 1992, parallel elections for a president and parliament were held in which 900,000 people voted.

This phase of nonviolent struggle (1990–3) surpassed all expectations: uniting the Albanian community (Muslim and Catholic, traditionalist and modernist); pinning responsibility for violence on Belgrade; and establishing a base of self-organization. The people, it seemed, were united, determined, and organized, refusing to be provoked into violence despite the brutality of the Serbian police force and its paramilitary auxiliaries. Whenever there was an incident of violence, such as a police raid on a village, experienced activists – either from the LDK or from the Council for the Defence of Human Rights and Freedoms in Kosovo – would arrive, interceding if the police were still there, to try to calm the situation and document what happened, and also to explain that this attempt to provoke violence should be resisted. The LDK's Ibrahim Rugova "presided" over a rudimentary state, with education, health, tax, and information departments. It seemed the whole population was "on message" in support of the nonviolent struggle, and those with doubts either joined in, doing what they could, or went into exile.

Although Kosovo had lost its traditional allies against Serbia when Slovenia and Croatia achieved independence and agreed not to interfere in rump Yugoslavia's "internal issues," Kosovo made new international alliances through mobilizing the diaspora and participating in transnational networks. If Albania was the only state to recognize the

Republic of Kosova, by the end of 1992 there were clear gains internationally. The CSCE (the Conference for Security and Cooperation in Europe, forerunner of the OSCE) established a mission in Kosovo and undertook to mediate negotiations on education, while in December the US unilaterally threatened military action if Belgrade launched a new human rights crackdown, a threat repeated by the Clinton administration in February 1993.

The general perception among Kosovo Albanians was that they could do little to affect the situation in Serbia proper. Various contacts were maintained with democratic oppositionists in Serbia, while there was little hope that oppositionists in Serbia would exercise significant influence. There were signs in the mid-1990s that Serbia was growing weary of war and even that sections of the Serbian elite in Belgrade were resigned to losing Kosovo, though not yet ready to take the political risk of making this public. In Kosovo itself, however, there were rising complaints of "stagnation" in the struggle, and there was widespread frustration that the 1995 Dayton agreements (that ended the war in Bosnia) offered Kosovo nothing.

Ibrahim Rugova was not alone in interpreting the refusal to be provoked as "don't take risks," but he faced mounting criticism for his "passive" approach, especially on two questions. The demobilization of Kosovars can be dated back to a moratorium on demonstrations; inside Kosovo, this was explained as "a strategic pause." However, it was not lifted for five long years. Rugova also made nonsense of the parallel parliamentary elections of May 1992 by not convening the parliament. Those illegal elections had been an empowering experience. Yet, instead of escalating from that to pose to Milošević the dilemma of "let this parliament function or show the brutality of direct rule from Belgrade," Rugova retreated. Those most exposed would have been the 130 parliamentarians, the people who had competed to be named the people's representatives and who therefore should have been most willing to shoulder that risk.

Even on constructive activities, the prevailing attitude was overcautious. Although the Mother Teresa healthcare network was constantly expanding and improving and began to access international funding, the education system was stuck: overcrowded facilities were common, and outdated curricula led to frustration. Another critical problem was the hemorrhaging of money spent on importing goods that could have been produced in Kosovo. In contrast to the centrality of Gandhi's promotion of *swadeshi* (homespun production) or the Palestinians' widespread "household economy" policy during the first *intifada*, only one small group (Home Economics, cooperating with the Rural Women's Network) initiated income-generating activities. Various other practical proposals were simply ignored or delayed until it was too late.

An active nonviolent movement has perpetually to explore the spaces for action. Instead, after the 1992 parallel elections, the Coordinating Council of Political Parties became irrelevant, the LDK monopolized leadership, Rugova himself became more remote, and anyone invoking "unity" was likely to be stifling diversity and initiative. Women were central to the constructive work around education and health and campaigned with energy and initiative, yet only two women became prominent through the LDK, and they were not part of Rugova's inner circle. Meanwhile, the LDK youth organization (upper age limit thirty) was excluded from representation on the party's governing council. This was a recipe for how to *diminish* strategic capacity: "increase homogeneity, reduce accountability to constituents, suppress deliberative dissent, and disrupt cycles of learning" (Ganz 2009, p. 19).

In 1997, however, something different did happen. The Kosovo Albanian students' union UPSUP defied the moratorium on demonstrations to organize a march to "reclaim" university buildings. Summoned to see Rugova, they refused politely but firmly to change their plan, saying that as Kosovars they respected him as their president, but as students they insisted on having the human right to education. They invited supporters to quietly join the customary evening promenade on Pristina's main street. The response was so great that it alarmed the diplomatic community in Belgrade. The highest-ranking delegation yet to visit Kosovo – twelve ambassadors – asked UPSUP to desist, inadvertently confirming the latter's belief that the way to make the world notice was not to follow the "softly, softly" advice that diplomats gave Rugova but to stir things up.

For the opening of the university year, October 1, students carefully planned a nonviolent march to the university buildings, consisting of 15,000 students in white shirts or sweaters, following a code of nonviolent discipline, with some 30,000 supporters at the roadside. When it reached the police line the march halted, but the participants refused to disperse. When the police attacked with truncheons and tear gas, the front rows stayed on their feet as long as they could – their courage impressing onlookers, including the international and Serbian press.

Suddenly, UPSUP students were the heroes of Kosovo. Even Rugova praised them. The diplomats too changed tack, some inviting UPSUP to send delegations to their countries. In Serbia new potential allies came forward: there had already been discreet contacts between

UPSUP and Belgrade students, but now Belgrade students issued a public declaration supporting the human right to education and promising to travel to Pristina to observe the next UPSUP protest.

Unfortunately, this revitalization of nonviolent struggle happened too late to prevent war – the Kosovo Liberation Army was already organizing and, following the Drenica massacres a few months later in February–March 1998, would be joined by many students. These massacres included the slaughter not just of the extended family of KLA founder Adem Jashari but also of unarmed families following the earlier nonviolent policy – sit quietly at home without weapons. Such brutal slayings ended hope in nonviolent action, although there continued to be urban nonviolent protests as an adjunct to the fighting elsewhere.

The students' "active nonviolence" indicated a potential never fulfilled. The necessary shift from cautious defense to a nonviolent counter-offensive did not occur. This could have aimed to sow doubts among those carrying out repression, to exploit divisions within Serbia, and to convert international lip-service to human rights into effective measures of support.

There was a widespread assumption, shared in the early 1990s by Kosovo Albanians, that nonviolence is more likely than armed struggle to attract international support. This seemed to be the case for Kosovo when the US threatened air strikes against Serbia in 1992–3, and certainly Kosovar nonviolence was vital in convincing international bodies to denounce Serbian human rights violations. However, what became increasingly apparent was that – as the student protests would make plain – the West's goal was to keep Kosovo quiet, and there was no intention to support a persecuted people in a just nonviolent struggle. The US threats of 1992–3 coincided with the Kosovar moratorium on protests, and during the next five years, in which Kosovo was not protesting, far from rewarding Kosovars for their endurance and refusal to be provoked, neither the US nor any of its allies offered aid to the Kosovar parallel institutions. Instead, Western diplomats until 1998 lectured Kosovar leaders to abandon the demand for self-determination and accept autonomy under Serbia. In contrast, once the war began in 1998, they switched from denouncing the KLA as terrorist to treating it as a prospective ally, and in 1999 independence was suddenly on the international agenda. Regardless of any qualms about the criminal tendencies within the KLA, NATO saw no option other than to build it into its ally on the ground in the war with Serbia (Gow 2003, pp. 260–4).

Dealing with violence

One of the keys to success in nonviolent struggle is dealing with the opponent's willingness to use violence. Authors such as Sharp argue that a regime's violence against a resolute nonviolent movement can be brought to rebound against it – an effect he terms "political jiu-jitsu", and which Brian Martin more recently has incorporated into the concept of "backfire" (Martin 2007). In the events discussed here, this happened spectacularly with the UPSUP protest in October 1997, the only occasion when Kosovar activists deliberately courted brutal violence. A core group of UPSUP members were well prepared, standing side by side with people they trusted, and calculated that the police violence would "backfire" against the regime – as indeed it did. The subsequent images of police brutality and of the bloodstained white shirts of the students not only brought international condemnation, but even the patriarch of the Serbian Orthodox Church – the Serbian body most determined to preserve what is Serbian in Kosovo – for the first time condemned police brutality.

A strategy of nonviolent struggle might well include such confrontations to dramatize a long-term injustice. However, most nonviolent actions do not involve courting violence but rather seek to find ways to restrain regime violence and reduce its impact on the movement. This can entail adapting tactics to limit regime violence, recording the regime violence, supporting those subject to regime violence, or weakening the chain of repression. At the same time, the movement must strengthen its own capacity to maintain nonviolent discipline and adopt patterns of work that overcome fear.

Adapting tactics pragmatically to limit police violence has many dimensions. In moving from "unobtrusive" action to open defiance, it is common to look at relatively safe spaces – be that in a crowd at a sporting event, in a mass funeral, or sheltering in the relatively "protected" space of an institution such as a church; indeed, the first protests in Chile took place on church grounds. The timing of an action – both when it takes place and how long it lasts – can also affect the degree of police violence. The MCTSA planned its lightning actions for times when the maximum number of people would see them. Each action was planned to last just a few minutes, which did not eliminate police violence but at least rendered it gratuitous – unnecessary to disperse the protesters.

Documenting the violence can arouse moral outrage, rebounding against the opponent, costing them loss of public support, loss of legitimacy with allies, and even defections from the regime. The very process of documentation can convert attempted intimidation into a weapon against the regime and a source of strength. *Supporting those subject to attack* in Chile involved developing therapeutic responses to torture, distinct from conventional "trauma" treatment, and included supporting those whose loved ones had been detained or disappeared. Part of *weakening the chain of repression* is prompting questioning among agents of repression and seeking allies capable of inhibiting them.

Conclusion: movements that learn

Movements are not born fully fledged; they grow, adapt to their context (and its changes), and learn. In this chapter, we have seen movements pass through phases – of gestation, emergence, growth, repression, frustration – and regimes too pass through phases, from the reign of terror to attempts to regain legitimacy and consent. These contexts make distinct demands on movements, requiring an adaptability and a perpetual interaction between experience on the ground and the strategic choices made by the groups that constitute the movement.

The slogan "unity is strength" has largely been echoed in the literature on nonviolent action. Certainly, unity can be a source of strength, but movements also face the issue of how to organize themselves in ways that are open to innovation and experimentation. On the one hand lies the danger of "fragmentation," which, argues Wendy Pearlman (2012), referring mainly to Palestine, can make it impossible to pursue a coherent policy of nonviolence (see also Norman 2010). On the other lies the warning of Kosovo, where what I call "the dead hand of unity" of the LDK bred conformity, sidelined people with initiative – whether they were proposing protest, dialogue, or constructive activity – and postponed issues about the future organization of society. Pearlman suggests the term "cohesion," which lends itself better to the self-motivated and bottom-up cohering of various social forces.

As we have seen, the process of cohesion can begin when there is only "submerged" or "unobtrusive" opposition, as it did with the Chilean *arpilleristas*. For Gandhi, constructive work was a central means to cohesion: an expression of common purpose, a collective way of addressing everyday problems, and a pointer toward a future of self-rule. He especially turned to this as a form of organizational development when he found that issuing guidelines on nonviolence was not enough to establish a nonviolent discipline for protest. There was a sense, too, of cultural change, with practical and constructive nonviolent initiatives continually expanding to embrace new facets

– a process we also saw both in Chile and in the early years of the non-violent movement in Kosovo.

Neither the Chilean *arpilleras* and the subsequent MCTSA nor the Kosovo Albanian students of 1997 were in the mainstream of their respective movements. They were highly motivated groups who succeeded in harnessing emotional and moral indignation into concerted action. From their particular circumstances, they made a significant impact on their situations, in stimulating creativity and in raising the curtain of fear. They discovered untapped potentials and new points of leverage, becoming learning experiences not just for participants but for a much wider body of citizens and supporters.

Questions for discussion

1 How can a nonviolent movement balance unity with diversity?
2 The chapter discusses the importance of "constructive work" and building foundations for a sustainable movement. How do movement leaders and organizers decide when to move from low-level preparations to more confrontational tactics? What kinds of pressures might they encounter?
3 The MCTSA included activists from Marxist groups favoring armed struggle. How would you have viewed their participation?
4 It is often claimed that nonviolence helps attract international support. Yet the NATO states were not prepared to discuss Kosovo's independence until there was war. What does this tell us?

Suggestions for further reading and research

Burrowes, Robert (1996) *The Strategy of Nonviolent Defense: A Gandhian Approach.* Albany, NY: State University of New York Press.

Carter, April (2012) *People Power and Political Change: Key Issues and Concepts.* Abingdon: Routledge.

Ganz, Marshall (2009) *Why David Sometimes Wins: Leadership, Organization, and Strategy in the California Farm Worker Movement.* Oxford: Oxford University Press.

CHAPTER 5

Questions of Strategy

Stephen Zunes

Primarily nonviolent "people power" movements have played a significant role in the overthrow of authoritarian regimes in dozens of countries over the past three decades, forced substantial reforms in even more, and seriously challenged repressive or unjust systems in still others. These nonviolent insurrections are distinguished from armed struggles in that they are carried out by organized activists who, either consciously or by necessity, eschew the use of weapons of modern warfare. Nonviolent activists also distinguish themselves from participants in more conventional political movements by using tactics outside the normal political process, including strikes, boycotts, mass demonstrations, contestation of public space, tax refusal, destruction of symbols of government authority (such as official identification cards), refusal to obey official orders (such as curfew restrictions), and the creation of alternative institutions for recognizing political legitimacy and fostering social organization.

Until fairly recently, the assumption was that, while nonviolent action could be an effective strategy in challenging injustices within Western democracies – such as the civil rights struggle in the United States in the 1950s and 1960s – it was incapable of actually overthrowing a government or changing an entire political system, particularly if it involved toppling entrenched autocratic regimes that were willing to use force against peaceful demonstrators. Ousting such dictatorships seemed particularly challenging when they were supported by the United States, the Soviet Union, or other major powers. Most Western opponents of communist dictatorships as well as opponents of right-wing dictatorships assumed that repressive regimes could only be brought down through armed revolution or foreign invasion. History, however, has demonstrated that most dictatorships overthrown and replaced by more democratic systems have come as a result of movements by civil society engaging in strategic nonviolent action (Karatnycky and Ackerman 2005).

This chapter looks at successful and ongoing struggles by pro-democratic movements in the Global South. In particular, it examines two African anti-colonial struggles in which the national liberation movements, despite initially assuming victory would come through guerrilla warfare, turned to nonviolent action as the predominant form of resistance: South Africa, which suffered under the internal colonialism of a ruling white minority under the apartheid system, in which the resistance struggle was ultimately successful; and Western Sahara, initially under Spanish and later under Moroccan occupation, which is experiencing an ongoing struggle for independence. Most anti-colonial struggles, even those led by armed movements – such as those in Algeria and Mozambique – also had significant nonviolent components, though these are often lost in the historical narratives put forward by the victorious revolutionary vanguard parties (Bartkowski 2013b). South Africa and Western Sahara, however, are among the relatively few where there was a move from a reliance primarily on armed struggle to an engagement primarily in nonviolent struggle. They also serve as examples of movements which never espoused a commitment to principled nonviolence and never renounced their right to armed struggle, but recognized their chances of success would be enhanced through civil resistance rather than guerrilla warfare.

Anti-imperialist struggles

Colonialism and imperialism are, by their nature, violent. Imperialism comes through the guns, ships, planes, missiles, drones, and foreign troops of imperialist powers, as well as local collaborators. Challenging imperialist forces through conventional military means has virtually never worked for the peoples of Africa, Asia, Latin America, the Middle East, and other parts of the world subjected to imperialist aggression. As a result, the doctrine of asymmetrical warfare came into practice in the form of guerrilla warfare, where civil resistance movements, though they could not draw on stronger firepower, could rely on strong popular support. Chinese revolutionary leader Mao Zedong (1961, ch. 6) argued that revolutionaries needed to be to the people what fish are to the ocean. In the Vietnam War, the Vietnamese were able to win against enormous odds because the National Liberation Front (the "Vietcong") had the support of the vast majority of the people in the South Vietnamese countryside. The difficulty the United States was having in attempting to overcome them led Che Guevara (1967) to advocate for the launching of additional revolutionary movements that would likewise frustrate US hegemonic aspirations, calling for the creation of "two, three, many Vietnams."

There was a strong sense by anti-imperialists during this period that a popular armed revolution could never be defeated. However, there have always been real costs to these victories. In Vietnam, as many as 3 million people, primarily civilians, died during what they call the American War. Up to 7 million Vietnamese became internal refugees, most of the urban areas of the north were bombed to rubble, and bomb craters made whole sections of the countryside look like the surface of the moon. Defoliants destroyed millions of hectares of rainforest and farmland, leaving a toxic legacy through poisoned soil, deformed children, and chronic illness. Indeed, most countries which have undergone armed revolutions, even when the insurgency is victorious, are faced with large segments of the population being displaced, farms and villages destroyed, much of the nation's infrastructure severely damaged, the economy wrecked, and widespread environmental devastation. Vietnam, for example, is still affected greatly by the damage to its infrastructure and environment from the war that ended forty years ago, and the people are still suffering from its political, economic, social, and psychological consequences. The net result has been an increasing realization by those seeking revolutionary change that the benefits of waging an armed insurrection may not be worth the costs. And the methods of counter-insurgency warfare are even more deadly and effective today than they were forty years ago.

Another problem with armed struggle is that, once in power, victorious movements against dictatorships often fail to establish pluralistic, democratic, and independent political systems capable of supporting social and economic development and promoting human rights. Often these shortcomings result in part from counter-revolution, foreign intervention, trade embargoes, and other circumstances beyond a victorious popular movement's control. However, the choice of armed struggle as a means of securing power tends to exacerbate these problems and creates troubles of its own.

For one, armed struggle often promotes the ethos of a secret elite vanguard and a strict military hierarchy. Often disagreements that could be resolved peaceably in non-militarized institutions lead to bloody factional fighting. In some countries, such as Algeria and Guinea-Bissau, the more progressive elements of the revolutionary leadership fell victim to military coups not long after armed movements ousted European colonialists, and the new governments abandoned many of their progressive ideals and slid into authoritarianism. Other victorious armed anti-imperialist struggles, such as those in Angola and Mozambique, transformed into bloody civil wars.

Like any military organization, armed liberation movements are organized on an authoritarian model based upon martial values and an ability to impose their will through force. It is no accident that many guerrilla commanders, when they become civilian leaders of a new government, continue to lead in a similar autocratic manner. Empirical research has shown that the majority of dictatorships brought down by nonviolent struggle evolve into stable democracies within a few years, while dictatorships overthrown through armed struggle, in the vast majority of cases, tend to become further dictatorships, often with continued violence and instability (Chenoweth and Stephan 2011). To win any genuinely democratic struggle, the development of broad coalitions is critical. Unlike violent movements, a mass nonviolent movement cannot succeed without the support of the majority of the population. There has to be give and take within a movement in order to mobilize the broad constituency necessary to wage a collective struggle on such magnitude. In order to build that kind of support, it requires utilizing a pluralistic model of organization that could serve as a basis of more democratic and representative governance.

Nonviolent activists refuse to engage the repressive apparatus on the state's terms. Rather than staging a military confrontation, in which government forces would generally have a clear advantage, nonviolent insurgents choose their "weapons systems" with an eye toward winning popular support and making the regime's exercise of its power advantage a liability. Their efforts are aided by the fact that it is easier to mobilize people to demonstrate nonviolently than it is to ask them to pick up a gun or a hand grenade, a reality that creates a disequilibrium in which the unarmed group finds it easier to recruit supporters than does the government. Indeed, in a study on civil resistance of more than 300 struggles against autocratic regimes and foreign occupations or in support of secession over the past century, Erica Chenoweth and Maria Stephan (2011) noted that nonviolent struggles were more than twice as likely to succeed as armed struggles and, on average, in a far shorter period of time.

Although nonviolent conflict shares much with its violent counterpart, the differences between the two have an important impact on both the means and the consequences of a conflict. The theoretical assumptions underlying nonviolent struggle are significant and provide a challenge to a great deal of conventional thinking in the social sciences. The relative success of so many nonviolent social movements implies, as Gene Sharp noted, that political power is ultimately "fragile because it depends on many groups for reinforcement of its power sources" (Sharp 1973, Vol. 1, p. 8). Because "nonviolent action cuts off sources of [the regime's] power rather than simply combating the final power products of these sources," it poses a much more severe threat to a regime's authority than does armed rebellion (ibid., Vol. 3, p. 454). Furthermore, the success of nonviolent movements implies that power is more pluralistic. For example, even if the state has a monopoly on the tools of repression, it cannot successfully subjugate the population if they refuse to obey its dictates or recognize its authority. To the extent that this is true, it means that even the most oppressive regime rules to some degree by consent, particularly by actors such as police and soldiers. This assumption suggests that revolutions/revolts grow out of the disintegration of consent, not simply through the agitation of armed rebels.

However, some scholars familiar with civil resistance in authoritarian settings have argued that Sharp's theory of power relies too heavily on individual and voluntaristic behavior (Burrowes 1996; Martin 1989). For example, Souad Dajani (1995), in her pioneering study of the Palestinian *intifada*, acknowledges that nonviolent action can be a powerful and effective means of overcoming oppression, but she also argues that there are processes of marginalization, dependency, and integration that need to be taken into account. As a result, power sources within established social patterns and structures must be identified and described before people can effectively discredit them and mobilize opposition to repressive regimes. In short, Dajani and others consider Sharp's theory of "withdrawal of consent" an unsatisfactory explanation for why nonviolent movements succeed because it does not invite analysis of the structural roots of power in society.

According to Dajani, in order to tell the story of a movement, one must account for such factors as the roots of social movements, the power and resources available to the regime and the resistance, and the means available for changing power relationships. Cases show that only practitioners able to identify the structural and/or ideological sources of their opponents' power, as well as the political, social, economic, and ideological sources of power and methods available to them to target these sources of power, can conduct the kinds of successful nonviolent campaigns Sharp envisioned. Since there is so often an asymmetry of power between nonviolent activists and their opponents, it may be strategically necessary to target the political will of the opponent rather than its structures of control.

For example, leaders of the white minority in apartheid South Africa could have held on to power much longer than they did, but they recognized that the costs of doing so in the face of massive civil resistance in the black townships and international sanctions in support of the popular uprising outweighed the benefits of doing so indefinitely. Understanding the location and operation of power permits social movement leaders to better design and implement tactics of civilian resistance and better assess those tactics' efficacy.

Strategies, tactics, and dynamics of strategic nonviolent resistance

Much of the world's media attention on unarmed insurrections has tended to focus on the final days of a protracted struggle, when millions take to the streets or occupy a central square. However, these dramatic displays are usually the culmination of many years of organizing. Nonviolent struggle, like armed struggle, will succeed only if the resistance uses effective strategies and tactics. A guerrilla army cannot expect instant success through a frontal assault on the capital. They know they need to engage initially in small low-risk operations, such as hit and run attacks, and take the time to mobilize their base in peripheral areas before they have a chance of defeating the well-armed military forces of the state. Similarly, it may not make sense for a nonviolent movement to rely primarily on the tactic of massive street demonstrations in the early phases of a movement, but rather to diversify their tactics, understand and apply their own strengths, and exploit opportunities to mobilize support and increase the pressure on the regime.

Most successful unarmed insurrections have focused upon identifying and undermining the pillars of support for the regime. For example, in some cases these could include the ruling party, crony capitalists, the security services, the media, a particular demographic, and an allied foreign government. A movement need not destroy every pillar to bring down the government; if enough were simply weakened, they would no longer be able to withstand widespread popular resistance.

Recent years have demonstrated a growing awareness that nonviolent methods are far more effective in weakening such pillars of support and mobilizing the population in opposition. History has repeatedly demonstrated that armed resistance tends to solidify the pillars of the regime and alienate undecided elements of the population, who then seek security in the government. When facing a violent insurgency, a government can easily justify its repression. But force used against unarmed resistance movements usually creates greater sympathy for the government's opponents, whereby an opposition movement leverages state repression to advance the movement's ends.

This effect was seen repeatedly in the anti-apartheid struggle in South Africa, during which most of the white population was united against acts of "terrorism" committed by the armed wing of the African National Congress (ANC) but recoiled at the sight of unarmed black protesters being shot and brutally beaten. In addition, unarmed campaigns involve far more participants, taking advantage of a popular movement's majority support. The indigenous population of Western Sahara living under Moroccan occupation has recognized that they cannot just wait and hope for a renewal of the armed struggle by the Polisario Front (the exiled national liberation movement) or place their faith in stalled diplomatic efforts, but must actively resist the policies of the occupiers themselves. Yet another factor is that unarmed resistance also encourages the creation of alternative institutions, which further undermine the repressive status quo and form the basis for a new independent and democratic order, such as when residents of South Africa's black townships organized their own municipal governments, court system, and municipal services in place of those imposed by the apartheid regime.

Armed resistance often backfires by legitimizing the use of repressive tactics by the state. Violence from the opposition is often welcomed by authoritarian governments and even encouraged through the use of agents provocateurs, because it then justifies state repression. By contrast, state violence unleashed on unarmed dissidents often triggers a turning point in nonviolent struggles. A government attack against peaceful demonstrators can be the spark that transforms periodic protests into a full-scale insurrection. Even if the repression takes the form of a massacre that temporarily frightens oppositionists into pulling back from direct confrontation, it can undermine the credibility of the government, broaden the base of opposition nationally and internationally, and lay the basis for the reemergence of a movement later on. Encouraging defections from the government's side is important. Such defections are far more likely when troops are ordered to gun down unarmed protesters than when they are being shot at. Defection, however, is rarely a physical act of soldiers spontaneously throwing down their arms, crossing the battlefield, and joining the other side. Not everyone can do that. Sometimes defections come in the form of bureaucrats or officers degrading the effectiveness of the regime through quiet acts of non-cooperation, such as failing to carry out orders, causing key paperwork to disappear, deleting computer files, or leaking information to the other side.

Indeed, unarmed resistance movements also tend to sow divisions within pro-government circles for a number of reasons. First, disagreements surface internally regarding how to deal effectively with the resistance, since few governments are as prepared to deal with unarmed revolts as they are to quash armed ones. Violent repression of a peaceful movement can often alter popular and elite perceptions of the legitimacy of power, which is why state officials usually treat nonviolent movements less harshly. Second, some pro-government elements become less concerned about the consequences of a compromise with insurgents if their resistance is nonviolent. Unarmed movements increase the likelihood of defections and non-cooperation by unmotivated police and military personnel, whereas armed revolts legitimize the role of the government's coercive apparatus, enhancing its self-perception as the protector of civil society. The moral power of nonviolence is crucial in the ability of an opposition movement to reframe the perceptions of key parties – the public, political elites, and the military – most of whom have no difficulty supporting the use of violence against violent insurrections.

The efficacy of nonviolent resistance in dividing supporters of the status quo is apparent not just in rendering government troops less effective but also in challenging the attitudes of an entire nation and even foreign actors, as in the South African struggle against apartheid. Pictures of peaceful protesters – including whites, members of the clergy, and other "upstanding citizens" – broadcast on television worldwide lent legitimacy to anti-apartheid forces and undermined the South African government in a way that the armed rebellion was unable to do. As nonviolent resistance within the country escalated, external pressure in the form of economic sanctions and other solidarity tactics by the international community raised the costs of maintaining the apartheid system.

Due to increased global interdependence, the non-local audience for a conflict may be just as important as the immediate community. Just as Gandhi played to British citizens in Manchester and London, organizers of the civil rights movement in the American South were communicating to the entire nation, especially to the Kennedy administration, as well as to the rest of the world. Insurgency against the Soviet bloc was disseminated by television broadcasts that spread the news from country to country, legitimating local protests that no longer seemed like isolated events organized by unstable dissidents. The prominent role of the global media during the anti-Marcos "people power" movement in 1986 was instrumental in forcing the US government to scale back its support of the Philippine dictator. Israeli repression of the largely nonviolent protests by Palestinians during the late 1980s had a similar effect on Americans, whose perception is significant given the role of both private citizens and the US government in sustaining Israel's military and economic infrastructure. As Rashid Khalidi (1988, p. 507) observed, the Palestinians had "succeeded at last in conveying the reality of their victimization to world public opinion."

Regardless of the level of international support, nonviolent resistance movements can help create alternative structures which provide both a moral and a practical underpinning for efforts aimed at bringing about fundamental social change, even well before the downfall of a regime. In the course of a popular struggle, political authority may be wrested from the state and invested in civil society, as these parallel institutions grow in effectiveness and legitimacy. The state may become increasingly irrelevant, as parallel nongovernmental bodies take over an increasing portion of the tasks of governing a society, providing services to the populace, and creating functional equivalents to the institutions of the state. (For example, see chapter 4 on Kosovo.)

Parallel structures in civil society may render state control increasingly impotent, as in Eastern Europe before the fall of communism, when underground presses bypassed government censorship, avant-garde theater and rock bands helped create an alternative cultural scene, and millions of Poles joined the independent trade union movement Solidarity, which quickly eclipsed the official communist-led unions. In the Philippines, the dictator Ferdinand Marcos lost power not through the defeat of his troops and the storming of the Malacañang Palace but from the withdrawal of sufficient support for his authority. With millions of Filipinos taking to the streets in defiance of curfew restrictions and soldiers refusing his orders to shoot them, the palace became the only part of the country that he effectively controlled. On the same day that Marcos was officially sworn in for another term as president in an "official" but private ceremony inside his palace, Corazon Aquino was symbolically sworn in as the people's president in a public ceremony. Given that most Filipinos saw Marcos's recent election victory as fraudulent, the vast majority offered its allegiance to Aquino, his opponent, as the legitimate president. The transfer of allegiance from one source of authority and legitimacy to another is a key element of a successful nonviolent uprising.

In many respects, nonviolent action is the ultimate asymmetrical warfare. It takes the principles of guerrilla struggle and brings them to a higher and more effective level. In the face of severe repression, rather than being confronted directly, the oppressive apparatus can be mocked in such a way that shows that the subjected population is not only unafraid but willing to expose the absurdity of the restrictions imposed upon them. One tactic is to place authorities in a dilemma where they either allow a display of defiance to be openly expressed or appear petty and rather silly in suppressing it. For example, the Moroccan authorities strictly ban any display of the Western Sahara flag. One evening, pro-independence activists tied paper flags to scores of feral cats in the occupied capital of El-Aaiún, forcing soldiers in full riot gear to chase them through the alleys the following morning in their frantic efforts to catch the cats and remove the flag. These small acts of disruption and defiance can complement or lay the foundations for more visible, large-scale actions.

South Africa and the struggle against apartheid[1]

Against enormous odds, nonviolent action proved to be a major factor in the downfall of apartheid and the establishment of a democratic black majority government. This came despite the fact that movements working for fundamental change in South Africa faced unprecedented obstacles. Never had such a powerful and highly industrialized state been overthrown from within. Opponents of apartheid faced a complex web of regulations which produced a most rigid stratification system that severely limited dissent by the oppressed majority. Apartheid South Africa defied most traditional political analyses on account of its unique social, political, economic, and strategic position. It practiced one of history's most elaborate systems of internal colonialism, with a white minority composed of less than one-fifth of the population in absolute control. The ruling party was led by racialists who also possessed an unusual amount of political sophistication. They controlled some of the world's richest mineral deposits, including one-third of the earth's known gold reserves. A modern military machine stood ready in an area which was void of any other large conventional force. Its internal security system was elaborate and repressive. As a modern industrialized state in an undeveloped region, South Africa had a degree of economic hegemony despite almost universal non-recognition of its legitimacy. It was a pariah of international diplomacy, yet economically – and to a lesser extent strategically – it was well integrated into the Western system.

It was this paradoxical situation, of the state being both extraordinarily powerful and highly vulnerable, that gave nonviolent resistance its power. Despite the country's great mineral wealth and an increasing industrial capacity, South Africa's white minority regime found itself dependent on its black majority, its southern African neighbors, and the industrialized West to maintain its repressive political system and its high level of modernization. Indeed, the resistance movement in South Africa has been referred to as "probably the largest grassroots eruption of diverse nonviolent strategies in a single struggle in human history" (Wink 1987). This nonviolent movement, which consisted both of internal resistance and of solidarity work outside the country, was largely successful in its strategy, which avoided challenging the South African state where it was strong and concentrated its attacks on where it was weak. While many Western governments argued that the supposedly benevolent influence of Western capital would gradually force an end to South Africa's apartheid system, and many on the left argued that liberation would come only through armed revolution, in fact it was largely unarmed resistance by the black majority and its supporters, both within South Africa and abroad, which brought the end of white minority rule.

The anti-apartheid struggle had largely been nonviolent until 1960, when the Sharpeville Massacre and subsequent banning of leading anti-apartheid organizations led to the African National Congress (ANC) forming an armed wing, which ended up basing its operations in exile along with underground political and military cells. However, despite occasional acts of sabotage, the armed struggle never succeeded in launching a full-scale revolution. In the 1970s, the Black Consciousness movement emerged, stressing the empowerment of the black majority, which was joined by a revitalized labor movement. When popular resistance emerged in the 1980s, it was centered not on an armed uprising but on massive non-cooperation. As described in an editorial in the *Weekly Argus* on August 19, 1989, "the intimidatory powers of the state have waned; the veneration of the law has diminished with the erosion of the rule of law. Inevitably that meek acquiescence of yesteryear has evaporated and SA is now witnessing an open, deliberate and organised campaign of defiance."

Though it is easy to think of apartheid South African society in terms of radical polarization, a model that would tend to support armed struggle as a means of change, the high degree of interdependence – albeit on unfair terms imposed by the ruling white minority – allowed greater latitude for manipulation through nonviolent means than is possible in classically polarized societies. About half of the country's Africans lived in areas allocated to South Africa's whites, including all the ports, major cities, industry, mines, and optimal agricultural land, as did virtually all of the coloreds and Asians. The white minority existed from day to day with a high level of dependence on the black majority, not just for their high standard of living but for their very survival. Nonviolent action constituted a more direct challenge to the system of apartheid than did violence.

The shift to a largely nonviolent orientation lured white popular opinion away from those seeking continued white domination. Nonviolent action threw the regime off-balance politically. A related factor was that the largely nonviolent struggle of the 1980s made the prospects of living under black majority rule less frightening. Though the prospects of giving up their privileges was not particularly welcomed by most whites, the use of nonviolence by the black majority against their white oppressors was seen as indicative of a tolerant attitude not likely to result in the previously anticipated reprisals upon seizing power. The use of armed struggle as the primary means of resistance, even if white civilian casualties were kept at a minimum, would have led many whites to fear for the worst.

One consequence of the divisions created within the white community was resistance to military conscription, which began in the 1970s by white youth opposing South Africa's occupation of Namibia and invasion of Angola and later developed into the End Conscription campaign. It grew dramatically in the mid-1980s when the regular armed forces moved into the black townships to suppress the uprising. As many as 1,000 new open resisters surfaced in 1989 alone, and thousands more evaded the draft in less public ways. Resistance included voluntary exile, going underground, or voluntarily submitting to arrest and imprisonment for refusal to be drafted into the army. While some were religious pacifists, most resisted on political grounds. Even those who did not actively participate in anti-apartheid activism undermined the system's survival by reducing the numbers of soldiers called upon to enforce it.

Active resistance by previously unsympathetic whites in support of the nonviolent defense of a number of squatter settlements threatened with destruction by authorities, such as the Crossroads community near Cape Town, created a climate of divisiveness within the ruling order which was then exploited by the black resistance. Nonviolent action allowed far greater potential for creating cleavages among the privileged white minority, such as how to respond to the resistance, how long to resist the inevitable changes demanded by the revolutionaries, and at what cost.

While maintaining their commitment to pursue armed struggle, both in principle and as a strategy of disrupting normal operations of the repressive state, the South African opposition became gradually aware by the early 1980s that armed struggle was to be just one element of the resistance, along with international isolation, an open mass movement, and an underground network to link them together. The armed struggle needed to be integrated with the unarmed struggle in order to be successful, melding the two into a "protracted people's war" or a popular insurrection. Despite the romantic rhetoric of a victorious ANC army marching to Pretoria, the ANC never saw armed struggle as the sole or even the primary means for bringing down the apartheid regime (Price 1991, p. 9). Strategic analyst Thomas Karis noted that, "despite a commitment to 'armed struggle,' the ANC has considered sabotage and guerrilla attacks to be only a minor strand in a multifaceted strategy consisting mainly of politically inspired demonstrations, strikes and defiance" (1986, p. 134). By the 1980s, the ANC saw strikes and boycotts as "a main element in the organization's strategy for liberation," emphasizing that the armed struggle was only "one strand" in the fabric of resistance strategies which included civil disobedience (Uhlig 1986, pp. 168–70). The ANC even acknowledged that most of its acts of sabotage and small-scale guerrilla attacks were no more than "armed propaganda" (Karis 1986). Indeed, during the anti-Republic Day campaign of 1981, where hundreds of thousands of people took part in protest rallies all around the country and a successful general strike demonstrated the level at which the opposition could mount a successful mobilization, the ANC launched about a half dozen attacks against strategic targets across the country in a well-coordinated manifestation of popular support for a campaign of mass resistance.

While many ANC activists still believed that the armed resistance would eventually escalate and play a more significant role, in practice it had become a means of providing moral support for the unarmed resistance, rather than – what many had anticipated – an unarmed resistance being used primarily to support the armed struggle. According to journalist Julie Frederikse (1986, p. 178),

> While the African National Congress is known for its anti-government guerrilla attacks, its leaders also seem wary about any over-emphasis on military rather than political activity. The ANC President's first public statement of 1984 exhorted all South Africans to "create conditions in which the country will become increasingly ungovernable."

Eventually, the ANC recognized that the non-cooperation of the people was key and that it was ungovernability of the country by the apartheid regime, and not its physical overthrow, which would end apartheid. It was taking advantage of the government's weaknesses, not the ANC's limited strengths, which would prove to be decisive. The most important pillar upon which the apartheid system rested was the cheap black labor which gave white South Africans one of the highest standards of living in the world. Virtually every sector of the economy was predicated on a system in which the black majority would work for the white minority. If the blacks were no longer willing to work reliably under such a system, the system could no longer function.

The shift to a largely nonviolent strategy in the anti-apartheid strug-

---

Box 5.1 The Black Consciousness movement and the question of violence

A major factor in the revitalization of the South African resistance was the Black Consciousness movement, which was launched in the early 1970s, stressing self-reliance and nonviolent resistance. Though inspired in part by Frantz Fanon's ideas of empowerment and conscientization, the Black Consciousness movement stressed that black pride need not come only through violence. Sam Nolutshungu (1982, pp. 183–4) observed,

> Although Fanon's writings were widely read and his ideas of alienation in colonial society had much influence on many of the theorists of black consciousness, there is little evidence that his ideas on violence were much discussed, and none that they were widely shared. It is nowhere seen as being in itself a mentally liberating process; rather its instrumental role properly comes only when consciousness has been achieved by other means.

Similarly, Gail Gerhart, writing about the internal resistance movement of the 1970s, adds, "The aim of Black Consciousness as an ideology was not to trigger a spontaneous Fanonesque eruption of the masses into violent action, but rather to rebuild and recondition the mind of the oppressed in such a way that eventually they would be ready forcefully to demand what was rightfully theirs" (1978, pp. 285–6).

Black Consciousness movement leader Steve Biko, who was tortured to death while in police custody in 1977, and other internal resistance leaders stressed the need for nonviolence, at least in the early stage of the struggle, and criticized the armed groups' "reckless rush to confrontation when circumstance did not favor a black victory" (Gerhart 1978, p. 285). Some activists saw the public espousal of nonviolence as a tactical recognition of the need to postpone government repression of the anti-apartheid group's public activities, and that there needed to be a "second phase" following conscientization – that of armed struggle. Preliminary clandestine committees were set up by black consciousness leaders to explore that very possibility, but these were set aside as advances in the internal and largely nonviolent resistance became apparent. There was some pressure from militants both in leadership and among the grassroots about moving to an active armed resistance, but the tactical advantages of nonviolent resistance, regardless of the sincerity of its initial advocates, had meanwhile won widespread support.

gle, then, was not the result of an ethical transformation but was born out of necessity. The black South Africans' overwhelming numerical majority made the use of nonviolent action particularly effective when they started to mobilize in large numbers in the mid-1980s. Nonviolent action, despite its requirements of discipline and bravery in the face of repression, allowed participation by a far greater percentage of the population than would a guerrilla army, thus optimizing the blacks' majority. Rather than ungovernability of the townships by the white authorities creating liberated zones which would become a beachhead for an armed assault against white South Africa, as many predicted, it was their ungovernability in itself – combined with effective alternative institutions – which helped force the government to recognize the need for negotiations.

Western Sahara and the struggle for self-determination[2]

In 1975, on the verge of its promised independence from Spain, Western Sahara – a sparsely populated desert country about the size of the state of Colorado – was invaded by its powerful neighbor Morocco. Following sixteen years of guerrilla warfare against Moroccan occupation forces waged by the pro-independence Polisario Front, a ceasefire took place with the promise that the United Nations would conduct a referendum on the fate of the territory. Morocco, however, refused to allow the referendum to proceed and has maintained its occupation of 85 percent of the territory, moving in tens of thousands of Moroccan settlers and suppressing any kind of pro-independence activism. Despite this, sporadic nonviolent resistance has emerged in the occupied territory.

The transition from armed to unarmed insurgency was not the result of a deliberate strategy on the part of the Polisario, nor is it widely considered necessarily an optimal means of waging a struggle for independence. Unarmed strategies of resistance by Sahrawi nationalists are largely tools of necessity, not tools of choice. Further complicating the situation is that, while a slight majority of Sahrawis live under Moroccan occupation inside Western Sahara, the rest have languished in refugee camps in Algeria since 1976. It is from these camps that Polisario launched its war of national liberation against Morocco (1975–91), and it is from these camps that it continues to wage its international diplomatic war for independent statehood. Unarmed resistance to the occupation has instead been the purview of the Sahrawis living in the areas of Western Sahara under Moroccan control. What emerges is a picture of a political movement with widespread popular support but one that lacks strategic vision, defensively adapting itself to new global environments.

The emergence of a nonviolent resistance movement within the occupied territory was facilitated by the combination of the slight political opening made possible by the ceasefire, along with new communication technologies that made it easier to inform the outside world of the resistance efforts and Moroccan repression. Indeed, little is known about the tactics of unarmed resistance used during the years of war in Western Sahara. For the most part, it is assumed that the Sahrawis living under occupation were focused on assisting Polisario's diplomatic and military campaign in any way possible. In 1987, in preparation for a UN technical mission to lay the groundwork for the proposed referendum, Sahrawis began to prepare signs and banners. However, the Moroccan authorities quickly arrested any Sahrawi who appeared to be coming out to protest. Several of those imprisoned were held incommunicado for years, including Aminatou Haidar, who would later emerge as the most internationally prominent activist of the 2005 Sahrawi *intifada*, and who was recognized in 2008 as the recipient of the Robert F. Kennedy Human Rights Award.

The next noteworthy step in the evolution of unarmed Sahrawi resistance came in 1995 when, again, a UN delegation was visiting Western Sahara. By that time, the United Nations Mission for the Referendum in Western Sahara (known by its French acronym MINURSO) was already well established on the ground, but its mission was primarily to monitor the ceasefire and organize a vote. For a brief period, there was a strong hope among Western Saharan nationalists that the UN mission would not only deliver a referendum on independence but would also expose and take action against Morocco's severe and ongoing human rights violations. Due to French objections, however, MINURSO is the only UN peacekeeping force denied a human rights mandate; with constant Moroccan interference, it has been unable to monitor human rights inside the occupied Western Sahara (Human Rights Watch 1995). Even with the presence of UN peacekeepers and voter identification personnel, Western Saharan nationalists had a difficult time drawing international attention to the grave human rights situation and the denial of self-determination, as Moroccan authorities detained, abused, and imprisoned many activists. Polisario made the detention of these activists an issue at the negotiating table, where the UN Secretariat was desperately trying to keep the referendum process going.

The next round of major Sahrawi protests, which began in 1999, were different from previous eruptions of nationalist sentiment, insofar as they were much larger and not geared toward international audiences. Just two months after the ascension of King Mohammed VI, Sahrawi students and laborers erected a protest camp in the center of El-Aaiún to test the new ruler on his promises of economic and political reform. Initial Moroccan efforts to break up the camp only backfired, producing some of the largest Sahrawi demonstrations ever witnessed in the occupied zone. While some of the student and labor organizers admit having intentionally and provocatively set the stage for this kind of confrontation, the outpouring of anger directed at the Moroccan authorities took most by surprise, particularly so early into Morocco's brief honeymoon period with the new king. These demonstrations were also significant because they signaled the arrival of a new generation of young Sahrawi activists who had come of age during the Moroccan occupation and thus knew little about either Spanish colonialism or Polisario's leadership (Stephan and Mundy 2006). The 1999 protests not only indicated strong Sahrawi passions for independence but were also testimony to the failed legacy of Hassan II to win Western Saharan hearts and minds (Mundy 2011a).

Mohammed VI has likewise failed to win over significant numbers of Sahrawi nationalists. His first trip to the occupied Western Sahara in 2002 was met with protests, arrests, and the torture of nationalists. While the human rights picture inside Morocco proper improved slightly under Mohammed VI, Western Sahara remained a space of exception. Moreover, the king's explicit rejection of a referendum for Western Sahara (a position his father had adopted in 1981) further alienated Western Saharan nationalists, as did the regime's efforts to promote regional autonomy by renewing the Royal Advisory Council for Saharan Affairs (CORCAS – Conseil royal consultatif pour les affaires sahariennes), a body composed of Sahrawi loyalists, economic clients of the regime, and Polisario defectors. At the international level, the Western Sahara peace process, which had been heading toward a referendum in 1999, came to a complete standstill in 2004 with the resignation of James Baker as the UN Secretary-General's personal envoy. While Polisario was insisting that Morocco accept the parameters Baker outlined in 2003 (including a referendum with the option of independence), Morocco was insisting that a negotiated solution based on limited autonomy under Moroccan sovereignty was the only possible solution.

In this context, one of international and local stagnation, Western Sahara again erupted in May 2005. The 2005 protests were far less organized than the demonstration camp erected in 1999; the former grew largely out of an escalating cycle of protest and repression initiated by a small demonstration against arbitrary detention. The

May 2005 protests (or Sahrawi *intifada*) were symbolically interesting because they coincided roughly with the thirty-second anniversary of Polisario's founding on May 10. To a certain extent this was accidental, but it has nonetheless played into Western Saharan nationalists' narratives quite well, with the May *intifada* now constituting one of the most important events in the history of Sahrawis' fight for self-determination.

The 2005 events are important not only because they galvanized a new generation of young activists who had come of age during the years of false promises of protection and self-determination from the United Nations, but also because they were among the most digitally recorded and circulated events in the history of the Moroccan occupied Western Sahara. Whereas almost no images of the 1987, 1995, and 1999 protests ever emerged internationally, the 2005 protests were documented and rebroadcast widely. Images and videos of violent confrontations, tortured Sahrawi bodies, and police brutality had a conscience-shocking effect worldwide, particularly in Spain, where the majority of the population supports Western Saharan independence. Just as new media and communication technologies were helping to connect Sahrawis between the occupied zone, the refugee camps, and in the diaspora (notably in Spain), such technologies were also bringing their case to the attention of the international community. A noteworthy effect of the May 2005 protests was its galvanizing effect on the UN Secretariat, which increased its efforts to revive the negotiations process in the wake of the demonstrations, the harsh Moroccan crackdown, and the international outcry that followed (International Crisis Group 2007).

After the 2005 demonstrations, the situation inside Western Sahara was never the same again. A new culture of resistance among Sahrawi youth grew more and more fearless, even as Moroccan techniques of repression also became more sophisticated. Established Sahrawi human rights activists known outside the country could count on international pressure to keep them out of prison, but younger activists continued to face daily harassment, arbitrary detention, and torture, including sexual torture (Human Rights Watch 2008). After the Moroccan authorities' use of force to break up the larger and prolonged demonstrations in 2005–6, the resistance opted mainly for smaller protests, some of which were planned and some of which were spontaneous. A typical protest would begin on a street corner or a plaza, where a Sahrawi flag would be unfurled, women would start ululating, and people would begin chanting pro-independence slogans. Within a few minutes, soldiers and police would arrive, and the crowd would quickly scatter. Among other tactics have been leaf-leting, graffiti (including tagging the homes of collaborators), and cultural celebrations with political overtones. Such nonviolent actions, while broadly supported by the people, appear to have been less a part of coordinated resistance than a result of action by individuals.

While demonstrating creative tactics and enormous courage in the face of repression, the Western Sahara resistance has largely been lacking in overall strategy. With Moroccan settlers now greatly out-numbering the indigenous Sahrawi population in the territory, they are not dependent on Sahrawi labor to the extent that the white South Africans were. Support for the Moroccan monarchy from France, the United States, and other Western nations remains strong. Perhaps the most critical form of nonviolent resistance is not the sporadic protests but the determination of the Sahrawis – who have a distinct ethnic identity, dialect, culture, and history from those of their occupiers – to refuse to assimilate into Moroccan society. To whatever extent Moroccan occupation troops and settlers control the land, as long as they do not control the hearts and minds of the Sahrawis, they have not yet won. Indeed, the Moroccan government's regular use of violent repression to subdue the Sahrawi-led nonviolent protests suggests that civil resistance is seen as a threat to Moroccan control.

Strengths and limitations of nonviolence

Obstacles to the success of nonviolent action in support of self-determination and democracy are still formidable despite the remark-able record of such campaigns in recent decades. Authoritarian governments use legal restrictions, terror, and their monopolization of news media to make it very difficult to mobilize effective popular support for mass action. Decades of repression engender in citizens a sense of despair and a lack of empowerment. Members of ethnic minorities or peoples under occupation feel this acutely because they have particular difficulty winning majority support for their efforts against government repression.

In impoverished societies controlled by authoritarian regimes, many basic necessities are in short supply and access to them is controlled by local elites and foreigners. Where survival is people's greatest concern, unarmed groups simply may not be able to hold out long enough against their oppressors to succeed. In addition, governments with outside economic support can survive the near total collapse of their countries' domestic economies. For example, the Salvadorean junta withstood a series of general strikes in the early 1980s because

Box 5.2 Occupying a piece of desert

Moroccan colonists and Sahrawi collaborators are given preference where housing and employment are concerned, while most of the indigenous population receives virtually no benefits from their country's rich fisheries and phosphate deposits. In response, in September 2010, Sahrawi activists erected a tent city about 15 kilometers outside of El-Aaiún known as Gdaym Izik. By November, the nonviolent protest had swelled to close to 10,000 people, which – relative to the population – was much larger than the protests in Egypt's Tahrir Square three months later. Since any protests calling for self-determination, independence, or enforcement of UN Security Council resolutions are brutally suppressed, the demonstrators point-edly avoided such provocative calls, instead simply demanding economic justice.

The logic of the Gdaym Izik protest camp was multifaceted. It defied Morocco's incredible matrix of security inside the occupied cities in an unexpected move that the Moroccan security forces could not disrupt before it gained a critical mass. In the years leading up to 2010, Sahrawi youths had often built impromptu protest camps on the beach during the summer months when residents would vacation on the coast to escape the heat. The Moroccan response to these beach protests was to outlaw overnight camping on the coast and to increase the size of its police presence there in the summer months.

The Gdaym Izik camp also symbolized the history of the Sahrawi struggle in terms of the culture's nomadic past, the refugees living in camps in Algeria since 1976, and the 1999 protest camp in El-Aaiún. Not only were Sahrawis in Gdaym Izik renewing their grievances about joblessness and the hardships faced by uni-versity students, who must travel to northern Morocco for studies, they were also suggesting that their lives would be better if they lived in the refugee camps in Algeria. While this symbolic effort to escape the Moroccan occupation was coded in a language of economic and social grievance, there was a deliberate effort among camp organizers not to make it a political issue, fearing that any sign of pro-independence sentiment would hasten the Moroccan government crackdown.

Even this was too much for the Moroccan monarchy, however, which was determined to crush this nonviolent act of mass defiance. The Moroccans tight-ened the siege in early October, attacking vehicles bringing food, water, and medical supplies to the camp, resulting in scores of injuries and the death of a fourteen-year-old boy. Finally, on November 8, the Moroccans attacked the camp, driving protesters out with tear gas and hoses, beating those who did not flee fast enough, and killing up to two dozen. In a dramatic departure from the overwhelm-ing nonviolent protests which have characterized the Sahrawi resistance, the violent destruction of the camp set off a wave of rioting, which in turn triggered the burning and pillaging of Sahrawis' homes and shops, with occupation forces shooting or arresting suspected activists, hundreds of whom disappeared after the outbreak of violence (Zunes 2010). This episode represented the most intense period of Sahrawi–Moroccan clashes yet witnessed in the history of the occupied Western Sahara (Mundy 2011b). While these events initially drew unprecedented international attention to the nonviolent resistance struggle for self-determination, the massive protests which emerged shortly thereafter in Tunisia and Egypt soon eclipsed Western Sahara's early contribution to the Arab Spring.

the United States government committed enough aid to finance most of the regime's budget. Threats of a veto by France have prevented the United Nations from even providing MINURSO with a human rights mandate, much less demanding that Morocco live up to its promise to allow the people of Western Sahara the right of self-determination through an internationally supervised referendum.

Repressive regimes assured of substantial foreign assistance may be less likely to refrain from using violence to suppress dissent for fear of fatally damaging their legitimacy, though they still must be sensitive to how human rights abuses against nonviolent dissent may affect such support. In recognition that openly attacking their own citizens would cost them dearly, a number of regimes – such as those in Colombia, Honduras, and Iraq – have pursued a kind of privatization of the repressive apparatus. In such countries, higher-ranking government officials have tacitly condoned the formation of pro-government vigilante forces, which often operate with the direct support of the police and the military. The goals of these death squads are to assassinate or otherwise silence leaders and participants in nonviolent movements and to terrorize the population into submission. Despite being quietly supported by some key segments of the government, such vigilante groups are far enough outside the official chain of command that government and military officials can plausibly deny responsibility for or knowledge of their actions. While most of the nonviolent activists still blame the regime, some elements of the population and foreign backers may accept the regime's portrayal of itself as a moderate force doing its best to curb violence and extremism on all sides. When this happens, calls to stop government-sponsored violence will go unheeded.

Privatization of the repressive apparatus follows from adoption of the "low-intensity conflict" (LIC) counter-insurgency strategy developed by the US military. A comprehensive strategy that comprises economic development programs, propaganda, and anti-guerrilla military campaigns, LIC was implemented in El Salvador, Guatemala, Colombia, the Philippines, and elsewhere beginning in the early 1980s. Recognizing that shooting into crowds merely strengthens opposition, US strategists began working with foreign officials to develop means to combine repression with nominal civilian control of the national government aimed at converting the population from insurgents to supporters of the regime. The purpose of LIC is to neutralize dissent, not simply to kill dissenters. With this end in mind, American advisors trained and cleaned up the local armed forces in order to restore respectability to the most visible government institution. At the same time, they encouraged government officials to neutralize trade union, academic, and religious leaders; identify and silence grassroots supporters of the opposition; and limit and repress independent human rights groups.

American military trainers emphasized responsible crowd-control methods but also gave instruction in other forms of violence (see McClintock 1984). A Central Intelligence Agency report, initially secret, to Nicaraguan Contra units advocated "the selective use of violence" by paramilitary units as preferable to "indiscriminate" repression as a means of "decapitating" the leadership of the opposition (Neier and Omang 1985). The privatization of the repressive apparatus has had a chilling effect on the prospects of successful advancement of human rights. For example, in Sri Lanka during the 1990s, when the nominally democratic government was faced with two simultaneous insurrections, efforts by human rights activists and others to salvage some semblance of rule of law were met with widespread death squad activity.

Fortunately, "nonviolent intervention" by teams of international volunteers organized by Peace Brigades International (PBI) and similar groups has been somewhat effective in protecting activists. Growing out of the Gandhian tradition, PBI and similar groups have sent teams to Guatemala, El Salvador, Sri Lanka, Colombia, and the West Bank to accompany prominent nonviolent activists as, essentially, unarmed bodyguards. Because leaders of even the most repressive regimes do not want to deal with the diplomatic fallout from international observers (particularly North Americans or Europeans) being casualties of – or even just witnessing – death squad attacks, PBI teams have served as successful deterrents to some of the worst activities (Mahoney and Eguren 1997). These efforts have been extremely limited thus far. Yet, while they have yet to evolve to the degree that would constitute an effective means for ending the threat from death squads, there is certainly some potential for further development.

When repression is severe, whether it comes directly through the government or through its surrogates, gaining international support is critical. Despite verbal condemnation of its racial policies, the Western industrialized world gave South Africa consistent support over the years in the form of trade, industrial development, technological assistance, infusion of capital, and arms. South Africa would not have become the economic and military power it did without the massive aid it received from the West over forty years of apartheid rule. Before the imposition of sanctions in the mid-1980s, there was over $13 billion worth of annual trade between South Africa and the West, which, combined with $30 billion in foreign investment, supplied the country with the vast majority of such basic commodities as transportation equipment, electrical equipment and machinery, nuclear technology, telecommunications facilities and services, computer technology, chemicals and related products, paper and manufactures, and other goods essential to the maintenance of a modern industrialized state. In addition, the West supported the South African regime through outstanding bank loans and credits totaling $6.5 billion, much of which went to government entities with no restrictions.

As a result, it became apparent that not only was it necessary to undermine the pillars of support for the regime within a country, it was critical to undermine the foreign sources of support as well. When the United Nations Security Council threatened sanctions and other punitive measures against South Africa, the United States, Great Britain, and France cast vetoes as a result of their own important economic and political interests. By the mid- to late 1980s, however, not only were strikes, boycotts, and other forms of increasingly disruptive resistance having an impact within South Africa, images shown in the global media of brutal repression by South African police and military against largely nonviolent protesters spurred ultimately successful campaigns to impose international sanctions. Labor unions, church groups, students, and leftist organizations made business as usual with the apartheid government impossible. This upsurge in solidarity work came as a result of the largely nonviolent resistance in South Africa during the 1980s and the repression from the government which resulted. In contrast, had the primary mode of resistance been armed struggle, it is unlikely the same level of sympathy and the resulting mass mobilization would have been enough to make the sanctions movement so successful.

While advanced industrialized countries contributed indirectly to maintaining white minority rule in South Africa, they have played an even more direct role in supporting the Moroccan occupation of Western Sahara. Morocco has been able to persist in flouting its international legal obligations toward Western Sahara largely because France and the United States have continued to arm the occupation forces and block the enforcement of resolutions in the UN Security Council, demanding that Morocco allow for self-determination or even simply the stationing of unarmed human rights monitors in the occupied country. So now, in addition to the nonviolent resistance by Sahrawis, it is important to consider the potential of nonviolent action by the citizens of France, the United States, and other countries that enable Morocco to maintain its occupation. Such campaigns played a major role in forcing Australia, Great Britain, and the United States to end their support for Indonesia's occupation of East Timor (Zunes 2001). However, while Western Sahara has received far more support from the world's governments and international organizations in its struggle against Moroccan occupation as compared with East Timor and its fight against the Indonesian occupation, it has failed to result in a comparable mobilizing of global civil society.

Conclusion

For the vast majority of those living under repressive regimes, who are not pacifists, the decisions about violence and nonviolence are utilitarian, not ethical. Whether a particular pro-democracy struggle is successful or unsuccessful depends not on whether it is violent or nonviolent, but whether the movement can develop effective strategies and tactics, mobilize its base of support, and undermine the pillars upholding the regime. However, the empirical evidence clearly demonstrates that nonviolent strategies are almost always more effective and have fewer negative consequences. History has shown that even if a government has a monopoly of military force, and even if a government has the support of powerful international actors, it is still ultimately powerless if the people refuse to recognize its authority. Through general strikes, filling the streets, mass refusal to obey official orders, and other forms of nonviolent resistance, even the most autocratic regime cannot survive.

Though many analysts see the liberation of Western Sahara as particularly challenging, there was a time when the prospects of liberating South Africa through strategic nonviolent action appeared similarly bleak. Despite the revolutionary rhetoric of the exiled liberation movements, armed struggle neither is nor was a realistic option in either case. While those in advanced industrialized democracies should not pass moral judgment against oppressed peoples of the Global South who feel a need to take up arms in their defense, there should be little hesitation in encouraging the widespread dissemination of the burgeoning knowledge of the history and dynamics of strategic nonviolent action.

Finally, it is important that those in the advanced industrialized countries acknowledge that it is their governments that provide most of the military, diplomatic, and economic support to the world's remaining dictatorial regimes and occupation armies, suggesting that more attention be given to campaigns against the arms trade and the transfer of technologies used to monitor and suppress dissent. While strategic nonviolent action is the most effective form of pro-democratic and anti-imperialist struggle for those in the Global South, those supporting such struggles should acknowledge that the countries most in need of large-scale strategic nonviolent action are the advanced industrialized nations of the global North that continue to support repressive regimes.

Questions for discussion

1 For many years, there was a romantic attachment by anti-colonial and anti-imperialist advocates regarding armed struggle. Why has that changed?
2 What are the main distinctions between advocacy of nonviolent methods on ethical grounds and advocacy of nonviolent methods on utilitarian grounds?
3 What are the similarities and differences in the strategies used in Western Sahara and South Africa? What factors influenced the decision to use nonviolent methods?
4 What makes the prospects of success by a largely nonviolent struggle against the Moroccan occupation of Western Sahara more challenging than the success of the largely nonviolent struggle against the apartheid regime in South Africa?

Suggestions for further reading and research

Association de soutien à un référendum libre et régulier au Sahara Occidental (ARSO), *Western Sahara*, www.arso.org.
Smuts, Dene, Westcott, Shauna, and Nash, Margaret (1991) *The Purple Shall Govern: A South African A to Z of Nonviolent Action*. Oxford: Oxford University Press.
Zunes, Stephen, and Mundy, Jacob (2010) *Western Sahara: War, Nationalism and Conflict Irresolution*. Syracuse, NY: Syracuse University Press.

CHAPTER 6

New Media and Advocacy

Srdja Popovic and Marcella Alvarez[1]

Much has been written during the past decade on nonviolent revolutions driven by "people power" movements all over the world, from the wave of "Color Revolutions" that swept the former Soviet bloc to the "Arab Spring" of 2011, which resulted directly in the ousting of long-time autocrats such as Tunisia's Zine El Abidine Ben Ali, Egypt's Hosni Mubarak, and Libya's Muammar Gaddafi. Nonviolent social movements proved that long-held assumptions about the power of the state can be fundamentally altered when masses of people are able to rally in the name of their rights. And, while many decried the outcomes of these movements, nonviolent resistance seems only to be gaining ever more traction, with citizens taking to the streets to protest government policies sparked by such varied causes as urban development (Turkey), hikes in bus fares (Brazil), and the lack of identification numbers for infants (Bosnia and Herzegovina). All of these movements represent a new kind of middle-class awakening and lead to broader calls for social, political, and economic change.

Regardless of vastly different contexts and cultures, there have been several common denominators among nonviolent social movements that have emerged over the past decade. First, they were started mainly by grassroots civilian-led groups (non-established political "outsiders"), and young people – teenagers and young adults under thirty-five – have been instrumental in pushing the struggles forward. Second, they all significantly utilized new media – and this is not a coincidence.

New media and social networking sites have been instrumental in disseminating messages, mobilizing supporters, and documenting and publishing human rights violations and state-sponsored violence. Even before the "Arab Spring," news media were overwhelmed with titles about "Facebook–Twitter revolutions," as in the case of the Green movement during the Iranian post-election crisis of 2009, when President Mahmoud Ahmadinejad was widely accused of stealing votes. On the other hand, media experts as well as activists warn us not to over-exaggerate the actual role of social media in such movements, astutely pointing out that struggles for freedom, social justice, and democracy can only really be won in the real world, not in the virtual one.

The phenomenon of media and technology in nonviolent struggle is not new (Martin and Varney 2003). It is clear that nonviolent resistance utilizes an incredibly wide spectrum of communications. From the use of low-tech communication in the rural areas of Mali, where people sang and told tales to get messages across to fellow resisters, to the secret underground printing facilities organized by the Polish Solidarity movement during the 1980s, to the downloading and dissemination of the list of "198 Methods of Nonviolent Struggle" composed by Gene Sharp, it is clear that, as technologies develop, so the tactics for knowledge dissemination about nonviolent civil resistance will only continue to grow.

The use of web-based "new media" in nonviolent campaigns arguably began with the students' resistance movement during the struggle against Yugoslav dictator Slobodan Milošević in the late 1990s. Members of Otpor! ("resistance") used emerging web and communication technologies not as an incisive tactic for subversion but because they had no alternative; in 2000, Serbia was still recovering both from economic sanctions imposed upon it by UN forces in the mid-1990s and from hyperinflation, which saw the printing of bills upwards of 100,000,000,000 Serbian dinars (the second highest inflation rate in the second half of the twentieth century). Given the crippled Serbian economy, youth members were forced to think of free and low-cost organizing tools to bolster their movement. The students created a web portal which served as a communication tool and used it to communicate covertly with members and followers.

Over the course of the movement and in the years to follow, Otpor! members learned that not only was new media cheap and effective, but it could be harnessed as a specific tool in and of itself – not simply as a cheap or stopgap replacement for better resources. Shortly after the Serbian revolution, other nonviolent movements low on funds came to former Otpor! members for advice about how best to harness new media for their own nonviolent movement. In 2003 Otpor! members founded the Centre for Applied Nonviolent Action and Strategies (CANVAS) as one way of training emerging activists in lessons in creative subversion that now incorporated new media technologies (and, incidentally, where the authors of this chapter are employed). Lessons about how to work with and use new media constitute an important workshop module in CANVAS training sessions.

The big challenge for those who are committed to learning and spreading knowledge about effective nonviolent struggle is to understand the evolution of social technology – that is, the way communications affect social interactions for political ends. And it is a mixed bag: while social media has forged many connections that would have been otherwise unlikely and has made communication undoubtedly quicker, the drawbacks of its usage – the tendency for opposition groups to rely on it too heavily and the relative ease of its penetrability by oppressive regimes – lead us to believe that social media has merely accelerated the implementation of great ideas that originate in face-to-face interaction. In this chapter, we give examples of how social media has been used for both positive and negative ends throughout the past decade of nonviolent struggle. Our experience and research show three major ways in which it significantly influences social movements, with both positive and negative effects:

- New media allows grassroots activists to broadcast their vision and reach a large swathe of people more quickly and cheaply than before, facilitating greater ease in gaining numbers and winning the crowd. However, activists must not rely solely on the "loose knit connections" typical of new media and have to keep their core activist subset, as research has shown how more effective movements utilize close interpersonal ties.
- New media is a powerful tool for recording and documenting human rights violations and bringing them to public scrutiny. Thus it is instrumental in gaining followers who have witnessed state-sponsored violence. However, autocrats and dictators have adapted and are now using new technologies to crack down on activists at a quicker rate than ever before.
- Using open-access media and internet technologies streamlines education of tactics and strategies, and theoretically opens the possibility for self-education about nonviolent resistance. However, this can lead to a problem of "clicktivism," in which "activism" becomes limited to sharing a link or watching an online video. The dissemination of knowledge about tactics does not in and of itself translate to practice, as it takes creativity and work as well as a keen eye to the specific context of each country from those living there to maximize success.

Foundation: how the rules of communication changed

Social media is an attractive topic because it allows us to do things that were unthinkable just a few decades ago: you can post a video documenting an act of violence committed by your country's regime, and your friends can not only forward it to their friends, but they can also add comments and links to related documents, supposedly making each viewer a shareholder in the issue at hand.

We agree with media scholar Clay Shirkey's definition of new media as a medium that has the ability to create both mass impact and interaction. According to Shirkey's narrative, before the advent of the internet, media was split into two distinct groups: broadcast media and communications media (Shirkey 2008, p. 86). Broadcast media served a "one to many" function, where a message was amplified by a sender to a wide range of receivers (such as a newspaper or television network). Communications media, on the other hand, encompassed technology that facilitates two-way conversations between individuals (such as the postal system, the telegram, and the telephone). What changed with "new media" is that now it is easier – rather than engaging in one-to-many or one-to-one communications – to hold many-to-many communications (Shirkey cites email as the first example of many-to-many communications). The effect is something that we are still experiencing – the beginning of the collapse of the barrier between broadcast and communications media.

As many-to-many communications began to take on different forms, they also (unintentionally) spread to the field of social organizing. While new media is not defined by its relation to social movements, a brief discussion of its progression as a tool for political subversion is useful for any student studying its effects on nonviolent civil resistance.

Again, according to Shirkey, the development of new media and nonviolent struggle has its roots in a fairly common entertainment – a flash mob (Shirkey 2008, p. 166). Flash mobs are crowds of people who gather together to engage in a common action, often utilizing the element of surprise for entertainment. While the internet is not necessary for their organization, flash mobs gained mass popular appeal only when videos of them were posted on video-sharing sites such as YouTube. A common example of a flash mob (and one of the first to be documented) was organized by an editor at *Harper's* magazine who wanted to conduct a social experiment and secretly sent out instructions, under the pseudonym "Bill from New York," for people to meet up in a specific spot in Macy's. Over one hundred people showed up next to a certain rug and, when asked what they needed, everyone claimed they needed a "love rug," perplexing the saleslady and causing amusement.

Shirkey cites one distinctive moment occurring in May 2006

when flash mobs as a social organizing platform became decidedly politicized. Belorussians tried to organize a flash mob in Minsk's Oktyabrskaya Square to join together and eat ice cream. They did this for fun, but the government took it as a threat against the bans against public social gatherings and intervened, arresting the bystanders. This moment is important for us as trackers of social movements because it introduced the idea that it is not about *what* people are doing once gathered through social networks, but about the physical *gathering* of people itself – something oppressive regimes try to prevent. And, although used for very different end goals, flash mobs and banned protests operate under much the same mechanisms in that they are organized in a digital space yet enacted in the real world. Furthermore, the relation of social movements and flash mobs gets to another key idea – creative tactics that result in both entertainment and subversion have the powerful ability to decrease fear, making it more likely people will join the cause.

Since the "Ice Cream Revolution" in Belarus, the technological field has expanded exponentially, and new technologies are more than ever tapping into the same gathering power of the flash mob phenomenon. From the quick diffusion of videos taken by monks in Myanmar in 2007, which led to the thousands-strong marches of the Saffron Revolution, to the arrest of Egyptian activists for performing the "Harlem Shake" video meme while calling for interim president Mohammed Morsi's resignation in February 2013, it is clear that, as technologies develop, civil resisters adapt their methods for protest along with them. And it is not only in highly oppressive countries that people are harnessing "people power" through new media – for example, the 2011 Occupy Wall Street movement took advantage of Twitter, Facebook, WordPress, Tumblr, and mapping technology to spread the word about its actions.

However, the intelligent use of social media is not the most important thing these movements have in common. When it comes down to it, successful nonviolent campaigns of the last decade have been built on three crucial building blocks: unity, planning, and nonviolent discipline. Social media can enhance specific aspects of a nonviolent movement's strategy, but it will never take the place of smart, deliberate action on the streets. Again the question arises – Why is there so much buzz around the new media? Examples of nonviolent struggles that rely on incredibly limited media or communications systems are not hard to find (Zunes 2012). The fact is that the world we live in now is ever more connected, with more than 2.8 billion of the global population tapped into online systems (*Measuring the Information Society*

2013). And, if the past ten years have been any example, it is the tech-savvy youth groups who will lead society in new and creative ways of nonviolent civil resistance.

We want to emphasize as we go through the following arguments that we see new media as simply an evolution of previous communication technologies and not limited simply to social networks such as Facebook or Twitter, although those inevitably garner the most attention. We feel that new media, as the subject of this chapter, is a continuation of other communications media, embracing the use of cell phones, videos and the internet. The following examples will illustrate different ways groups have harnessed and utilized the new technologies available them.

Winning the crowd: the online logistics of nonviolent revolution

"Gotov je!" said the message that kept thousands of Serbs' mobile phones beeping and buzzing on the nights leading up to Serbia's 2000 election. "Gotov je!," or "He's finished!," referred to then dictator Slobodan Milošević, whose eleven-year rule had brought Serbia wars, hyperinflation, and extreme levels of unemployment and poverty. The nonviolent opposition in its various forms had been trying to overthrow Milošević for nearly a decade, and it looked as if they were finally going to "finish" him off by ousting him from power. These text messages were a reminder to Serbian observers to remain vigilant and positive on the days leading up to the election.

In today's world of smartphones and high levels of web penetration, it is extraordinarily easy to transmit information quickly via email, Facebook, Twitter, YouTube, and countless other platforms. But in Serbia in 2000, mass text messaging was the most anonymous and far-reaching technology available. Most young Serbs owned mobile phones, and, by simply inserting an anonymously purchased SIM card in a computer and pressing a few buttons, one could send a message to up to 200 people. Then activists from the student group Otpor! threw the SIM card away, erasing all traces of the author and allowed phone trees to carry the message further. Had there been Facebook or Twitter, perhaps the cost of purchasing new SIM cards would have been alleviated and messages would have reached their respective constituencies with just as much efficacy.

This tactic efficiently fulfilled two goals: the message reached a mass of people in a fast and cheap manner and it enabled people to participate personally. Individuals forwarded exactly the same message they had received from movement organizers to important people in their own contact lists – often adding their own comments. When someone received a text about a planned action, they were sure that it was from a reliable source (somebody from their own contact list). Eventually, the regime was unable to locate the source of the message. After the initial few hundred times it was forwarded, it became so widely disseminated that it was absolutely impossible to locate, stop, or arrest the initiators. The phone itself facilitated two-way mass interaction, but the text message was more akin to a broadcast tool, thus utilizing new media's capacity for mass interaction and impact.

The Serbian Otpor! movement was highly efficient, but its members still spent thousands of hours collectively preparing for its events. In the year 2000 alone, Otpor! organized more than sixty anti-Milošević rallies and rock concerts throughout Serbia. Activists had to prepare, design, and print catchy, informative leaflets and posters to attract participants. This in itself required a significant amount of effort. Preparation for the rallies necessitated vast human and material resources and countless working hours. One of the biggest public rallies in Otpor!'s history was the celebration of Orthodox New Year on January 13, 2000. More than 100 activists worked for at least three weeks spreading 25,000 leaflets and more than 12,000 posters. As a result, 30,000 people were brought to the iconic Republic Square in Belgrade. At the rally, Otpor! made its point that, as long as Milošević was in power, there would be no reasons for celebration. With the slogan "2000 – this is the year!," they sent the powerful message that 2000 would be the year that "life" must win in Serbia. Event planning was then a considerably more time-consuming undertaking than it is today.

An impressive study of protests in Spain by Oxford University, in

Figure 6.1 *Otpor! printed pamphlet distributed in Belgrade, Serbia, 2000 (translation: "This is the Year.")*

Box 6.1 Bosnia's #JMBG movement

We can make a regional comparison between the Serbian Otpor! movement and Bosnia's #JMBG movement. Also known as the "Baby Revolution," it gained traction during the summer of 2013 and succeeded in bringing thousands of people to the streets in the biggest protests in the country's recent history. The hashtag in the name is already indicative of the importance Twitter had in its organization and denotes the difference between the avid web users of #JMBG and the street prowlers of Otpor!. Though #JMBG certainly organized a great deal of many effective rallies and protests, unlike Otpor!, most of this was via Twitter and Facebook rather than through café rendezvous and SMS. Its members cut down on printing costs by creating a Facebook album of materials for people to print at home. They used new media effectively while maintaining a determined, cohesive, and functioning operation. #JMBG activists were able to use new media to reduce the hours of necessary preparation but continued to be highly efficient, investing the hours they saved with new media in other important tasks and activities to broaden the scope of the movement.

Like Otpor!, however, #JMBG espoused a broad cause that could appeal to any Bosnian regardless of class or ethnicity: anticorruption. In fact the whole affair began as outrage over the failure by squabbling cantons to distribute JMBG numbers to recently born babies, thus limiting their legal rights and making it difficult to get a passport. (JMBG is an acronym for Jedinstveni Matični Broj Građana, or Unique Master Citizen Number.) The lack of identification numbers caused the death of two infants by making it impossible for them to be treated at hospitals for lethal diseases. This served as a catalyst for mobilizing many Bosnians who had endured for years blatantly corrupt practices by politicians, regardless of region, religion, or ethnicity.

The #JMBG movement, or the "Baby Revolution," was thus very united. To date, it has a following in most cities of Bosnia, crossing the ethnic and cantonal divisions that had so brutally divided the nation during the 1990s. With the help of new media it has united the global Bosnian community as well. In one of its Facebook campaigns, people would take a picture with a sign that simply stated "#JMBG." People would then upload this photo on the JMBG Facebook page, where others would respond with likes, comments, or similar photos. This prompted hundreds of photos from Bosnians but also rallied the international community around the cause – anyone who simply supported the movement could participate by writing "#JMBG" and taking a photo. Even though outsiders could not be present in the real-field campaigns, they were able to show their solidarity in a quick and efficient manner. Very rapidly people began to get creative with the pictures – finding local celebrities or taking pictures in interesting settings.

Much in the same way that people became personal stakeholders when they were able to comment and forward the "mass SMS" messages of Otpor!, the #JMBG movement allowed people to contribute personally and creatively with their images – generating mass impact *and* interaction, and bringing the Bosnian struggle to the attention of international players and partners.

collaboration with the University of Zaragoza, provides evidence that new media is a very powerful tool for cheap and fast public mobilization (González-Bailón et al. 2011) – similar to the quick and easy way that Bosnians from abroad were able to show their support by snapping a picture. The protests in Spain under the Movimiento 15-M were sparked by the political response to the financial crisis, resulting in demands for new forms of democratic representation. The main target of the campaign was an organized protest on May 15, 2011, which brought tens of thousands of people to the streets from fifty-nine cities all over the country. "Digital media has played an important role both in the recent wave of mobilizations in the Arab world and in protests across Western countries, such as the Occupy movement across cities worldwide," explains lead author Sandra Gonzalez-Bailon. After following the posting behavior of 87,569 users and tracking a total of 581,750 protest messages over a thirty-day period, she continues, "If people are exposed to many messages calling for action within a short time frame, they are more likely to respond to this apparent urgency and join in. This creates recruitment bursts that can translate into a global cascade with truly dramatic effects, as the massive demonstrations and the wave of occupations that followed shows" (University of Oxford 2011).

Let's assume that a present-day activist needs a minute or two to post a Twitter message and compare this with the effort Serbian activists needed to invest some thirteen years ago to reach a similar size audience and organize protests in sixty cities of Serbia. The impact is definitely impressive. With the help of email, Facebook and Twitter, groups with members in all time zones can gather in virtual space and create invitations in fifteen minutes, and they have a much greater reach. While we must not confuse the committed activists with those that may be willing to support the cause only from a distance, new media has definitely decreased the barriers of entry to into "low-level" participation.

Keeping the core: the bonds technology cannot replace

Paradoxically, one of the best things for the success of a mass collective action movement is having a small number of closely connected activists dedicated to a shared vision – not the "march of millions" that is so often seen as the sign of successful campaigns. According to sociologists Florence Passy and Marco Giugni, strong interpersonal ties within a movement are just as persuasive a reason to join and participate in a movement as are the person's interest in the issue

Box 6.2 Fundraising through social media

Some advocacy groups have seen a sizeable boost in donations after successfully implementing new media campaigns. Many of these groups used the technique of harnessing hundreds or thousands of small donations that add up to a big sum, frequently dubbed "crowd-sourcing" or "crowd-funding." Probably the best-known social movement website is www.avaaz.org – a petition and donation consolidation machine that claims to have organized over 10,000 rallies and raised over $15 million online.

Other sites such as www.kickstarter.com and www.indiegogo.com have become excellent fundraising tools for social justice causes, and even for producing films and books about nonviolent resistance. Aside from being able to raise funds using online media, these sites can simultaneously act as media platforms. Just the fact of getting featured on the Kickstarter or Indiegogo homepage has become a marketing tool in and of itself.[2] In other cases, activists have leveraged fundraising via social media to gain access to the mass media. For example, in the week June 2–9, 2013, the Turkish activist group Democracy in Action succeeded in securing $108,371 via Indiegogo to fund a full-page ad in the *New York Times* and raise international awareness about the situation in Turkey.

and perceived level of self-efficacy (Passy and Giugni 2001). Malcolm Gladwell (2010) illustrates this in his article about social movements when he discusses the lunch counter sit-ins in Greensboro, North Carolina, which began not with thousands of people, but instead by just four college freshmen who dared one another to order a cup of coffee in Woolworth's. In another civil rights movement anecdote, Gladwell discusses how, in 1964, the Mississippi Freedom Summer Project was spearheaded by four college freshmen who had been to high school together or lived together. They had witnessed friends who were beaten and arrested, and they knew, on a very personal level, the effects of the oppressive American system at the time.

As a point of comparison, we can look at how a quarter of the unpaid white student volunteers brought in from the North to raise civil rights awareness in the South deserted the project after three students were murdered by white supremacists. Doug McAdam (1983) explains that, while "*all* of the applicants – participants and withdrawals alike – emerge as highly committed, articulate supporters of the goals and values of the summer program," the difference was that the activists who remained in the South were more likely to have personal connections with Southern locals than the people who did not stay around. Violent groups show similar trends as nonviolent ones in this regard: 70 percent of Red Brigade recruits in 1970s Italy had at least one good friend already in the group (Gladwell 2010). There is ample evidence that preexisting social networks are a major contributing factor in the recruitment process (Jasper and Poulsen 1995; Munson 2008).

The Serbian Otpor! movement again serves as an example of this – the core founding members had all been friends in high school, attended anti-Milošević rallies in the 1990s, and shared close interpersonal connections. They would frequently stay at one another's houses, and joke and play pranks on one another. Even before it turned into a movement, the close interpersonal ties the members shared laid the foundation for the core activist group that would go on to plan the nationwide movement. This meant that the amount of time activists spent together strengthened the bonds between them and increased the likelihood of success. If an event did not succeed as planned, not only were individuals letting down the movement, but they were also letting down their friends and those to whom they had become close as a result of participation in the movement. This smaller cadre of committed activists – committed both to their cause *and* to one another's personal wellbeing – is, from what we've witnessed, an incredibly important basis for building a movement.

Learning that close personal ties through small numbers of people is a key component of mass mobilization movements, Otpor! activists created an educational organization to share the lessons they learned in Serbia with nonviolent movements around the world. The Centre for Applied Nonviolent Action and Strategies (CANVAS) has organized workshops for activists from fifty countries since 2002. Training is always limited to ten to twenty people per workshop, and friendship groups and those who have fought alongside one another are encouraged to apply together. If the participants are not already acquainted, often they become close during the course of the workshop, having dealt with the same types of regional struggles.

From its interactions with nonviolent revolutionaries and scholars, CANVAS has witnessed, first hand, the effects of new media on people power movements. Interestingly, though, throughout all the changes in communication technology, CANVAS's major successes have not been based on training people remotely through conference calls or emails, but in fact quite the opposite: real-field campaigns that facilitate a mentor–mentee relationship have been shown to be the most valuable. It is through in-the-field dialogues and interactions between veteran activists who know the inner workings of planning a movement and emerging activists trying to find the right way to implement their ideas for a future democratic society which prove the most productive. We will detail throughout the rest of this chapter how the activists we work with have maximized effectiveness of new media in campaigns and how the latter has undeniably changed nonviolent resistance. However, we must emphasize that real-field nonviolent resistance campaigns must take precedence in order for the effectiveness of social media to be maximized.

"We speak for ourselves!": the new power of public scrutiny

The sharing of visual media has made it difficult for regimes to commit acts of violence and get away with it. The accessibility of camera phones means that, with a quick enough eye, almost anything can be captured on video and distributed for the world to see, eluding traditional media outlets over which the state often has control. One case in which social media contributed to international condemnation of violence is Myanmar's 2007 Saffron Revolution. Myanmar's ruling junta, the State Peace and Development Council, removed fuel subsidies without notice in late summer of 2007. In response, in protest against rising fuel prices, citizens began marching that August to an unprecedented degree. Security forces immediately arrested civilians, and the process of marching and being arrested continued for another month before Buddhist monks joined the protests. Although Myanmar is widely considered to have high levels of censorship and low levels of technological innovation and internet penetration, "citizen journalists" managed to distribute videos internationally in order to hold the regime accountable.

Most Burmese citizens never posted videos to nationally based websites and blogs for fear of retribution from the junta. Instead, those working at the periphery – Burmese ex-pats living in neighboring countries – documented abuses and sent videos and audio to international human rights organizations such as the Burma Campaign UK, Amnesty International and Avaaz. The potent images of police abusing monks as they chanted Buddhist statements affected viewers, which led to public statements by human rights groups denouncing the junta's actions, as well as the direct implementation of sanctions on the country. These NGOs and civil-sector organizations coordinated an international protest called the Global Day of Action for Burma on October 6, 2007, consisting of rallies in over one hundred cities in more than thirty countries.

Although international pressure did not force the Burmese junta into hiding, it did elicit sanctions and condemnation from influential diplomats made aware of the Burmese people's plight, at which point government officials became involved. The junta reacted defensively and enacted an internet blackout – which actually brought people out into the streets. It has been argued that, without the internet-based campaigns that were so crucial to the Saffron Revolution, the government would have reacted even more harshly, and more protesters and monks would have died (Chowdhury 2008, p. 8). Websites such as www.free-burma.org helped to publicize the movement and served as invaluable resources.

An arguably more successful example of new media putting a price tag on state-sponsored violence is the 2009 case of Iran's Neda Agha-Soltan, a civilian activist who had been harassed by authorities but who was killed after stepping out of her car to attend a protest during the Green Revolution, a series of protests in response to alleged election fraud. This was the most watched death in recorded history (Fathi 2009). Unlike in the Burmese case, this footage was used both as a rallying point within the country itself and to draw international attention. The death was captured on three separate cameras and quickly became a unifying point for the Iranian opposition. In a press conference a few weeks later, US President Barack Obama addressed the video and the Iranian protests as a whole with the following statement:

> In 2009, no iron fist is strong enough to shut off the world from bearing witness to peaceful protests [sic] of justice. Despite the Iranian government's efforts to expel journalists and isolate itself, powerful images and poignant words have made their way to us through cell phones and computers, and so we've watched what the Iranian people are doing. (CBS 2009)

Some claim that the role of Twitter in the Iranian struggle has, by and large, been highly overstated (Esfandiari 2010). However, two years later, in Egypt, Facebook played a crucial role in the spreading of information that led to a revolution with the "We Are All Khaled Said" campaign. Khaled Said, a 26-year-old computer programmer living in Alexandria, posted video footage of police and drug dealers cooperating. In response, police snatched Said from an internet café and beat him to death in front of the owners of the café and some other eyewitnesses. Soon after, pictures of Said's mangled body were posted online and went viral. This event resonated with Egyptians because the victim could have been anyone. Said quickly became a martyr and both the face of the Egyptian opposition and a symbol of police brutality. Wael Ghonim, a computer engineer, started the "We Are All Khaled Said" Facebook group, on which he posted a call to protest on January 25, 2011 (Zunes 2011). The subsequent protests served as a crucial jumping-off point for the rest of the country.

Web trappers and great firewalls: how the autocrats adapted

On January 7, 2011, at 22:34:00 GMT, Renesys (the Internet Intelligence Authority) reported the "virtually simultaneous withdrawal of all routes to Egyptian networks in the Internet's global routing table." In sum, Egypt experienced a surprise internet outage lasting five consecutive days (Dainotti et al. 2011). On January 27, 80 million Egyptians were cut off from the web. Three days earlier, the government had ordered the blocking of Twitter. Such drastic measures were soon imitated by neighboring Libya and Syria. Crude yet straightforward site blocking, "denial of service" attacks (a targeted interruption of internet service), and the more drastic outages employed by Mubarak, Gaddafi, and Assad's administrations were a trademark of early attempts by such regimes to quell the upsurge of internet use to organize the local revolts against authorities. Caught by surprise, and apparently lacking the time to attempt more sophisticated tools of censorship, such regimes panicked and pulled the plug on the internet, only to find that, by the time they had done so, it was already too late and the protesters no longer required the internet to mobilize large numbers of people on the streets. None of these drastic measures, not even the mobilization of unrestrained state violence against the growing opposition, prevented Mubarak's removal from power by the army in February or the death of Gaddafi in October that same year.[3] Syrian autocrat Bashar al-Assad – perhaps learning from these pitfalls – did not follow the same trajectory, however.

In May 2011, the Syrian Electronic Army was founded as the first Arab internet army and was used to great effect by launching sophisticated cyber-attacks and spamming campaigns on dissident websites, foreign news, local media, and even Western government pages (Noman 2011). Claiming to be a team of young Syrian patriots who did not want to stay passive "towards the fabrication of facts on the events in Syria" (though in reality under the supervision of the Syrian Computer Society, an organization founded in 1995 by Bashar al-Assad's own brother, Bassel al-Assad), the Syrian Electronic Army has proven to be one of the first and most active attempts by governments to organize a young, internet-savvy, and loyalist counterweight to those who would perceive the internet as a safer avenue through which to criticize and mobilize support against the regime.

The Syrian Computer Society shows that, rather than stick with the awkward site-blocking and internet outages (that were easily traceable to the government), regime loyalists are adapting and attempting to find more creative ways to use new media against them and ultimately to turn the tables on who maintains the balance of power in cyberspace.

Perhaps the most notorious evidence that authoritarian regimes are catching up with democratic activists in terms of the application of new media is something informally known as the "Great Firewall of China." In 2011, the published Chinese budget for security and surveillance leapt by nearly 14 percent, to a total of $95 billion, compared to $91.5 billion in military expenditures (Dobson 2012, p. 281). The Chinese authorities, usually on the local level, find diverse ways of dissuading criticism against the Communist Party, though, on a national level, the Great Firewall succeeds for the most part in automatically filtering out particular keywords and URLs at the internet service provider (ISP) level. This allows companies working within China to block subversive and illegal content. In fact, most of the censorship at this level is undertaken by private corporations carrying out government regulations – not the government itself. Even foreign companies such as Yahoo, MSN, and (for a while) Google act as censors of a sort within China to avoid the Chinese government meddling in their affairs. Most of the techniques used by the Chinese authorities are similar to those used in democratic nations to filter age-appropriate content in households or to filter work-appropriate sites in offices. Thus, since politically controversial results do not even turn up in search engines, users do not know that such sites exist at all. Furthermore, social networking sites such as Facebook and Twitter either do not exist in China or have more closely monitored Chinese counterparts.

The Chinese government is taking even more clever steps than simply coercing new media providers to carry out their rules and regulations at the router and ISP level. The Communist Party itself uses new media to reach out to the Chinese people in order to gauge opinion and weigh their grievances. Recently, the Open Decision Making Program in the massive port of Hangzhou began broadcasting government meetings and public hearings to encourage public participation, after which the city saw a 12 percent drop in public grievances after the first year (Dobson 2012, p. 260). In fact, Chinese citizens could be said to have access to more and better information than ever before. On the internet, the average web-surfing citizen shops online, plays video games, and checks their favorite sites, allowed to go about their business unhindered as long as they don't cross the line of threatening the party's monopoly on power. The party learned how to co-opt the internet for its own purposes, exhibiting its responsiveness to whatever frustrations its people air online as long as they remain on a local level, focused on economic or social issues (especially issues of corruption) and in no way demanding large-scale political change in the system.

Other governments are much more aggressive in how they use the internet to foil activists, creating fake accounts on Facebook or Twitter and sending links to opposition members. Censors have become adept at impersonating other people. During the Arab Spring uprisings in 2011 in Bahrain, the accounts of arrested Bahrainis were used to set up false links with internet protocol (IP) addresses with tracking traps attached, meaning that those who clicked on the links suffered consequences ranging from house raids to losing their jobs. According to Eric King, head of research at Privacy International, "Bahrain particularly has been at the forefront of this, using FinFisher and Trovicor, both intelligence gathering software that some have compared to malware, and now this method of IP tracking, to identify, arrest and mistreat those who challenge their authority" (Brewster 2013).

Such attacks on activists through imposter sites are focused not only on individuals but on media sites as well and are carried out frequently in the countries of Iran, Bahrain, Belarus, and Vietnam. Among this group, Iran stands out as using particularly draconian methods of regulating internet use; in 2012, Mahmoud Ahmadinejad's conservative government attempted to accelerate the implementation of a plan that had been on the back burner for the past decade: an independent Iranian internet. While he succeeded in imposing new laws concerning cyber cafés and developed a national email to streamline contact between government officials and Iranian citizens, on account of the financial and technical difficulties of implementation the national internet has yet to be launched. Regardless, it does represent one of the most extreme methods authoritarian regimes may use in the future not only to regulate activists within their boundaries by removing any sense of anonymity from web users but also to regulate communication with the outside world, possibly even blocking foreign browsers.

This is evidence of a trend that shows how autocratic regimes might make use of new media for oppressive aims. It is clear that the "Facebook/Twitter Revolutions" can no longer be reproduced with the same degree of ease or element of surprise. And the fight is no longer one-sided. Now, rather than being limited to defense, governments have greater offensive capabilities than ever – from the comforting paternalism of the Chinese Open Decision Making Program to the more venomous cyber-attacks of the new Syrian Electronic Army and its regional counterparts. Autocrats have certainly learned their lesson. Activists should no longer expect that they will be able to subvert authoritarian regimes simply by utilizing new technologies.

... And knowledge for all: self-teaching revolution

Theoretical information, such as general training manuals and the philosophy and practice of nonviolence, are now extremely easy to transmit thanks to websites, social media, and other online sources through "open-access" and "open-source" resources – which have clear benefits for nonviolent civil resisters.

The term "open access" has today come to refer to anything that is available for free online, on the assumption that it has been deemed common knowledge or important for the wider society. Similarly, the term "open source" was coined in 1998 by software developers who advocated such processes that were technically advantageous for the development of software in general, but it also has social implications that are often overlooked. The Free Software Movement was launched officially in 1983 to achieve the goals of freedom to use, study, modify, and redistribute software. The social benefits of free software are outlined in the GNU Manifesto[4] (published in 1985) and read as an impressive statement of the relationship between emerging technologies and social good – an issue that is increasingly coming to the forefront of political civil resistance.

Open-access materials about nonviolent resistance create the possibility for people to teach themselves. While manuals will never be a substitute for face-to-face education or training, they can streamline the learning process so that people who have the drive and will may be able at least to glean the most appropriate tactics for themselves. We believe that it is possible to teach nonviolent tactics and strategies to anyone who may want to use them in their own home-grown struggles.

Here at CANVAS we endeavor to make all of our materials open access by having our publications and research papers available for free download through our website. We spread and disseminate printed books to our workshop participants free of charge. Starting in 2009 with the post-election unrest in Iran, the number of books downloaded skyrocketed, and we learned that the sheer fact of their availability may have helped guide resisters in their struggles. It would cost an exorbitant amount of time and money to spread 17,000 copies of

CANVAS's flagship publication *Nonviolent Struggle: 50 Crucial Points* from our Belgrade office to, say, Tehran. However, that number of copies of the book were downloaded (in Farsi) from the CANVAS website in July 2009 alone.

Furthermore, free social media websites have drastically changed the way we are connected to activists. In 2003, at the beginning of our international engagement, activists from around the world used mostly mutual contacts and telephones – email, if we were lucky – to reach us. In 2011 and 2012, more than 75 percent of the people who contacted us did so through Facebook or Twitter accounts – citing the number of likes their campaign has garnered or "our mutual friends" as proof of their involvement in strategic nonviolent resistance. Although open-access materials are a valuable means of connecting with people and spreading knowledge, we use them only when appropriate; in Egypt, activists used both email and photocopy machines to circulate a handbook called "How to Protest Intelligently" during the winter 2011 revolution. The originators asked distributors to avoid Twitter and Facebook because Egyptian authorities were monitoring the sites (Black 2011).

CANVAS often gets press because the Otpor! symbol has shown up in different movements worldwide, and occasionally autocrats have used this as evidence of our involvement in their region, whether or not we have trained people there. We have been blamed publicly by authorities who find our materials in the hands of activists and cannot comprehend that they simply went online and downloaded them. Sometimes movements have grown and prospered independently of a CANVAS training; however, movement organizers were able to implement similar tactics because they had free access to materials. We use this as evidence of the fact that open-access media can make the resources for nonviolent social change available to those who will use them in a productive way in their own domestic struggles.

Clicktivism: the dangers of online activism

From the point of view of CANVAS, the major advantages of new media are that it makes things faster and cheaper, it puts a price tag on state-sponsored violence, and it allows for people to educate themselves about nonviolent resistance to an unprecedented degree. However, online space can become saturated; when seeing many pleas for action glaring from their computer screens, internet users can become apathetic, in a contemporary manifestation of "compassion fatigue" (Moeller 1999). Furthermore, opposition groups must keep in mind that virtual "people power" does not equate to real "people power." The combination of mass impact and mass interaction has also given birth to a new type of online advocacy, deemed "clicktivism" by those who consider it a lackadaisical measure with little potential to spark a real revolution.

For a good example of clicktivism we might look at the documentary "Kony 2012," which accumulated more than 100 million views in the first six days of its release, becoming among the most viral videos in YouTube history. It was put out on March 5, 2012, by the activist group Invisible Children and sought to raise awareness about the Ugandan rebel leader Joseph Kony and his practice of recruiting child soldiers for the Lord's Resistance Army (LRA). The video created attention and buzz in its own right. By March 7, 2012, two days later, there had been 2,448,227 tweets about Kony, a figure that increased to 5,469,696 for the whole of 2012. Of those tweets, 868,209 were positive and 694,881 were negative. Inevitably, however, there was a significant drop in sentiment by the end of the year. Invisible Children was accused by local Ugandans of marketing Kony's image in a highly inappropriate fashion that upset actual victims of the LRA. For other groups, such as the Uhuru Solidarity Movement, the premise of Invisible Children was blatantly colonialist in spirit. It characterized the organization as consisting of "white hipsters traveling to Africa to draw sympathy for African children while not doing anything constructive to help them" (Fox 2013).

There is a fine balance between exaggerating your support for a righteous purpose and basing your membership on the amount of comments or tweets you have – a "low-level" commitment that may be useful in gaining the crowd but not keeping the core. Nobody can deny that gaining international attention to an issue is a critical turning point for a movement; the Free Burma Campaign from 2007 serves as a good model of how to engage with the international community after a grassroots movement has taken hold. However, social changes are spurred by radical thinking and paradigm shifts. Social media may make information-sharing much easier, but it does not inherently encourage productive conversation or innovative ideas, particularly in the early stages. In fact it encourages organizations to think of their supporters as numbers, as activist campaigns start increasingly to resemble advertising campaigns, which don't necessarily translate into success.

The Serbian Otpor! movement did not begin with millions of people on the streets – in fact some of the early campaigns were carried out simply by a couple of core activists with a creative vision. One of the movement's most effective tactics was a dilemma action – an event or prank that puts the opposing forces in a lose–lose situation (Sørensen and Martin 2014). For example, two Otpor! members painted Slobodan Milošević's face on a barrel and set it up in front of the Belgrade National Theater. They offered passersby the chance to pay a "Dime for Change" – to hit Milošević's head on the barrel with a baseball bat. The members managed to slip away before the prank was carried away by its own momentum. Eventually police responded and were faced with the dilemma of either doing nothing or arresting the barrel. They arrested the barrel, and the next day it was front-page news all across Serbia. Some sort of news communication service was necessary in order to spread the word about what had happened, but it was a *news-generating event in itself* that was the brainchild of two people and needed some amount of secrecy to be pulled off. In a high-risk situation in which two people could not have met in public and dragged a barrel to a public square, social media might have been another outlet for a similar prank, but it would not have replaced its effectiveness.

The largest problem with clicktivism is not that it uses digital platforms in and of itself, but rather that it assumes that using an online medium replaces innovative, creative action. Clicktivism boils down to intellectual or creative laziness, using new technologies *in place of* deliberate action.

One further issue with clicktivism is that it tends to whitewash culturally specific issues that are always involved in real-field campaigns. Grassroots actions such as the "Dime for Change" are based largely on the cultural context of a country's domestic activists but also on the physical space in which the actions occur – something that is best understood by familiarity with the culture *and* the context of people living there. For example, when Otpor! activists created the "Dime for Change" campaign, they thought about Serbians' hard-edged sense of humor, which would find it funny to bat Milošević squarely in the face, as well as the fact that the barrel should be placed in the middle of the highest density walking zone in the city. They even anticipated that the police would do something silly like arrest the barrel and thus came equipped with cameras. There were no Facebook pages or Twitter feeds, but the effect was not diminished. And, despite the change in communications technology, the real act of creativity was not one related to communications but instead the seed of the idea itself to use country-specific humor in a high-traffic area. It is the creative activists themselves who know what is truly subversive – which may or may not include the tool of new media. Education of tactics is important because activists may then maximize the tools and adapt them to their own struggles where appropriate.

We see more and more how people use pranks and jokes to garner a high media payoff. It is usually effective precisely because it invokes a culturally specific situation. The more important question for civil resisters, then, must be one not of how to reach a wide swathe of people but one of what activists can do that will be both relevant and pertinent so that media outlets will respond positively. For activists living in the twenty-first century, to disregard new media would be to disregard a key communication tool. If we relate back to the example of how Democracy in Action placed a full-page ad on www.indiegogo.com to publicize the Gezi Park protests, we can see that the real creativity was in using a nontraditional source of news (indiegogo) to publicize and call attention to the fact that traditional news outlets (such as the *New York Times*) were not giving due attention to the mass civil protests occurring there. This was an especially relevant issue, as one of the main grievances of Turkish protesters was that the traditional news outlets refused to portray the scale of the protests accurately. We are not claiming that using new media or digital platforms for activist causes leads in and of itself to "clicktivism" – simply that one should be aware of its pitfalls.

Media of our time: new means to the same ends

In 2013, with the results of the Arab Spring still in confusion in Egypt and Syria and with no tangible concessions achieved in the wake of the Occupy movements, we are reminded that new media, even with its new speed, affordability, and broader reach, is no replacement for true action and creative subversion. The trap of overreliance on loose-knit networks and the pitfall of what we call "clicktivism" cannot be underestimated. However, we must observe that new media has irreparably damaged the confidence of authoritarian governments and opened up the possibility for new forms of civil dissent.

The use of technology has spawned countless varying narratives about whether it has done more to help or to harm nonviolent civil resistance. One thing we can be sure of: in people-powered struggles, both democrats and autocrats have learned to benefit from the speed and efficiency of new media. Both have progressively found out how to raid for information, shield their own, and share their information with each other at their convenience. What originally was touted as an easy avenue for social mobilization is clearly much more complex.

The Arab Spring may have alerted the world to the power of Facebook and Twitter, but it also kicked off impressive developments in the art of surveying and filtering what is shared on such sites. War is, increasingly, organized from remote places, behind screens and keyboards, with malware attacks on Iranian nuclear facilities and university student websites alike, recruitment in chat rooms, and propaganda on video-sharing sites. Similarly, the people-power phenomenon present in both flash mobs and political protests is relying more and more on internet technologies.

But how much has it really changed? So what if the police attack protesters with a computer virus as much as they attack with the traditional club? So what if activists now communicate through Facebook groups instead of by telephone? Conflict is not won with information alone. The Chinese Communist Party does not maintain its still ironclad control merely because it monitors the internet, and the 2011 revolution in Egypt was not won by the activists in Tahrir Square by those whose support was limited to clicking "share" on Facebook. It was the people who exposed themselves to the same risks, punishments, and ordeals as nonviolent protesters generations before them. The industry that has developed around social media gives itself far too much credit, and by patting them too much on the back we are in danger of forgetting the essentials: resistance against autocracy will always depend on the endurance and adaptability of the democrats and the errors and gaffes of the autocrats.

Nonviolent civil resistance is won through unity, planning, and nonviolent discipline. Where new media is interesting is that it has changed the game in how both resisters and regimes communicate among themselves, fundraise, recruit, propagate messages to the public, and spy on one another. It is not a weapon in and of itself. An analogous comparison would be the installation of radar in fighter planes, which revolutionized air combat forever, or the invention of the telegraph, which changed the rules of battle over wide swathes of land and negated the distance between commanding officers. But radar could not have saved a pilot if he did not have a fighter plane or the skill to maneuver it, and a telegraph could not have saved a commander if he did not have the ability to react properly in a timely and strategically sound manner. Of course, in a broader sense, Shirkey is correct: the combination of communications and broadcast media makes new media a revolutionary innovation and has heavily affected human interaction. But when it comes to conflict, violent or nonviolent, new technology can still only be a means to an end.

Questions for discussion

1 How do you see the term "creative activism?" What is it and what is its relation to nonviolent resistance and/or social movements? Think of examples when activists used creative techniques for getting their message heard.

2 Consider the 'laughtivist' example of when Otpor! members painted Slobodan Milošević's face on a barrel and had people hit it with a bat. Some would consider this an aggressive act that borders on violence. What defines the line between nonviolent and violent techniques? Do you agree that this was a nonviolent action? Where does one draw the line between using aggression in a nonviolent manner and using aggression in a violent way?

3 People such as Julian Assange, the founder of WikiLeaks, and whistleblowers Chelsea (Bradley) Manning and Edward Snowden have thrust the issues of leaking and whistleblowing into the middle of the debate about civil resistance. How do these individuals fit into the discussion of new media and nonviolent struggle? Is their role different from that of other types of nonviolent activists mentioned in this text?

4 Throughout the chapter, the term "social movement" is referred to, and often the authors use it explicitly in the context of nonviolent action. How are social movements and nonviolent resistance connected? Is it possible to have a mass movement that utilizes violence? What would this look like, and how is it different than armed conflict or guerrilla warfare?

Suggestions for further reading and research

Boyd, Andrew (2012) *Beautiful Trouble: A Toolbox for Revolution*. London: OR Books.

Centre for Applied Nonviolent Action and Strategies (CANVAS) www.canvasopedia.org.

Jasper, James M. (1997) *The Art of Moral Protest: Culture, Biography, and Creativity in Social Movements*. Chicago: University of Chicago Press.

Sørensen, Majken Jul (2008) "Humor as a Serious Strategy of Nonviolent Resistance to Oppression," *Peace & Change*, 33(2): 167–190.

PART III

Contexts

CHAPTER 7

Civil Rights and Domestic Policy

Amanda D. Clark and Patrick G. Coy[1]

People have disagreed over politics and policies for centuries, waging conflicts with each other in order to further their preferred structures and policies. The questions for this book and for this chapter are the means that are chosen to further one's goals. Movements that rely upon violence to bring about change frequently construct the conflict as an "us vs. them" experience. There is little room for compromise or acceptance of competing ideas, and intense alienation between the parties often results, no matter who triumphs. There are, however, other viable approaches to accomplish social and political change.

The twentieth century brought an increased use of nonviolent tactics to effect change to revolutionary systems and also to reform existing systems. One of the many advantages that nonviolent action delivers in any change campaign is that the opponent is not turned into an "other" and vanquished. As we will see in this chapter, such an approach is particularly important in domestic policy conflicts, as disputing parties still need to live and work together in the same community long after a campaign is completed and the conflict is "resolved." Nonviolent campaigns reject a dichotomous either/or and us/them approach that objectifies the opponent. Instead, campaigners construct the issue as a shared problem facing their community and seek to create a sense of "we" as they highlight the unfair practices and injustices that are holding their community back. All of these dynamics are well illustrated in the nonviolent movement that challenged and changed segregation policies and practices in Nashville, Tennessee, in the US in 1960.

In the 1950s in the Southern US, segregation of whites and blacks was still the official and unofficial law of the land. But this American-style apartheid, known as the "Jim Crow system," was soon to change, albeit grudgingly. Several key events, including the bus boycott in Baton Rouge, Louisiana (1953), the *Brown* vs. *Board of Education* Supreme Court decision ending racial segregation in public schools (1954), the bus boycott in Montgomery, Alabama (1955–6), and President Eisenhower's intervention in the integration of a high school in Little

Rock, Arkansas (1957), proved that the time had come to fight against inequality. The success of bus boycotts had demonstrated that the nonviolent techniques utilized by Gandhi's followers to gain Indian independence in 1948 could also work in the American South.

In the winter of 1959–60, Nashville, Tennessee, became an important stop on the road to civil rights. College students staged sit-ins at the segregated lunch counters of major downtown department stores. Although these department stores would allow black customers to shop, blacks were forced to use separate bathrooms and were not allowed to eat in the store restaurants. The relentless humiliation that came with segregation helped these students decide it was time to actively resist. As 19-year-old James Bevel put it, "I'm sick and tired of waiting" (Morris 1984, p. 206).

economic impact of nonviolent action

An important component of the disciplined focus on nonviolent action was economic. Businesses that depended upon black consumers could not afford disruption of day-to-day business or prolonged boycotts. As demonstrated in the case study that follows, success in Nashville depended on this disciplined focus on the political, social, and even economic dimensions of nonviolent action. The case also provides an opportunity to examine the steps involved in a nonviolent campaign. In particular, we will apply Adam Curle's conflict progression matrix as a framework to analyze the Nashville campaign.

Background

examples

During the early months of 1960, sit-ins and related acts of nonviolent resistance to segregation blossomed across the South. The Nashville sit-ins serve as a prime example of the organization, disciplined execution, and rigorous adherence to the principles of nonviolent action required to achieve the end result of policy changes. The action campaign in Nashville was strategic, requiring months of education in nonviolent tactics, the identification of targets, and test sit-ins. It was important to the movement for a number of reasons. First, it was not led by Martin Luther King, Jr., and thus proved that others following the principles of nonviolent action could succeed unaided by the power of a famous name and the resources that came with it. The case is also important because the students involved became important leaders in the civil rights movement for years to come.

Nashville provided a distinctive setting for a civil rights battle. Although segregation was a fact of daily life in the city, it was carried out "not with the passion of angry racist officials, but more as a cultural leftover from the past" (Halberstam 1998, p. 110). The white residents of the city, self-titled "the Athens of the South," thought themselves reasoned and progressive. The mayor, Ben West, was a moderate; he had increased the number of blacks in the police and fire departments and had helped integrate the restaurant at the Nashville airport. The *Nashville Tennessean* was a liberal newspaper that frequently covered civil rights issues and supported the end of the discriminatory poll tax. Unusual for the times, there were even black representatives on the city council, and Nashville had a large group of educated black elites (Ackerman and Duvall 2000).

Although this case is grounded on student activism in the face of daunting odds, many adults were critical to the success of the Nashville sit-ins. The students received months of training in workshops on nonviolent action by Reverend James Lawson, Jr., a conscientious objector who had been imprisoned for eleven months for his refusal to register for the draft during the Korean War. Paroled to do Methodist mission work, he spent three years in India, where he learned about Gandhian nonviolence. After returning to the US he enrolled in a master's program in theology at Oberlin College in Ohio, where he met King at a speaking event. King was impressed with Lawson's knowledge of nonviolence and urged him to move south immediately to promote nonviolent change. Employed by the Fellowship of Reconciliation (FOR) as a Southern "field secretary" to promote racial justice through nonviolent action, Lawson went to Nashville and enrolled in the Divinity School at Vanderbilt University.

In 1958, Lawson initially held workshops on nonviolence in the basement of the church pastored by Reverend Kelly Miller Smith, who had founded the Nashville Christian Leadership Council (NCLC) earlier that same year. Smith's acceptance of Lawson into the community immediately gave his message about the power of nonviolent resistance increased credibility (Halberstam 1998). Use of the church also gave the sit-in movement a built-in communication conduit and base of support in the community, a common role played by black churches throughout the civil rights movement.

Participants in Lawson's earliest workshops were mostly black adults. After learning about nonviolent resistance, they discussed how to apply it in the Nashville context. It was mothers who provided the target:

> They told of how [when shopping downtown] they and their children were exhausted and had no place to stop, except to sit down in the street. They talked about how painful it was to be in the children's clothing floor at Harvey's where there was a carousel where children could play while mothers

had coffee. They talked about having to tell a child you can't play on that but they see other children on it. And so as a result of those descriptions, I knew by the end of the workshops we had to go after downtown and we had to begin with pulling down those signs and with restaurants and lunch counters. (Lawson, cited in Lee 2010, p. 134)

The lunch counters were tactical targets with a larger strategic goal, since they were seen as an "opening wedge" (Isaac et al. 2012, p. 167). In effect, they were a soft target susceptible to being pried open, making it possible to lay bare the entire Jim Crow system. The lunch counters were a good place to start for several reasons. The student protesters would quickly have the support and backing of the adult black females in the community since the downtown stores and the lunch counters were so important to mothers. In the workshops, DeLois Wilkenson told of visits to downtown stores and her pain and humiliation at having to lie to her children about being in too much of a hurry to eat there after shopping. Another black mother said that, when her son climbed onto a counter stool, a clerk ordered her to "Get that nigger kid off of that stool" (Limbo 2006, p. 165). Such regular indignities made the black women of Nashville natural allies of the student activists. The lunch counters were also high profile yet focused targets, and they were located within stores that already served the black community. How could storeowners take money for other goods sold in the stores while refusing to serve a 25-cent ham-burger to the same patrons? Many whites could also easily see the irony of the injustice.

Student mobilization can be an effective strategy for nonviolent action because students often have flexible schedules, most do not have families to support, and many are willing to take risks for social change (Morris 1981). In the fall of 1958, Lawson moved his non-violence workshops to a church closer to Fisk University and started recruiting students. Since the Nashville area was home to four black colleges – Fisk University, Tennessee State College, American Baptist Theological Seminary and Meharry Medical School – it provided a pool of ready recruits. The city also had a high number of black college graduates, who created "an enlightened new black middle class" (Halberstam 1998, p. 109). The mobilization of this "enlightened" com-munity would later prove to be integral during the height of the sit-ins. This was possible because of the early cooperation between adults and students in identifying shared goals, thereby avoiding the compe-tition and "turf wars" that bedeviled sit-in campaigns in other cities.

Diane Nash, a Chicago-raised freshman at Fisk University in 1959, had never experienced the overt segregation of the South. What she encountered as a student in Nashville, however, soon propelled her to the workshops because she "felt stifled and boxed in since so many areas of living were restricted" (Carson 1981, p. 21). James Bevel, Bernard LaFayette, and James Lewis were students at American Baptist Theological Seminary. All three had been born in the South and were eager for change. These students later became dynamic leaders of the civil rights movement, participating in sit-ins across the South, the Freedom Rides, and the March on Washington. In the fall of 1959, however, they had defined targets in downtown Nashville, and they began to strategize to desegregate lunch counters in earnest. Figure 7.1 shows a timeline of the major events of the Nashville sit-in campaign.

Actors and forms of power

Participants in nonviolent action need to identify "pillars of support," both for their own group and for their opponents. Earlier research has focused mainly on the support system that keeps the oppressors in place; however, this case presents an opportunity to apply the concept to the support needed by the opposition. Pillars of support are the institutions and organizations that are sources of power for either side; weakening the pillars of support for one's opponents erodes their power and may even cause collapse of the status quo (Helvey 2004, p. 8). On the other hand, strengthening relations with one's own support pillars increases one's own clout and ability to act effectively. Lawson and his group of nonviolent activists leveraged several pillars of support in their fight against segregation, including the concentration of black colleges in and around Nashville, national and local religious institutions, influential white sympathizers, Nashville's black adult community, the training in nonviolent action provided by established civil rights and peace movements groups, and a sympathetic media presence in the form of the *Nashville Tennessean* and, eventually, national media coverage (see figure 7.2).

The larger civil rights movement was successful in part on account of the power and influence of black churches. The black community had little influence in the traditional institutional centers of power such as the police force, local government, and business and trade associations. Black churches provided the organization, financial management, and leadership skills that whites were receiving from such sources (Morris 1984). The student movement had great support among the religious community, white and black, in Nashville. For

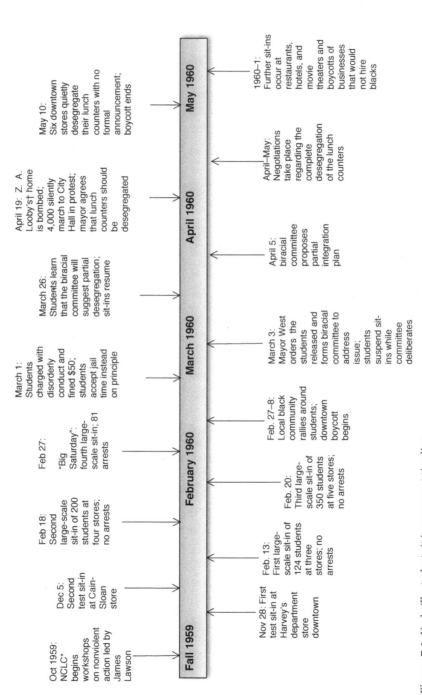

Figure 7.1 *Nashville student sit-in movement timeline*

Notes:

*NCLC: Nashville Christian Leadership Council

†Z. A. Looby: prominent African-American attorney in Nashville

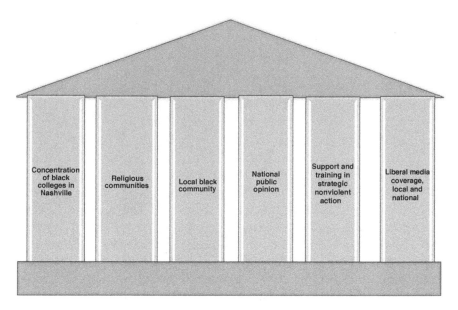

Figure 7.2 *The pillars of support of the Nashville nonviolent movement*

example, the First Baptist Church led by Reverend Smith, in addition to hosting Lawson's workshops, regularly reached out to the congregation and the broader adult black community to raise awareness of the sit-in campaign and collected money for bail in the event of arrests.

Will Campbell, a white Baptist minister working with the National Council of Churches, was a staunch supporter of Reverend Smith and James Lawson. His connections to prominent white community members in Nashville would become crucial during the height of the sit-ins. In addition, a young white reporter from *The Tennesean*, John Seigenthaler, wrote many articles explaining the injustices surrounding white reaction to the sit-ins, drawing regional and national media attention, and influencing the choices made by some white Nashville residents. For example, during the height of the black community's boycott of the downtown shopping area, several white female shoppers turned in their store credit to show their disdain for the storeowners' stance on the situation (Lewis and D'Orso 1998).

Mobilization of the adult black community would become integral to the success of the sit-ins as well. Smith regularly called the college students "the children" in his sermons and meetings, both as a term of endearment and as a way of underscoring their integral part of the community, even though many had been raised elsewhere. Smith wanted to remind the congregation that these were comparatively young people taking risks for the entire black community of Nashville and, as such, were deserving of their support and protection. This regular imagery of "the children" gave the adults the impetus to support the students as they could imagine that they were their own offspring. For example, when the police finally cracked down during the third sit-in and massive arrests were made, the adults closed ranks behind these students, whom they considered as members of their own families. In fact, Smith said that he had "never seen the black community so united" (Halberstam 1998, p. 177).

The Nashville nonviolent movement consisted of two subgroups: the Student Central Committee and the NCLC. The Student Central Committee conducted the sit-ins, while the NCLC took care of financial and logistical support throughout the greater community. The NCLC working groups participated in painting protest signs and handling the funds collected. Local black attorneys, including Z. Alexander Looby, offered their services to the arrested students; teachers and students from Meharry Medical School provided medical care to those injured during the sit-ins (Morris 1981). The adult black community also began a boycott of the downtown shopping area after the third sit-in resulted in mass arrests of the peaceful black students and no arrests among their white attackers (the boycott will be discussed in more detail below). Radio stations, ministers, and groups of women quickly spread the news about the boycott, which shortly reached nearly complete participation in the black community.

The students' focus on remaining nonviolent became an important source of power for them as well. Through their training, they learned to maintain their decorum and never fought back, even when physically attacked themselves. They did not resist arrest but went quietly and proudly to jail and refused to pay fines, opting instead to serve time in the county workhouse. The images of the best and brightest black students in Nashville unjustly jailed for wanting to be served a simple meal increased the pressure on the authorities.

The media, in particular, played an interesting role in Nashville on both sides of the conflict. Of the city's two main newspapers, the *Nashville Tennessean* and *The Banner*, the more liberal of the two was the *Tennessean*, which had a history of supporting liberal issues, such as the abolition of the poll tax, and had a large base of readers in the black community. Mayor West also had taken liberal positions on racial relations. Apart from helping integrate the airport restaurant he had supported a law that allowed councilmen to be chosen by local residents while he was a state senator, thus enabling black city councilmen to be elected. However, despite their similar leanings on racial issues, because of a long history of animosity over election outcomes, the mayor and the *Tennessean* "hated each other" (Halberstam 1998, p. 113). This rift caused the mayor to depend on the segregationist Jimmy Stahlman and his newspaper, *The Banner*, for political support. Being tied to the conservative Stahlman caused the mayor to change his tactics in dealing with the students and probably drew the process out for a longer time. Nevertheless, the movement's pillars of support extended far beyond Nashville. National pressure, including a telegram from former First Lady Eleanor Roosevelt, began to bear down on the mayor in response to the treatment of the students (Ackerman and Duvall 2000).

The stages of nonviolent conflict

The case of the Nashville student sit-ins is an excellent example of how nonviolent action can be used to move a long-simmering injustice and latent conflict from the back burner to the front, forcing it finally to boil over and making it impossible for community members to continue to ignore or to acquiesce to the injustice. In the process, a nonviolent action campaign can redistribute power within a community, bringing about greater justice and increasing the possibility of a sustainable peace. Analyzing the campaign's strategies and the reactions of Nashville's white power structures through Adam Curle's conflict progression theory will shed light on how this process works longitudinally – i.e., over time in the life of a nonviolent action campaign.

[handwritten marginalia: ① redistribution of power w/in a community ② justice ③ possibility of peace]

Based in part on his experiences working as a mediator behind the scenes in African and Asian liberation conflicts, Adam Curle devised a matrix upon which social conflicts can be usefully charted to recognize and understand the stages they go through. The matrix compares the levels of power the parties possess and the levels of awareness of the conflict and the action campaign. It provides a useful way to analyze the nonviolent dynamics of the Nashville case, and the remainder of this chapter will be structured according the primary stages in the matrix (see figure 7.3).

Stage 1: Education

Curle's social conflict matrix has four stages, the first stage being education. Injustice and conflict can be occurring, but it is latent and unrecognized by too many people. Lawson's workshops on nonviolent action were not only a place for training on nonviolent tactics; they

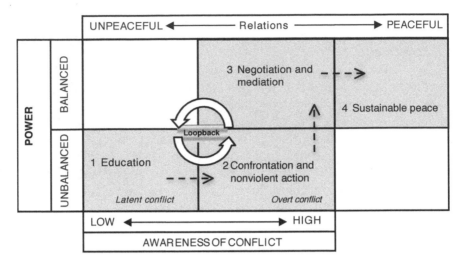

Figure 7.3 *Curle's conflict progression model*

also became a safe social and political place for like-minded people to gather and discuss their own experiences with segregation and their desires to confront it. People shared personal stories of injustice and realized they were not alone. Consciousness was raised, which is an integral dimension of the first stage in the matrix.

As Angeline Butler, a student at the workshops, remarked, "It had been six years since the Supreme Court had ruled on *Brown* and nothing had happened in any of their lives. *Nothing*" (Halberstam 1998, p. 76). The students were no longer willing to accept the status quo as their parents had and wanted to see change in their daily lives. As another student put it, "We weren't having it anymore ... We're trying to eradicate the whole stigma of being inferior" (Doyle 1985, p. 87). Learning occurred at multiple levels: workshop participants were developing shared understandings about why ongoing segregation was unacceptable in 1959 Nashville; they were learning how to confront the conflict in a nonviolent way; and they were discovering together their shared power in and through nonviolent action.

The workshops were based on a synthesis of Christian nonviolence and Gandhian philosophy. Many of the attendees were black students and members of the local black community; however, there were several white students involved as well. Lawson's calm and methodical manner turned some of the students off at first. However, as he connected the Gandhian training with the students' religious and cultural traditions, they began to believe not just in their purpose and mission but also in the nonviolent methods he was proposing (Halberstam

1998). In what was at the time a somewhat novel approach to education and training, Lawson created what turned out to be remarkably realistic and prescient simulations, with some students playing the parts of the protesters and some the parts of angry antagonizers. It was a no holds barred simulation because Lawson wanted the young people to be prepared for the significant mental and physical abuse they would encounter during the actual sit-ins. The activists were taught how to protect their vital organs from punches and kicks by curling into a ball when they were torn out from their seats. They also had to learn the hard-won self-discipline required not to fight back when lighted cigarettes were stubbed out on their necks and not to respond verbally if someone got in their face and tried to provoke them. Most important, they were taught always to get back up and resume their rightful place at the lunch counter, and to do this with a quiet dignity that was designed to win the grudging respect of their oppressors. Joe Goldthreate, a student at the workshops, said:

> We went to the meetings and we started to learn how to be nonviolent, people knocking you around . . . I could handle everything but spitting, the white guy walked by and spit in my face, if you want to be a part of the program at that time, you couldn't fight back. You put everyone in jeopardy of getting hurt or killed. So I had to accept it if I wanted to be a part . . . Don't give them a reason to turn to violence. That was the number one thing that was preaching. I guess when they knocked me out of the chair and spit on me and drug me, I was prepared for that because I'd been trained day in and day out. (Isaac et al. 2012, p. 173)

The training required the students to develop alternative understandings of the nature both of courage and of power. These activists were being educated not just in the technical aspects of nonviolent tactics before using them but also in the philosophical and psychological underpinnings of a nonviolent approach to securing social and political change. The longer the group prepared through the workshops, the more their individual and collective confidence levels grew. They soon created a new organization called the Nashville Student Movement. Bernard Lafayette encapsulated the educational and preparatory aspects of the workshop when he insightfully called them "a nonviolent academy, equivalent to West Point" (Ackerman and Duvall 2000, p. 316). This volunteer troop was being prepared for the next stage of the conflict – i.e., to wage a nonviolent battle confronting the injustice by escalating the conflict nonviolently and thereby making it impossible for the Nashville community to continue to carry on segregated business as usual. For Jim Lawson, whose studies in India had convinced him of the need to take risks in order to secure social and political change, the sit-ins were also "a judgment upon the middle-class conventional, half-way efforts to deal with radical social evil" (Carson 1981, p. 23).

Lawson and his students conducted two test sit-ins in November and December of 1959. The small integrated teams went into the department stores, made minor purchases to establish their credentials as paying customers, and attempted to sit at the lunch counters and order. They were extremely polite and, when refused service, simply asked for the manager and to have the policy explained to them. The student teams were doing reconnaissance – gauging the mood and level of resistance in each store before starting the actual battle. The staff in some stores, such as Harvey's, were polite to the students and seemed uncomfortable with their employer's national policy. Others, such as those in Cain-Sloan, treated the students with contempt and stood fully behind the segregation policy. This intelligence would be vital when the real sit-ins occurred because the students knew which stores might need to be targeted with more forceful resistance (Halberstam 1998).

The education stage of a campaign lays a foundation upon which later stages are built. As such, it is critical. Yet since activists wage non-violent conflicts because they are motivated to end injustices, there is often a sense of urgency. Consequently, it is easy for a campaign to give insufficient time to stage 1, the educational stage, and move too quickly to stage 2, confrontation. But doing so can have perilous results if the activists are not fully prepared for the rigors and risks of nonviolent action. Absent proper preparation, resisters may answer violence with violence, turning potential supporters away. If improperly prepared for the severe repression they will face, activists may also drop out of the campaign and recruitment of replacement resisters is made more difficult. Finally, the education stage is important because it can prepare activists and the larger community of supporters to weather the inevitable ups and downs of a strategic campaign that is focused on both short- and long-term goals. In short, proper preparation keeps hope and vision alive no matter what happens in the confrontation stage. Angelina Butler describes the Nashville movement's patient education stage:

> Students in Nashville were testing downtown area restaurants in small groups, going back to the workshops, reporting what happened to them on the journey, reporting how they felt about the interaction where the people had threw something at them on a counter or put a cigarette butt out on their back, or whether a person spat on them for sitting at the counter. But [initially] the

[handwritten margin note: Importance of preparation]

idea was not to get arrested, it was to go back to the workshops when threatened with arrest and now let's talk about what happened, because that's part of the training for preparedness of having a nonviolent demonstration and movement. So we'd not only go back and talk about it, we would then place ourselves [in role plays and simulations] in a position of pretending to be on the demonstration where now people would do even worse things to you than had happened to you on that day that you went downtown to practice . . . Now the problem is how do you feel, what's your reaction, this is how it's going to be. (Isaac et al. 2012, pp. 171–2)

As Butler describes, the test sit-in period blended the education and the confrontation stages of the conflict. In order to understand the dynamics of a nonviolent conflict it is helpful to break it down into its key parts or stages, as Curle's matrix does. But we still must remember that each stage is a complicated process, not an episode or a one-time event, and the boundaries between the stages are somewhat fluid. A campaign may also engage in more than one stage at a time, as we saw with the Nashville movement when the students were testing the store policies and small groups without risking arrest and returning to the workshops and meetings to engage in debriefing and education. The overall process and the progression between stages may seem to be linear, but there are often loop-backs; such is the nature of all complex multi-party social conflicts.

For example, throughout the sit-ins, the activists were also attending nonviolent action training and community meetings. These meetings (weekly at times, nightly at other periods) were open to the whole community and held in Reverend Smith's church, ensuring that the adults understood the motivations and techniques the students were using. The meetings emphasized the strategic, long-term nature of the campaign for change and prepared the activists for the momentary setbacks that are present in every campaign. This regularized education not only kept the students committed to their tactics, it also solidified the support of the adult black community. For example, after the first round of negotiations failed to net a satisfactory result, the students were able to overcome their disappointment and quickly move back into confrontation in part because of the ongoing education component and the emphasis on the long-term goal.

Stage 2: Confrontation

The second stage of Curle's conflict progression is nonviolent confrontation. For the oppressed low-power party, this stage is all about their

Box 7.1 Self-discipline in the Nashville sit-ins

The Nashville students were not breaking any laws by sitting at the lunch counters. They were challenging the status quo and local policies. The fact that they did so with the utmost respect and regard for the employees and property of the stores only heightened injustice and therefore the paradox of repression. Before they sat in at the lunch counters, these students put on their best clothes; once there, they opened their schoolbooks and studied quietly. They did not resort to violence or bad behavior against anyone to illustrate their point. Those who participated agreed to abide by the following guidelines:

DO NOT
1 strike back nor curse if abused;
2 laugh out;
3 hold conversations with floor walker;
4 leave your seat until your leader has given you permission to do so;
5 block entrances to stores outside or the aisles inside.
DO
1 show yourself friendly and courteous at all times;
2 sit straight – always face the counter;
3 report all serious incidents to your leader;
4 refer information seekers to your leader in a polite manner;
5 remember the teachings of Jesus Christ, Mahatma Gandhi, and Martin Luther King: love and nonviolence is the way.

When their detractors resorted to violence and beatings, the students did not retaliate or even defend themselves, further heightening the injustice of the situation. Even supporters of Southern segregation such as James J. Kilpatrick, the editor of the *Richmond News Leader*, remarked on the stark contrasts these nonviolent tactics created with the local white toughs who arrived to harass the black students:

Here were the colored students, in coats, white shirts, ties, and one of them was reading Goethe and one was taking notes from a biology text. And here, on the sidewalk outside was a gang of white boys come to heckle, a ragtail rabble, slack-jawed, black-jacketed, grinning fit to kill, and some of them, God save the mark, were waving the proud and honored flag of the Southern states in the last war fought by gentlemen. Eheu! It gives one pause. (Quoted in Cozzens 1998)

empowerment, about demonstrating to themselves and others the power at their disposal. Yet deciding when to move from the education stage to overt confrontation is always a delicate decision, one dependent on local dynamics and context. An important strategic decision in this case was to hold off on large-scale sit-ins until after the Christmas holiday. The organizers felt that disrupting the traditional

Christmas holiday shopping season – which was both economically and symbolically important to white Nashville – would evoke an unnecessary backlash and take attention away from the main goal. A key aspect of successful nonviolent campaigns is reaching out to non-participants on the multiple "sides" of the conflict, gaining their sympathy, and eventually their support and involvement. In Nashville in 1959, doing too much too fast could alienate the bystander public in both the black and the white communities rather than making them potential allies and even active supporters. In addition, holding off until February gave the movement more time to prepare and slated the sit-ins for a less busy time of the year, both socially and economically.

The first large-scale sit-in occurred on February 13, 1960, moving the campaign into the confrontation stage. Following best practices in nonviolent conflict, Lawson and the students paid attention to minute details, including the power of symbols and of disciplined targeting. For example, each student was dressed in their best Sunday clothes, making it doubly difficult for them to be dismissed by their white oppressors in the Jim Crow South as uppity rabble-rousers. Black and white pairs were also not mixed by gender, since the issue being confronted in this campaign was racial segregation at the lunch counters, not mixed dating or marriage. Over one hundred well-dressed, quiet students took their places at the lunch counters of several downtown stores. After they were refused service, they remained at the counters, some quietly studying, thereby sending another symbolic message that they were deserving of respect and service. The white storeowners, not knowing how to respond, closed the counters. No arrests or violence occurred. The success of the first sit-in buoyed the spirits of all the students. As they returned to the church that night to debrief and to plot strategy, John Lewis said, "It was like New Year's Eve – whooping, cheering, hugging, laughing, singing" (Lewis and d'Orso 1998, p. 96).

A second and third sit-in occurred within the next week, following a similar pattern of response from the stores. However, storeowners were getting increasingly nervous and did not like the instability and cost that even the test sit-ins were creating. City officials had quietly begun talks with prominent black clergy members about the situation. By the third sit-in, white counter-protesters began to increase in number and the threat of violence against the students was escalating. Several members of the clergy, worried about the possibility of actual violence against the students, had tried to talk them into suspending the sit-ins while negotiations between city officials, local business owners, and black community leaders could be worked out, but the students were not going to settle for just talk (Stollman 2006). This is a common danger to which many campaigns fall prey: moving too quickly from the confrontation stage to the negotiation stage. If resisters go to the negotiating stage too quickly – i.e., before they have fully demonstrated their considerable power through nonviolent action – they risk co-optation and demobilization, which leads to unachieved goals (Coy and Hedeen 2005). In this case, the students showed more strategic wisdom than their more timid elders.

On February 27, 1960, the fourth sit-in and its aftermath became the turning point in how white Nashville responded to the situation. Will Campbell had heard through his connections to City Hall that the police in the downtown area would be pulled back on that Saturday to allow the white protesters to harass the students both verbally and physically (Houston 2007). Then the police would return and arrest the students. Over 300 students participated in "Big Saturday," as it became known. Groups of white protesters verbally abused and physically attacked many students that day, but not one took the bait and fought back. Student protesters were knocked off their chairs and kicked, some had cigarettes stubbed out on their bodies, and others had ketchup and mustard emptied on their heads. Through it all, they remained true to their training and were disciplined and outwardly calm. Nonviolent tactics used that day included a human wave technique similar to that deployed by Gandhian *satyagrahis* at the Dharasana Salt Works in 1930 during the Indian independence campaign. As soon as one group of students was arrested, another group would take their place at the counters. Eighty-one completely nonviolent students were arrested, but not one violent white attacker.

In nonviolent theory, the "paradox of repression" refers to the fact that, when a dominant repressive force uses its power violently or destructively against a nonviolent opponent, support for the opponents is increased (thereby reducing relative power).[2] Excessive repression may result in many consequences that advantage the challengers – for example, previously uncommitted bystanders may rally to the cause of the nonviolent underdogs, who are perceived to be undeserving of the overreaction or violent repression; defections may occur within the repressive force; public opinion may turn against the repressor; movement activists may be confirmed in their cause and further emboldened to do more; and power may shift from the dominant oppressor to the nonviolent challenger.

In a classic example of the paradox of repression, the spectacle of Nashville jail cells filled with educated, respectful, well-dressed young black students – who were the pride of the black community, and who merely wanted to purchase a sandwich at a public lunch counter – was a public relations nightmare. Mayor West reduced bail to $5, but the students refused to cooperate with the injustice of the situation and would not pay the fine; they were released that night without bail. Two days later the students were fined but, again declining to cooperate with injustice, refused to pay. They instead opted for thirty-day sentences in the county workhouse, using the paradox of repression to highlight the inequity of the situation. Years later, John Lewis reflected on his first arrest for nonviolent civil disobedience: "I had never had that much dignity before. It was exhilarating – it was something I had earned, the sense of the independence that comes to a free person" (Halberstam 1988, p. 140).

Mayor West, realizing that increased negative national attention was hurting the reputation of the city of Nashville, released the students from their sentences within two days. He based his decision on the condition that the students would suspend the sit-ins while he created a biracial committee to address the situation. While the biracial committee included local white business leaders, the mayor, and several black university presidents, it did not involve any of the student leaders. Further seeking to defuse the conflict, Mayor West also met with about seventy-five black ministers who were angry that the Nashville police had not protected the nonviolent students from abuse. All of these developments show that the confrontation stage of the conflict was working: the whole of Nashville – white and black – was now highly aware of the conflict, power was beginning to be rebalanced, and the adult black community was also about to escalate the conflict significantly.

Stage 3: Negotiation (with loopbacks)

The campaign then entered the third phase of Curle's conflict progression: negotiation. As Curle theorized with his conflict matrix, education and disciplined nonviolent confrontation had somewhat equalized the historic imbalance of power. The backlash from violence perpetrated against the nonviolent students had forced the issue into the open, revealed the movement's considerable strengths, and pressured the city into negotiations. As frequently happens in nonviolent movements, this campaign moved back and forth between confrontation and negotiation.

The beatings the students endured and their subsequent arrests mobilized many adults in the black community. If these students, epitomizing the community's best and brightest members, were willing to take such risks, the adults would support them further and bring more pressure to bear for desegregation by launching a total boycott of all the downtown stores, even while the mayor's biracial committee was negotiating.

Although several myths abound about how the idea of a shopping boycott of the downtown area began, the clearest account is articulated by Bevel. He states that Fisk University's economic department head, Dr Vivian Henderson, brought up the idea at one of the regular evening meetings at Reverend Smith's church (Morris 1981). The economic losses incurred as a result of the boycott, coupled with white avoidance of the downtown area because of the violence of white protesters, pushed the business community into a more amenable stance towards negotiation. Reverend Smith reported that, shortly after the boycott began, white merchants started showing up at his home wanting to "talk" (Morris 1984).

Then, on March 16, Diane Nash and a few other students sat in at the lunch counter of the Greyhound bus station, a locale not covered by their agreement with the mayor. They were served without incident. This tactic not only kept up pressure on the mayor but also represented sound strategic thinking, as it expanded the field of action onto the national legal level by challenging unlawful segregation in interstate commerce facilities.

The students heard through their contacts that the biracial committee was going to suggest only a partial integration plan for the lunch counters: one half would be for white customers, the other open to black customers. This unacceptable outcome caused the movement to reconvene the sit-ins at downtown stores on March 26, 1960. Since the students suspected that John Sloan was blocking a settlement sought by other stores, 120 students sat in at his store. As suspected, the biracial committee report was released on April 5, calling only for partial integration.

The failure of the negotiations, coupled with the ongoing boycott and the restarting of the sit-ins, represent a complete loopback to the second Curle phase: confrontation. By this time, the downtown shopping area boycott had firmly taken hold. Businesses that were already bleeding financially from the boycott now faced the prospect of also losing important Easter holiday dollars. As Bernard LaFayette stated, "It was a ghost town down there . . . the only people you saw were the demonstrators" (Ackerman and Duvall 2000, p. 324).

The situation remained at a stalemate for nearly another month, with the sit-ins and the boycott continuing. All this changed dramatically on April 19, 1960. Early that morning, the home of Z. A. Looby, the prominent and well-respected black attorney who was one of two blacks serving on City Council, was blown apart by dynamite. Attorney Looby had been helping the students after their arrest and during their court appearances. He and his wife were unharmed, but the powerful bombing (which blew out windows across the neighborhood) shocked the people of Nashville. According to Will Campbell, its backlash extended even to Nashville residents who supported segregation. "Mr. Looby, my God, he was a Republican. He wasn't a dangerous radical . . . People, even a lot of the racists, would say, now, 'dynamiting a man's home, you know, that's his castle.' That did help some [in shocking the larger white community into supporting the students and wanting an end to the violence]" (Houston 2007).

Campbell's analysis is an understatement. Indeed, the bombing undercut any political legitimacy still protecting the immoralities of segregation. The movement used it as an opportunity to exploit the paradox of repression, show their strength, and further escalate the conflict nonviolently by silently marching to City Hall that same day. There was no singing, no chanting, just the soft but steady steps of thousands of determined marchers. While no previous demonstration had exceeded 400 participants, 1,500 people started the march, and by the time they reached City Hall there were over 3,000, both students and adults. Only then did they commence singing. The student leaders were met on the steps by Mayor West. After several minutes of debate and conversation, during which the mayor agreed it was wrong and immoral to discriminate, Diane Nash asked the crucial question: "Then, mayor, do you recommend that the lunch counters be desegregated?" The mayor simply answered, "Yes," and soon Nashville was never the same (Halberstam 1998).

With that answer, the mayor of Nashville, along with the white business owners and student leaders, entered into the negotiation stage again. After several weeks of negotiations, the business owners and the movement agreed that full desegregation of the lunch counters would occur on May 10, 1960. However, no public announcements were made regarding the plan, and the students agreed that, in the beginning, only small numbers of black people would ask to be served. These concessions enabled the white business owners to save face and feel protected from the backlash from white segregationists (Ackerman and Duvall 2000). In a little over six months, the stringently nonviolent campaign had achieved its primary goal.

Stage 4: Sustainable peace

After the confrontation on the steps of City Hall and the following negotiations that opened the lunch counters to all, the campaign approached but never fully achieved the final stage of Curle's conflict progression chart: sustainable peace. The campaign's declared and disciplined goals were fully met via negotiations wherein the black community was a full partner with demonstrable power. Significant power shifts occurred that would reverberate for years to come. But, as in so many protracted social conflicts, the lunch counter conflict was nested inside a larger conflict over segregation and racial injustice more generally, and this larger conflict was still to be waged in innumerable ways, both in Nashville and beyond. In this way, sustainable peace was not fully achieved even in Nashville. But something equally important was accomplished because the success there – especially the demonstration of effective nonviolent power – spurred Nashville activists and the larger movement to confront other aspects of racial discrimination in the city and across the country. Moreover, these subsequent campaigns occurred in multiple social arenas, from housing to employment to schooling to transportation. This case therefore demonstrates the dynamic nature of social conflicts in that even the successful resolution of one conflict may prime the pump for other related conflicts to be engaged and waged nonviolently.

Outcomes

The success of the student-led sit-in movement to integrate the downtown lunch counters in Nashville is a strong example of how nonviolent direct action can lead to substantial change. However, the students' victory was only the first step in the long battle for equal rights. Other dimensions of segregation were later confronted, and Curle's conflict progression began again numerous times in many places, including in Nashville. After the lunch counter sit-ins, the Nashville community was aware of the segregation system's vulnerability to challenge, and further demonstrations occurred. Sit-ins took place at restaurants and cafeterias outside the downtown area; "sleep-ins" were staged at hotels and "stand-ins" in movie theaters (Ackerman and Duvall 2000). People protested and even expanded the boycott tactic to stores on the basis of their hiring practices. Some stores hired African Americans for the first time in positions other than menial workers (Morris 1984).

Step by step, other institutions of segregation fell across Nashville and across the country until the Civil Rights Act of 1964 finally made segregation in public places illegal. Nash recalled hearing the news that other student groups across the country were also holding sit-ins; the growth of the movement made her feel powerful, not alone, and validated the importance of the Nashville campaign: "So when we heard these newscasts, that other cities had demonstrations, it really helped. Because there were more of us. And it was very important" (Hampton et al. 1990, p. 58).

The downtown shopping environment of Nashville was not the only thing that changed as a result of the sit-ins. The history of Vanderbilt University was forever changed as a result of the events in early 1960. Due to pressure from Jimmy Stahlman, editor of the conservative newspaper *The Banner*, and the university's board of trustees, James Lawson had been expelled from the Divinity School on March 3, 1960, for his part in organizing the sit-ins. This expulsion immediately precipitated a backlash from the faculty and students at Vanderbilt. Eight of the sixteen Divinity School professors handed in their resignations when their proposal to readmit Lawson was rejected by Vanderbilt Chancellor Harvie Branscomb. Resignations of faculty in other departments followed, including several from the Medical School, which threatened the university's research funds and standing (Waddle 2002). Branscomb knew he had to get the faculty back, but the board would not allow Lawson's reinstatement. Finally, the stalemate between the chancellor, the board, and the faculty was resolved after Branscomb told the board he would quit if he could not reinstate the faculty. The board relented and allowed the faculty to be reinstated along with Lawson. However, Lawson had already moved to Boston University to complete his degree.

Many feel that Lawson's expulsion allowed Chancellor Branscomb to push his integration plans for the entire university much sooner than he had originally wanted, while others feel that it at least brought a serious conversation about race and student relationships to the forefront at Vanderbilt (Waddle 2002). Although its Divinity School had been quietly desegregating since 1953, Vanderbilt University itself did not become fully integrated until 1962, and black students did not begin enrolling until 1964. Many years later, demonstrating the transformative power of a social conflict waged nonviolently, Vanderbilt publicly apologized to Lawson and welcomed him back to campus as a distinguished university professor.

Many scholars have researched why the use of nonviolent direct action was so successful in Nashville. One of those reasons was the group of young, unknown students there who were leading the sit-ins.

Their high level of commitment both to Lawson's training on nonviolent action and to challenging the system of segregation contributed to their success. They were willing to risk their reputations and their lives in order to end lunch counter segregation. Furthermore, their campaign focused on one target that had resonance in the broader adult African-American community, and they maintained a disciplined focus both on their target and in their manner. On account of all that they learned through the campaign and to the respect that their success accrued to them, the Nashville students later became some of the most influential leaders of the civil rights movement.

One of their important contributions was to the founding of the Student Nonviolent Coordinating Committee (SNCC) in April 1960 at Shaw University in Raleigh, North Carolina, during the Youth Leadership Conference organized by Ella Baker, a staff member of the Southern Christian Leadership Conference (SCLC). Many colleges sent student representatives to the conference, usually one or two; however, the Nashville contingent consisted of sixteen students. The SNCC committed itself to "militant nonviolence" and to participatory democracy, inspiring many other groups to form in Northern cities and among white students as well (Isaac et al. 2012).

The students of the SNCC lived up to their promise of militant nonviolence when they stepped in at a critical moment to continue the Freedom Rides campaign through the Deep Southern states of the US. The Freedom Rides consisted of biracial teams who rode together in the front seats of interstate buses, thereby challenging segregation in interstate travel. After extreme violence threatened the lives of the riders, the original sponsors, the older Congress of Racial Equality (CORE), suspended the rides in May 1961. Diane Nash stated, "The students [Nashville group] have decided that we can't let violence overcome ... If they stop us with violence, the movement is dead" (Arsenault 2006, p. 181). The SNCC was credited not only with the continuation of the Freedom Rides but with helping to keep the momentum of the civil rights movement itself going after the 1960 sit-ins. This was accomplished thanks in part to the Nashville activists' diffusion of Lawson's workshop training model in cities and campaigns across the South and beyond (Isaac et al. 2012) and to Diane Nash's movement-wide promotion of the "jail no bail" tactic used successfully in Nashville (Stollman 2006).

As a group, the students were a formidable force, but they were also individual warriors. Diane Nash became a field worker for the SNCC, directing its direct action wing and participating in numerous campaigns, notably at Rock Hill, South Carolina (1961), Jackson,

Mississippi (1962), and Birmingham, Alabama (1963). She actively participated in and helped plan the Freedom Rides in 1961 and the Selma marches in 1965. John Lewis became chairman of the SNCC, participated in the Freedom Rides and the Selma marches, and was recognized as one of the "Big Six" leaders of the civil rights movement. In 1985 he was elected to Congress from the state of Georgia, only the second black elected to Congress since Reconstruction. James Bevel has been credited with the idea of the march on Washington, which culminated with Martin Luther King's infamous "I Have a Dream" speech in 1963. He was also instrumental in building up the movement in Birmingham (Halberstam 1998). These young leaders all brought with them the lessons of nonviolent direct action learned in Lawson's workshops in Nashville. This is evidenced by the fact that the Nashville rules of conduct for staying disciplined and nonviolent became a model for future campaigns across the South (Carson 1981).

Another notable outcome spurred on by the sit-ins in particular and by the movement in general was the reversal of decades of black support for the Republican Party. Martin Luther King, Jr., and John F. Kennedy would cross paths during the 1960 presidential campaign. King was not an early supporter of Kennedy on account of the latter's somewhat lackluster civil rights record. In October 1960, King participated in a restaurant sit-in in Atlanta that was part of the wave of sit-ins that followed after Nashville, and he was arrested and incarcerated. Kennedy then made several key moves that changed the direction of his campaign and solidified his reputation as a civil rights supporter. His brother Robert Kennedy made a call to a judge in Atlanta to try to get King out of jail; meanwhile John Kennedy personally called King's wife, Coretta, to express his concern.

Kennedy's embrace of the sit-ins was unequivocal: "it is in the American tradition to stand up for one's rights – even if the new way to stand up for one's rights is to sit down" (Branch 1988, p. 314). On the other hand, Kennedy's opponent, the Republican presidential candidate and sitting vice president Richard Nixon, refused even to comment on King's arrest, alienating black voters. Although King did not participate actively in the presidential campaign, the significant shift in black votes toward the Democrats contributed to Kennedy's win in the Electoral College battleground states of Illinois, Michigan, New Jersey, New York, Pennsylvania, South Carolina, and Texas, and therefore the presidency (Branch 1988). This made it possible, in turn, for the Democratic presidencies of John Kennedy and Lyndon Johnson that transformed the civil rights policy arena in the United States.

Conclusion

The fields of nonviolent studies and conflict resolution have been disconnected for too long. This analysis of the Nashville case applies a classic theoretical framework from conflict resolution – Adam Curle's matrix describing the progressive stages of social conflicts – to an equally classic case of nonviolent action – the Nashville sit-in movement of 1960. This chapter not only builds bridges between the fields but also builds theory. This case demonstrates the utility of analyzing nonviolent campaigns in relatively discrete stages. It also shows that effective nonviolent strategy depends upon sound analysis that matches appropriate tactics to the various stages of the conflict – for example, initially using test sit-ins that moved back and forth between the confrontation and the education stages while the subsequent actual sit-ins escalated gradually and in a structured way. In addition, the non-cooperation and refusal to make bail, the mounting of the downtown economic boycott only after negotiations failed, and using a silent march to City Hall in response to the home bombing were all appropriate and effective tactics for the respective stage of the conflict and campaign. The graduated escalation of the campaign and expanding diversity of tactics throughout allowed the participants to engage wider circles of the Nashville community, demonstrating the compounding power of nonviolent approaches and their utility in campaigns for community justice.

The Nashville case also establishes the importance of education and preparation through training so that activists understand the dynamics of social conflicts and are able to maintain nonviolent discipline. Both are critical in order to benefit from the paradox of repression and to redress traditional power imbalances between challengers and authorities. This case further demonstrates that social conflicts waged nonviolently do not tend to travel in a straight line from one conflict stage to the next. Thus, we have adapted Curle's theory to include and specify the loopbacks that often occur in campaigns, such as looping back from unsuccessful negotiations to nonviolent confrontation and from confrontation to education and back again.[3]

The Nashville case demonstrates the particularly valuable contributions that nonviolent action can make to campaigns for civil rights and social justice. Nonviolent approaches to waging social conflict do not necessarily include objectifying one's opponents and thinking of them as the enemy to be summarily defeated and then rejected, since doing so may sow the seeds for setbacks and even future conflicts. Nonviolence is especially well suited to campaigns for change such as civil rights struggles, where the goal is continually to improve the community, making it a more just place for all. One's opponent in a particular struggle may be one's ally in another, provided no relational bridges have been burned. These are all lessons that can be adapted and applied in nonviolent action campaigns waged now and in the future in a wide variety of settings.

Questions for discussion

1 What do you see as the key factors influencing success in the Nashville case? Why were these factors so critical?
2 What is the relationship between the stage in a social conflict and the nonviolent tactics that movement participants choose to utilize? Provide examples from the Nashville case.
3 How can the pillars of support model be useful in planning out a nonviolent campaign?
4 What impact did the Nashville sit-ins have on the broader US civil rights movement?

Suggestions for further reading and research

Curle, Adam (1971) *Making Peace*. London: Tavistock.
Halberstam, David (1998) *The Children*. New York: Random House.

CHAPTER 8

Revolutions and Democratic Transitions

Maciej J. Bartkowski

This chapter investigates the rising phenomenon of nonviolent revolutions – or civil resistance[1] – for political recognition where ordinary people organize to reclaim their rights and freedoms from a statist system, be it a domestic authoritarian government, a dominant group or a majority that formally rule the country, or an occupying power. A successful nonviolent movement driven by the infinite creativity of the agency of people with a long tradition of peaceful, civilian-based organizing not only brings about a breakthrough – an end to the repressive system – but often institutionalizes a new, defused type of political power, in the movement's own image, and redefines the relationship between the state and a politicized society.

Although the primary case study will be the Polish Solidarity movement, this chapter will also make brief references to a number of additional examples – the 2011 Egyptian revolution and movements in India, Russia, Iran, the Basque country, and China. The richness of empirical cases will help to address a set of interrelated issues, beginning with the agency-driven and structure-focused explanations for when nonviolent revolutions happen and moving on to why people choose unarmed resistance in the struggle against brutal oppression, what drives its effectiveness, and what constitutes successful nonviolent resistance. The chapter will also discuss specific movement-centric drivers that turn civil resistance into a powerful force – a two-level battlefield strategy, the creation of alternative institutions, and small acts of resistance that are undertaken by individuals, by communities, or on a larger, national scale. Finally, the chapter will focus on how to conceptualize and better understand the role of civil resistance in the tumultuous processes of democratization and systemic transitions.

Structure-centered accounts of revolutions

In this chapter, nonviolent revolution is understood as a political conflict and an outcome of a civilian-based struggle. On one hand, nonviolent revolution signifies a contentious exercise of political power by ordinary people but without recourse to arms. On the other, it represents an extra-constitutional change in the form of an overthrow of a political regime by peaceful non-institutionalized collective actions followed by a fundamental political transition.

The agency of ordinary people is always an inextricable driver of nonviolent revolutions; popular revolutions occur as the result of people's decisions. First tens and hundreds of organizers, followed by thousands of activists and, finally, the mobilization of millions of supporters, through their disciplined actions, make revolutions possible and account for their eventual success. Consequently, this chapter argues that such upheavals occur more because of the organized citizenry than because of the surrounding conditions, institutions, or elites that typically oppose or hinder the change. Popular discourse about how revolutions erupt has either highlighted the power of change-resistant oppressive regimes to instill fear, apathy, and passivity in their societies or the force of change-inducing mega-socio-economic processes and structures such as modernization, urbanization, rising class-consciousness or economic development, and crises that lay down fundamentals for major social upheavals. Both, the impossibility of revolutions and their historical inevitability, have been the main opposing perspectives on the occurrence of revolutions – all rooted in the power of everything but the ordinary people.

Before most nonviolent revolutions of the past century took place, few believed the upheavals could happen at all or would happen when they did, and an even smaller number thought they would be successful. When nonviolent popular revolts ensued – the Russian Revolution of 1905, the Iranian constitutional revolution of 1906, the Iranian revolution of 1978–9, Poland in 1980, the Philippines in 1986, Central and Eastern Europe in 1989, Serbia in 2000, Georgia in 2003, Ukraine in 2004, the Cedar Revolution in Lebanon in 2005, to mention just a few – the majority of scholars and policymakers, including regional experts, were caught by surprise. In 2010, most political observers would have been equally astounded to learn that, a year later, seemingly irremovable authoritarian leaders in Tunisia, Egypt, Yemen, and Libya would all fall from power. The dominant discourse was centered on the endurance and survivability of the authoritarian regimes rather than on how and why ordinary people could challenge them effectively (Gause 2011, pp. 81–90).

After the "impossible" revolution becomes a fact of life, suddenly the pendulum swings in an opposite direction. The newly emerging view is that the regime can lose its capacity to repress and a rebellion against it is, in fact, very likely. The argument that revolutions ignite when a regime's behavior changes (i.e., when its grip on power and society relaxes) suffers from two problems. First, it continues favoring regime-centric and structure-focused perspectives to account for the phenomenon that is of people's own making. Furthermore, past revolutions are often studied with today's knowledge; however, that knowledge was not available to the revolutionaries, those who stood against them, or the public in general. In fact, at the time of the upheavals, participants of the revolutions and others affected by them have usually limited information about internal divisions within the regime or its depleting capacity to oppress. Often, a popular rebellion starts not because the authoritarian grip eases – that might not be either felt or known at a time of troubles – but because it may be triggered by a repression that produces a popular backlash (known as backfire or political jiu-jitsu).

Agency of popular revolutions

The explanations of either the impossibility of an uprising or the inevitability of rebellion due to structural factors ignore the power and agency of ordinary people and are ahistorical, as developments on the ground contradict their premises. In reality, the emergence of nonviolent resistance is neither impossible nor inevitable. Nonviolent rebellions come to life in places and times where few predict resistance to form, as a result initially of the work of committed organizers and later of the mobilization of participants. It is difficult to predict break-out, trajectories, and outcomes of nonviolent revolutions precisely because they are linked not solely to rigid power structures, cultural traditions, economic conditions, or monolithic elites but, rather, to more elusive, unpredictable, and uncontainable human ingenuity and creativity.

Revolution that is waged by mobilized people through nonviolent methods of civil resistance is a political struggle. This is not a physical or material contest, as the outcome of nonviolent resistance does not depend on arms, wealth, or other material resources of its member activists. It is a political contest because it depends on the power of ideas (DuVall 2013). Effective ideas propel the civilian-led struggle to develop and to deploy strategies and skills of planning, organizing, and mobilizing that are original and appealing to others while, at the same time, surprising to the opponent. They help increase the number of people engaged in non-cooperation with the regime while minimizing the risks for the movement and maximizing the costs imposed on the adversary. In contrast to violent struggle, anyone can be part of developing and implementing ideas, and consequently can join a non-violent conflict and participate in open or tacit forms of civil defiance.

Political nonviolent struggle has the potential to create a virtu-ous circle of revolutionary mobilization – a successful method or campaign of nonviolent resistance increases the number of people who join the movement. The more people involved, the greater the number of individuals available to undertake nonviolent actions and the more diverse and enriched the pull of intellectual potentials that can be called upon in order to devise a larger gamut of creative nonvio-lent methods. The more ways of waging nonviolent struggle, the more opportunities there are for an even greater assembly of participants to be drawn into resistance. In turn, participants bring in new ideas, boost creativity, and devise other methods for civic engagement.

These intellectual, participatory, and method multipliers increase legitimacy and representation of the movement, help resistance overcome significant adversarial conditions, and allow activists to impose multiple pressures on the regime and its allies (Barrell and Bartkowski, n.d.). The breadth and quality of participants in the strug-gle help the movement to challenge simultaneously multiple relation-ships that the opponent has with different businesses, military and religious institutions, and other allies. The regime is then forced to spread its resources thinly.

Why people choose nonviolent means to wage their revolutions

Revolutions are usually associated with "fundamental and violent change" (*Columbia Encyclopedia* 2009, p. 4106). Often, the youth behind revolutions are thought to fuel radicalism that is more easily suscep-tible to armed rebellion than to peaceful protests. But some studies show that many revolutions that were spearheaded by youth man-aged to remain in fact nonviolent. The young people strategically chose peaceful means to mount their extra-constitutional opposition (Nikolayenko, in Schock 2014; Bunce and Wolchik 2011).

Generally, little attention in the literature on revolutions has been paid to the nonviolent nature of people's uprisings and to the strategic dimension of peaceful resistance with its coordinated and dispersed tactics.[2] However, an impressive body of data on nonviolent resistance campaigns in the seemingly most violent conflicts, such as anti-dictatorship, anti-occupation struggles, and self-determination campaigns (so-called maximalist struggles), has been accumulated. Not only did the number of these campaigns reach more than a hundred in the last two centuries, they have also been steadily on the increase; documented nonviolent upheavals against dictatorships and occupations and for self-determination include six nonviolent struggles in the nineteenth century, nine in the first half of the twentieth century, sixty-five in the second half of the twentieth century, and already fifty in the first decade of the twenty-first century – an increase of almost four times in comparison with an average decade of the previous fifty years.[3]

The observed rise in the number and frequency as well as in the successful rate of nonviolent struggles and campaigns to achieve major political goals (Chenoweth and Stephan 2011, p. 8) might also help to account for what Steven Pinker, a Harvard psychologist, argues is the decrease in political violence in the past and more recent human history. Next to economic interdependence, globalization, lower profitability of territorial conquest, and the emergence of human rights norms that Pinker identified (Pinker 2011) as major factors that account for the decline in political violence, the rise in the use of mass-based nonviolent rebellions against state structures is an important factor that contributes to the decrease in political deaths and major atrocities in comparison with violent conflict.[4]

Certainly, violence will continue by challengers, but its relative ineffectiveness and costs vis-à-vis its nonviolent alternative – if only the latter is better understood and assessed – may ultimately favor peaceful contestation as a preferred weapon of choice against violence by regime. The current noticeable increase in the number of nonviolent insurrections and their growing effectiveness suggests that, in the future, maximalist conflicts will include at least one party that uses methods of nonviolent action.

Given a common-sense proclivity to mount violent resistance (often depicted as armed self-defense) against a brutal regime, why would people choose nonviolent methods to challenge the unjust system? Several reasons can be identified. Sometimes people choose nonviolent methods of struggle because it is seen as their last resort after all other means have been exhausted without resolution – e.g., the use of courts, elections, negotiations, or violent actions. The supporters of violent uprisings, such as the ANC in South Africa in the 1960s and the 1970s or Maoists in Nepal, eventually concluded that their military efforts had not brought about the expected results while other constitutional means of change remained unavailable to them. Consequently, the violent parties made space either to return to the only available alternative (as in South Africa in the 1980s) or to try the last remaining option (as in Nepal in 2006) – that of nonviolent political organizing, with an extraordinary degree of success (see Ackerman and DuVall 2000; Dudouet 2012, p. 407).

Nonviolent resistance might also be seen as a possible and available tool but before other means of pressuring the authorities are considered. As Nkrumah, the leader of the Ghanaian independence struggle, argued: "We had no guns but even if we had, the circumstances were such that nonviolent alternatives were open to us, and it was necessary to try them before resorting to other means" (Presbey, in Bartkowski 2013c, p. 60).

Some groups choose nonviolent means to propel their revolution because they recognize that this is the most effective instrument for undermining undemocratic power that will help them reach immediate goals (an end to political oppression) and longer-term objectives (building an open and pluralistic society). Young Serbian leaders of the Otpor! movement, their colleagues from the Georgian Khmara and the Ukrainian Pora! and the Egyptian April 6 movement were known to have been exposed to training in strategic nonviolent conflict and/or to have educated themselves in this strategy by reviewing relevant literature, notably writings by Gene Sharp, and, in the later movements, watching documentaries such as *A Force More Powerful* or *Bringing Down a Dictator* (Rosenberg 2011, including the conversation this author had with key activists).

Furthermore, real-life learning from violent conflicts in the region can offer important lessons for the dissidents and organizers in other countries. Poles learned from Hungarians who rose up in 1956 that violent resistance against the Soviets was futile and was likely to lead to disaster for the society and its overall dreams of democratization. As a result, the future leaders of the Solidarity movement rejected violence – on strategic and not on pacifist grounds – concluding they would be more effective in reaching their political objective with the use of peaceful though still coercive methods of mobilization and organizing.

Closely related to a learning process is imitation and diffusion of successful nonviolent uprisings. Ghanaians and Zambians learned from successful nonviolent resistance led by Mohandas Gandhi in India against the same colonial power they were facing – the British (Bartkowski 2013b). Prior to their unarmed revolt against their president Shevardnadze, Georgians learned from the young Serbs about their nonviolent struggle against Slobodan Milošević. Ukrainians learned their own lessons from Georgians and Serbs and challenged peacefully and successfully outgoing President Leonid Kuchma and his ally Viktor Yanukovych over the rigged presidential elections in the winter of 2004–5.

There have also been imitation processes at play across historical periods within a single country. Solidarity leaders in Poland learned from their nineteenth-century nonviolent progenitors who used constructive programs in the form of organic work to defy the denationalization and deculturalization policies of the partitioning powers. Almost a century later, the Polish dissidents used the experience of their compatriots to build parallel civic 'self-defense' institutions in order to break tight censorship imposed by the communist government. Similarly, the organizers of the Free South Africa movement in the United States in the mid-1980s utilized the previous and rich experience of the civil rights movement to come up with innovative tactics in order to draw media attention and mobilize the American public and the US Congress to support the economic sanctions against the apartheid regime.[5]

Effectiveness and success of revolutions propelled by civil resistance

Chenoweth and Stephan (2011), in their path-breaking book on the effectiveness of civil resistance, point to participation as the one necessary attribute of civil resistance movements that plays a crucial role in their ultimate success. The more people join nonviolent mobilization, the greater the chances for the successful outcome. The authors explain that participation in nonviolent revolutions tends to be greater than in violent resistance because unarmed insurrections have relatively lower physical, moral, psychological, and tactical barriers of entry. There is no need for bodily strength or combat training to participate in nonviolent revolutions; in fact, men and women of all backgrounds and ages, ranging from children to the elderly, have been leading activists of nonviolent rebellion.

In contrast to the orders to kill that may be given during armed resistance, possibly raising ethical inhibitions among many, the actions in nonviolent resistance are much less morally divisive and are thus acceptable to a larger number of people. By its nature, participation in an armed uprising requires a readiness to die. Nonviolent revolutions are in fact much more about life than death, and there is a wide variation regarding the level of sacrifice or risk that one is asked to take.

Psychologically, it is easier to join civil resistance because it does not necessarily demand giving up one's life, while its rich tactical repertoire allows people of all ages, genders, and backgrounds to choose among more or less risky actions, ranging from public protests and strikes (with a greater exposure to immediate government repression) to stay-at-home demonstrations, boycotts of government-organized events, or refusal to buy goods from businesses controlled by the regime (with a reduced level of risk).

In addition to participation, a nonviolent movement's success depends largely on the extent to which it remains resilient when faced with the regime's attempts to undermine its unity, discipline, and organization. The regime may try to sow discord within the movement and create or exploit existing divisions in a similar way in which the resistance wants to dislodge the regime's pillars of support. The opponent may also infiltrate the peaceful actions with its *agents provocateurs* in order to undermine nonviolent posture and provoke or instigate violence. This has the aim of branding the opposition as extremists or terrorists and of using this as a pretext and justification for greater violence to crush the resisters. Successful movements manage to counter this by internalizing nonviolent discipline in their resistance methods, isolating and removing violent radicals from the movement, and publicizing violence and disproportionate use of force by the security forces.

The regime may also attempt to undermine or ban any form of independent organizing, including jailing dissidents and imposing legal, financial, and social sanctions on individuals to disrupt the planning of anti-government campaigns and the development of autonomous institutions. In response to the government's repression – often used under the cover of martial law and a state of emergency – civil resistance may choose to go underground and, while being less visible and exposed to the regime's repressive policies, try to regroup and reorganize. The activists then extend their underground solidarity and mutual-aid networks to those arrested, their families, and those seeking shelter. They may also engage in planning for and executing indirect cultural and symbolic actions that would slowly but inevitably hollow out the remaining legitimacy of the regime.

The effectiveness of nonviolent revolutions, be it against a dictator, an occupier, or a majority that denies minority's rights, has to be measured against the outcomes, which might not necessarily be tangible, immediately apparent, or easily assessed. In addition to the successes of nonviolent revolutionary movements in bringing down seemingly indestructible oppressive structures and liberating the societies from domestic or foreign oppression, the positive outcome of these revolutions can be evaluated by a set of other no less important developments. Nonviolent revolutions, for example, prevented or delayed, at important historical moments, major calamities associated with violent struggle (e.g., the cases of Kosovo, Ghana, and Zambia; Bartkowski 2013c). They also contributed to raising national awareness and shared identity, making possible an ideational revolution in the minds of divided people who began to see themselves as part of a larger collective (e.g., the cases of Bangladesh, Poland, Egypt, Algeria, Zambia and Ghana; ibid.). In other cases, nonviolent, civilian-led resistance built new autonomous organizations in the emerging national communities strong enough to sustain independence once it was won from the occupying or colonial powers (e.g., the cases of Poland, Mozambique, Zambia or the United States; ibid.).

Sometimes, in the protracted struggles against authoritarian regimes, the fact that revolutionaries confined their methods of resistance (preferring nonviolent over violent means and limited over maximalist objectives) or their goals (bringing down the system but making all people – both opposition and opponents – part of that change) helped pave the way to negotiated (also known as pacted) transitions. These types of transitions are initiated when powerholders and representatives of a popular movement come together to negotiate a historic agreement that opens up a political system and starts democratization.

Finally, a seemingly defeated or failed civil resistance movement might in fact endure in a hibernated form and continue action that constrains and contains the regime years into the future. For example, the apparent unwillingness of Ayatollah Khamenei to falsify the results of the 2013 Iranian presidential elections that led to the victory of the most liberal of the candidates, Hassan Rouhani, has been directly linked to the seemingly dormant Green movement. At a time of increasing economic and social problems caused by international sanctions, Khamenei feared the repeat of the mass-based popular demonstrations that took place after the 2009 rigged presidential elections, which might have awakened a full-fledged civil resistance movement and thereby threatened the survival of the Islamic regime.[6]

How nonviolent struggles for recognition are won

Successful struggles against foreign or domestic regimes require effective strategies to undermine various pillars of support. Activists may go beyond direct forms of nonviolent methods such as strikes, demonstrations, protests, or civil disobedience to utilize other strategies and tactics. Indeed, the repertoire of nonviolent actions, particularly in very oppressive environments, may include the strategy of skillfully setting up and managing a two-level battlefield, as well as building alternative institutions and waging the struggle through small acts of resistance.

Dependency and the two-level battlefield

No political system, no matter how powerful and committed to the use of violence, can possess an unlimited capacity to oppress an entire population at all times and in all places. Even during the height of Nazi power and its territorial expansion, the German military commanders in 1942 reported from Belarus and Russia to their headquarters in Berlin that "German forces could not exercise effective control without enlisting the [local] population" and that they "can master the wide Russian expanse . . . only with the Russian and Ukrainians who live in it, never against their will" (Summy 1996, p. 127). Consequently, instead of relying on cost-incurring violent coercion, the regime must continually buy the loyalty of important segments of society and ideally enjoy a degree of voluntary following. In the latter two cases, the regime builds (willingly or not) dependency relationships between itself and selected societal groups – the business community, security forces, religious establishments, and different professional syndicates.

These dependency relationships are of mutual benefit. However, the proximity or close social distance between these sectors create potential vulnerabilities for the existing system of rule that skillful resisters can exploit. As long as the parties see specific material advantages coming out of these relationships, they continue supporting one another. But no sooner is the flow of the material benefits derailed – the intentional result of skillful nonviolent actions – than groups begin questioning the rationality behind their support for the regime. This, in turn, leads to internal splits within a seemingly monolithic system of rule and its eventual downfall.

At the same time, civil resisters are often forced to wage their struggle on two levels: domestic and international. This is because, in some cases, the social distance between them and the oppressor is relatively wide, meaning that the latter's powers do not depend on the cooperation of those whom it oppresses (e.g., Israel's occupation of Palestine). In other cases, social distance between regime and supporters is quite narrow because of the dominant unifying ideology across the society (e.g., Nazi ideology and Hitler's regime, or Chinese jingoistic rhetoric and the communist government's policy towards Uyghurs or Tibetans), because of its single-ethnic composition and a strong affinity within the group (e.g., Syrian Alawites and the Assad regime), or because of popular imperial culture (e.g., British public opinion that, throughout the country's colonial history, was largely supportive of its monarchy and government's foreign policies).

In such situations, the nonviolent challengers often strategize their resistance around a 'two-level game': trying to undermine the control of the repressive regime, be it indigenous or foreign, on a domestic level while, at the same time, broadening its campaigns beyond immediate borders onto the international level. The latter strategy would rely on reaching out to potential third-party allies – be they other governments, members of the occupier's society, the political and business classes, or the international community in general – who are seen as having some leverage over the opponent. Using economic non-cooperation based on nonexportation and nonimportation, the American colonists, for example, exerted effective pressure on the British government indirectly through a third party – British merchants. The latter were losing considerable trade and profits because of the colonists' economic boycott, and it was their intervention in the British parliament that was credited with the repeal of the Stamp Act that the colonists opposed (Conser 2013, pp. 311–12).

Likewise, in the early twentieth century, the nonviolent struggle of Polish society for its independence helped unite the community, but it also popularized Poles' aspirations for their independent country abroad. The international press published stories of the school strikes in Russian Poland and also reported on civil resistance against the German land grab, which faced disproportionate repression from the German authorities. This raised sympathy among the publics in Britain, France, and the United States and garnered international support for an independent state for Poles that was eventually articulated in President Woodrow Wilson's Fourteen Points speech in 1918 (Bartkowski 2013c, pp. 259–77).

Activists can also play the two-level game with the regime by exploiting the state's desire to present itself as a responsible actor in international relations. Such an actor oftentimes commits itself to certain norms included in the international conventions that it voluntarily signs. For example, the organizers of Charter 77 in Czechoslovakia used the fact that the regime voluntarily signed the Helsinki Final Act in 1975 to pressure the government to follow its international commitments with regard to human rights. Charter 08 and the people's network set up around the initiative put public pressure on the communist government in China to comply with its international commitments contained in the Universal Declaration of Human Rights and the International Covenant on Civil and Political Rights, which the Chinese government signed in the 1990s. Similarly, the Egyptian anti-corruption campaign shayfeen.com used the government's signature under the UN Convention against Corruption to press it to implement its legal provisions, which allowed the third parties to bring anti-corruption cases to court.[7]

Alternative institutions

Alternative institutions signify a variety of entities, ranging from informal or illegal networks or associations of people that exist in a real or – now – a virtual world, to more formal, semi-official, or legal organizations. Some examples of alternative institutions are schools, churches, clinics, publishing houses, media outlets, political parties, financial, economic, and social institutions, agricultural cooperatives, governing institutions, and community service organizations. In civil resistance struggles, alternative institutions are either built anew (e.g., underground media) by growing opposition towards the status quo or can originate from preexisting institutions (e.g., churches) that now help organize and shelter dissident activities. Consequently, these types of institutions can become an important part of resistance strategies. The resort to alternative institutions might be instinctive as a result of severe oppression or perceived impenetrability of the system. In such conditions, direct nonviolent actions may be seen as being too risky or ineffective.

Oftentimes, society cannot engage in direct civil resistance actions until its conditioning is at a level that allows it to do so. The innocuous organizing through institutions such as sport clubs, reading groups, or economic organizations provides for such conditioning by generating a powerful, long-term, politicizing force that initially might influence stronger communal bonds and networks, increase awareness of shared culture, history, common identity, or destiny, or help more clearly articulate grievance frames, demands, or solutions – what George Lakey (1969) calls "conscientization." These developments can eventually broaden citizen participation and spawn direct collective methods and are thus an important predicate of effective political actions. For example, in colonial Zambia, the seemingly apolitical indigenous welfare associations that worked for social and economic development of the black community at the same time raised awareness about discrimination, degrading treatment, and a lack of opportunities because of the white settlers' actions and policies. The associations performed in fact proto-political functions, politicized local populations, honed the organizational and professional skills of their participants, nurtured a new leadership of pro-independence

Zambian leaders, and led to the formation of a country-wide political party (Momba and Gadsden 2013, pp. 76–7).

In the struggle against communism, alternative institutions played an extremely important role. From the mid-1970s, Poles built legal, semi-legal, and illegal institutions, among them human rights organizations, informal workers' councils, and professional associations, and a flying university that offered lectures about Polish history and politics free of censorship. They also set up publishing houses and a printing press that translated and published thousands of unofficial or banned works (including the translation of George Orwell's *1984* and *Animal Farm* and a popular booklet on "What to Do in Contacts with Police").

According to Wiktor Kulerski, one of the Polish opposition members, the liberation of the society through its self-organization and building of parallel institutions had a very strategic dimension and aimed at creating the situation in which "authorities will control empty stores, but not the market; the employment of workers, but not their livelihood; the official media, but not the circulation of information; printing plants, but not the publishing movement; the mail and telephones, but not communication; and the school system, but not education" (Stokes 1993, p. 106). The self-organized society, as Adam Michnik observed, was a liberating experience that created "a real, day-to-day community of free people" (Ackerman and DuVall 2000, p. 123). The long-term objective of the self-managing society was simple – to wrest gradually and tacitly the power from the authoritarian state – or, in the words of one of the oppositionists, Stanislaw Fudakowski, "to confront the centralized power of the state without ever having to confront it directly. Little by little, authority will be transferred to the local level, until in the end the state will have lost most of its power" (Weschler 1982, p. 105).

Setting up alternative cultural institutions – be they libraries, reading circles, art exhibitions, makeshift theaters, public performances and plays or concerts, networks of semi-legal or illegal schools, or organizational committees for commemoration or celebration – can be an effective instrument of resistance. These types of institutions formed and reinforced the national consciousness of many nations: Estonians, Lithuanians, Kosovars, West Papuans, Algerians, Egyptians, Ghanaians, Zambians, and Poles, among others.[8] As for the Poles, in the second half of the nineteenth century they rejected violent uprisings and embarked on a long-term, social engineering project known as "organic work." It was a resistance-driven philosophy of self-improvement that included the establishment of indigenous financial institutions and social and economic cooperatives alongside educational and cultural organizations. Through economic growth and social development, organic work aimed to ensure national subsistence and self-sufficiency in the face of denationalization policies pursued by the occupiers (Bartkowski 2013c).

Alternative institutions often serve the purpose of everyday, collective self-defense and survival against oppression that had lasted for generations. Even in its protracted form, this type of struggle has a strategic dimension. Namely, alternative institutions ensure that getting through life – even mere physical survival, encompassed, for example, in the Palestinian saying "existence is resistance" – becomes a strategic process of defiance (often on a subliminal level) against destructively centrifugal forces. The Palestinian notion of *sumud* (steadfastness) is manifested, for example, in the Palestinians' determination to stay on and cultivate the land no matter the hardship and oppression. This idea can also be represented by the life of political prisoners incarcerated in various undemocratic countries, such as Burma, the Soviet Union, or China. Prisoners – even in the most horrific conditions – often establish informal networks not only to secure and smuggle basic goods but also to educate themselves, write, and plan and strategize their defiance, even when lacking physical freedom (Fink 2009, specifically the chapter on prison: 'Life University').

In a digital age, the internet and online social networks have opened up opportunities to create new kinds of alternative institutions – the virtual or digital ones. An example is the work of Russian activists who set up an opposition coordination council by organizing mixed virtual and on-the-ground elections in October 2012 in which more than 80,000 cast their votes, the majority online. The coordination council is now largely a day-to-day virtual network of people, gathered mainly on the council's Facebook page,[9] that mobilizes Russians and organizes protest actions.

Small acts of resistance

During protracted political struggles against undemocratic and violent regimes, activists often impose indirect costs on the regime. They undermine its already weakened authority and legitimacy through various symbolic, cultural, and humorous actions that also involve, somehow innocently, the public, who would either watch or participate in subtly versed anti-regime performances. These actions reflect and reinforce the dissident culture in the society. Small acts of resistance, similarly to alternative institutions, are either the reaction to

Box 8.1 Basque cooperatives as alternative institutions

Often, because of their seemingly amenable nature, which substitutes direct actions and confrontation for the mundane work of self-organizing, alternative institutions might not be seen by the authorities as a direct, tangible, menacing threat to their rule – or, for that matter, as a form of resistance. This leads the adversary (and often external observers) to fail to comprehend the significance of this type of action. But, in reality, alternative institutions can offer physical and psychological space for society to withdraw and strengthen its social fabric in order to fight its adversary in future confrontations.

One relevant example is the Basques, who, between the 1950s and the1970s, initiated work on alternative institutions that aimed at economic development but also at the preservation of Basque identity, culture, and language under the yoke of the authoritarian regime of General Franco. The Basque cooperatives were seen by the regime as rather non-threatening undertakings as they were linked with the Catholic Church, which made them acceptable to the Spanish right, while their philosophy was seen as corporativist enough to gain endorsement of the Falange Party that constituted the backbone of Franco's regime. The cooperatives played an important role in teaching Basques the value of self-sustenance, self-reliance, and self-organization and building solidarity across economic classes.

Together with *ikastolas*, underground schools that taught the Basque language, and political self-education in bars across the county, the Basque alternative institutions transformed the society from its ethnic-based roots toward a genuine political community (which also included Spanish immigrants that settled in the Basque country) – aware of its rights, inspirations, and power (Kasmir 1996, pp.74–5, 99–100, 107–8).

a high level of repression imposed by the state (usually in the form of emergency laws, including martial law) or a general apathy and fear that permeates the community, paralyzing it and leading to inactivity. In such circumstances, the active part of society becomes submerged from the direct view of the opponent. The organizers plan quietly their ways to surface at a time and place of their own choosing and to organize specific actions, only to disappear again and emerge with yet another campaign at a later time.

Other small acts of resistance aim at expropriating symbolic celebrations that are at the core of the regime's ideology. One of the most important festivals in communist countries is International Workers' Day (May 1), a celebration of workers and their labor. In Poland, as well as in other countries of the Soviet bloc, the streets on that day were full of parades watched by the local and national communist dignitaries, usually from an elevated podium. In the 1980s, Poland faced a dire economic situation, which deteriorated further with international economic sanctions imposed on the country after martial law was

Box 8.2 Actions to highlight absurdities

One of the important goals of small acts of resistance is to keep revealing to the people a striking contradiction between the state's rhetoric about living in a normal country and the reality of their existence. Activists often try to show the absurdity of the system that claims to rule according to ordinary laws by forcing it to act in a way that contradicts common sense and goes against an ordinary person's intellect.

For example, in February 2012, in the Siberian town of Barnaul, activists assembled Lego people and other cartoon toys that held banners protesting the rigged 2011 parliamentary elections in Russia. The signs read: "I'm for clean elections," "A thief should sit in jail, not in the Kremlin," and "I am for honest elections" (O'Flynn 2012). The local police promptly arrested the toys, as they considered their protest an "unsanctioned public event." This was followed by the authorities' decision not to allow future protests of this kind because the toys were not "citizens" and could not lead or participate in protests. The country that bans and arrests protesting toys exposes the absurdity of its own rule and laws – which was the very goal of this small act of resistance.

In another case, in 2011, online activists called on Chinese citizens to engage in the subtle technique of resistance known as *san bu*, an innocuous stroll in public places. There would not be any shouting or banners but just an innocent walk and smile. This form of action allowed people to circumvent the ban on public protest while remaining anonymous and forced the authorities to use extraordinary and costly measures of closing down public areas next to the popular places for eating out in Beijing and other cities. Such small actions of defiance were considered an effective tool of psychological warfare against a paranoid authoritarian system trying now to chase shadows (Demick and Pierson 2011).

Likewise, in Russia, in May 2012, during growing repression against activists, twelve well-known Russian writers announced that they would take a simple stroll from one square in Moscow to a nearby city park. Usually a demonstration would require a permit from the authorities. A call for a stroll was an inventive small tactic that was to test the authorities' resolve to ban and impose fines on organizers of any public gatherings and people's rejection of such repressive actions. Eventually, an ingenuous stroll brought more than 10,000 people onto the streets, turning subtle defiance into an open display of opposition (Barry 2012).

instituted in 1981. Workers, whom communist propaganda placed at the vanguard of the system, could barely support their families. In one city in Poland, the people decided to use May 1 to show the misery of the Polish workers. They let their communist bosses in the factories know that, unless they were allowed to boycott the event, they would go out on the streets to "celebrate" that day, but bare-footed. For the workers there was little, if anything, to rejoice about on "their" day. Faced with a real dilemma, the local Communist Party finally decided to let the workers boycott the holiday rather than have them walk without shoes in front of the officials (Crawshaw and Jackson 2010).

Similarly, the Orange Alternative – a surrealist student movement in the Polish city of Wrocław in the 1980s – organized street theater and satirical and humorous enactments of the major holidays that were celebrated by the Polish communist regime, including Militia Day, Army Day, and the day of the 1917 Great Socialist October Revolution. On these holidays, which were lionized by the regime, the members of the Orange Alternative would organize happenings that caricatured state propaganda and the nature of the celebrations.[10] The idea of "taking back" public holidays and using festivals as days for mobilization has been evident in other movements as well, including in Iran and Egypt.

Civil resistance in democratic transitions

The notion that the way one fights determines the nature of future rule has been encompassed succinctly and aptly in the words of Adam Michnik, the Polish political dissident who, in the midst of the struggle against the communist regime, reminded his compatriots: "Those who begin by storming the Bastille end up by building their own." Another resistance fighter, and an iconic figure of the civil rights movement who worked side by side with Martin Luther King, Jr., the Reverend James Lawson, said during a meeting with a group of international activists and civil society professionals that "civil resistance is about resolving oppression after which its force continues to move the nation forward."[11] The difference between these two political activists and a majority of scholarship on democratization is that the former instinctively felt that the practice of political participation begins well before political freedom is formally instituted as part of a democratic system, and that the legacy of nonviolent resistance plays an indispensable role in democratization and democratic transition long after civil resistance against dictatorship ends. This view differs sharply, for example, from some of the established opinions that "democratic regimes that last have seldom, if ever, been instituted by mass popular action" (Huntington 1984, p. 212).

Indeed, most democratization theories focus on structures, the role of elites, and macro-level forces of change such as modernization. The attention is thus given to building open and competitive electoral infrastructure, ensuring civilian control over the army, creating an independent judiciary, separating political power among different branches of the government, introducing decentralization reforms or market reforms that strengthen the middle class, building political parties, or developing free media or independent civic organizations.

Little attention has been given to the impact of popular nonviolent movements on the trajectories of democratic transitions. Sidney Tarrow noted, for example, that "most scholars of democratization have either ignored movements altogether or regarded them with suspicion as dangers to democracy . . . When [researchers] do turn to movements in less developed systems, it is frequently only to catalogue and condemn ethnic and nationalist movements" (Tarrow 1995, pp. 221–2).

Several studies try to rectify a general disregard for the impact of civil resistance on democratization. The Freedom House study on *How Freedom is Won* identifies sixty-seven transitions between 1972 and 2005; fifty of these were singled out as bottom-up transitions in which civil resistance was a major factor leading to the breakthrough after which transitions began, fourteen were classified as top-down transitions led by powerholders or violent change, and three involved external interventions. 64 percent of bottom-up transitions are in countries that are classified by Freedom House as "free." This fares much better than the 14 percent of top-down transitions that boast free political systems (Karatnycky and Ackerman 2005). A complementary study that focused on economic growth showed that bottom-up transitions experienced moderate and high economic growth in 80 percent of cases, versus 50 percent for top-down transitions (Johnstad 2010). Another important study assesses the probability that a country will be democratic five years after successful nonviolent resistance at 84 percent, compared to 15 percent after a "successful" violent campaign (Chenoweth and Stephan 2011, pp. 201–19).

These studies suggest that the force of civil resistance cannot be reduced to a formulaic technique of a regime change or a universal recipe for bringing down dictators, as some detractors, including the Chinese and Russian governments, warn. The impact of civil resistance has to be measured well beyond the proximate struggle of ending immediate oppression. Both the study and the genuine practice of civil resistance are in fact about a wholesale transformation of society. This begins with a new political order that is already being built during the protracted nonviolent struggle which redefines traditional power relations between ordinary people, state, and elites.[12]

One concept that might play an important role in reconceptualizing civil resistance beyond a simplified view of regime change is perhaps the elusive idea of "social capital." Some view civil resistance as generating "social capital on steroids" (Chenoweth 2013). Others consider the impact of civil resistance in generating all types of social capital, from *bonding* (interacting with similar people), to *bridging* (getting together with people with entirely different views and backgrounds), and, finally, to *linking* (reaching out to and dialoging or negotiating with people in power to win them over) (Bartkowski 2009, 2010). Civil resistance can facilitate the formation of all three types of social capital.

Some methods of civil resistance can be more helpful in generating social capital than others. For example, acts of commission – something that the state authority outlaws (e.g., petitions, strikes, demonstrations, sit-ins, occupations, building parallel institutions) – might have a high index of social capital formation as they involve greater and denser human interactions, building and running organizations, and a considerable amount of human and material resources that need to be mobilized to sustain the actions. In contrast, acts of omission – not doing something that the state authorities require or expect (e.g., conscription boycott, election boycott, tax refusal, boycott of official events) – might come with a relatively lower index of expected social capital, as such actions might be performed largely by individuals and involve a thinner web of human interactions, little institutionalization, and less necessity for capital-intensive endeavors for their implementation.

Many scholars note a positive impact of civil resistance on long-term democratic change by recognizing a prefigurative role of nonviolent struggle (Vinthagen 2011). In Poland, for example, the engagement of the anti-communist opposition helped generate the greater, denser, and more propitious social capital needed to transform the system.

First of all, Solidarity managed to internalize within the psyche of the movement and socialize the general public in what some scholars refer to as the idea of a self-limiting revolution. This type of revolution emphasizes the nonviolent nature of the popular revolt. The nonviolent discipline was encapsulated in the call of one of the opposition leaders, Jacek Kuroń, to "set up [people's] own committees instead of burning down party committees" (Smolar 2009, p. 133). Another strategic self-limitation on the part of the opposition movement was its pragmatic goal of pushing for the establishment of free trade unions and professional associations rather than the outright democratization of Poland, even after more than 10 million Poles (or 80 percent of the country's workforce) joined a legalized Solidarity trade union.

An important element of the Polish self-limiting revolution was its regular emphasis on openness to dialogue and negotiation with the regime once it acknowledged the legitimacy of the demands for democratization and recognized Solidarity as an equal partner in negotiations. Consequently, one of the first tangible impacts of civil resistance on democratization was the setting up of a stage for a grand bargain between the opposition and the regime, which took a concrete shape in the round table negotiations between February and April 1989. Eventually, the self-limiting nature of the Solidarity movement, combined with its potency to use powerful methods of resistance, helped bring about accommodation with the government and impacted the transition that followed the 1989 accords. At the UN General Assembly in fall of 2012, the Polish president, Bronisław Komorowski, gave due credit to the revolution and the 1989 accommodation by saying that, "In the long run, the ability to self-contain and the strength of a wise compromise make a much better solution than maximizing one's own demands and trying to advance one's own arguments by force."

Other important developments[13] in Poland after 1989 that were influenced by prior experience and practice of civil resistance can be seen in the effective organization of Solidarity's political campaign during the first free and open parliamentary elections in the country since 1946. A self-organizing experience that was mustered in the years of mobilizing and resisting gave Solidarity a clear advantage over the communists and ensured its electoral victory in June 1989 despite a relatively short time to prepare the campaign.

Soon after coming to power, Solidarity implemented one of the most important and arguably most successful changes: decentralization reforms. In fact, the nature of this technical reform was very much an ideational reflection of Solidarity itself – of its decentralized structures and its own understanding and practice of political power as an authority diffused throughout hundreds and thousands of autonomous entities close to ordinary people. As a consequence of this reform, 2,600 self-governing rural and urban communes were established and given considerable governing powers, including finances and legal status. The entity that was given the responsibility for training thousands of civil servants and local officials for the newly established structures was, not surprisingly, a civic education foundation independent of political affiliations.

Finally, the legacy of civil resistance during the Polish transition was vividly notable in what Ekiert and Kubik (2001) refer to as a "rebellious civil society" that emerged in Poland between 1989 and 1993. The authors show that, during the first years of transformation, Poland experienced the highest number of protests and strikes in Central Europe – more than 6,000 strike actions each year – but that their demands were also self-limiting. They did not question the democratic direction of the reforms and thus had a reformist rather than a destructive or anti-democratic character. The mobilized civil society – an inheritance of the nonviolent resistance before 1989 – reinforced democratization processes in the country and held the new political elite directly accountable to the public at a time when political parties and interest groups were weak and still forming.

There is a need for more rigorous studies on the long-term impact of civil resistance. It must be noted that the current literature on strategic nonviolent conflict (Chenoweth and Stephan 2011; Karatnycky and Ackerman 2005; Celestino and Gleditsch 2013) considers the impact of civil resistance on democratic transition while looking at the practice of civil resistance *before* the breakthrough and *before* the initiation of the transition itself. A major limitation of the studies is that their data excludes civilian-based mobilization and nonviolent actions *after* the breakthrough is achieved. At the same time, other studies that considered popular nonviolent mobilization *during* transition focused either on a single case (e.g., Poland, in Ekiert and Kubik 2001) or on single methods of contention (e.g., strikes or demonstrations, in Teorell 2010) or derived largely untested propositions about the impact that peaceful resistance has on the democratization process (ibid.).

Conclusion

While referring to various examples, including a special emphasis on the case study of Polish nonviolent resistance, this chapter highlights a number of relevant issues with regard to nonviolent rebellions that are waged for recognition of societies' rights and freedoms. Early on, the chapter pointed to the dominance of structural accounts in explaining popular upheavals or major political changes. More often than not, these approaches occlude the valuation of the role and force of the agency of ordinary people. And, although the external conditions and structures are important and cannot be ignored either by the scholars or, for that matter, by the practitioners, they are not determinative for the emergence or success of nonviolent movements (Marchant 2007).

Nonviolent movements against brutal regimes are on the rise, and there are a number of reasons why people decide to resort to nonviolent resistance. In general, it is easier for the population to join a nonviolent movement than a violent struggle and to make a meaningful and equally important contribution regardless of one's skills, wealth, age, or gender. Such diversity brings creativity and new ideas for action, which ideally inspire still others to join the movement.

The chapter also stressed that a strategic approach to waging a nonviolent struggle combined with thorough planning are crucial for the success of the movement. A reflection of the strategic approach to a conflict can be the efforts on the part of activists to extend their battlefield beyond an immediate arena of struggle and to reach out to potential international allies or societal groups in other countries to increase the pressure on their adversary. Other examples were building alternative institutions to ensure both the resilience of the struggle and a development of society, laying down the economic, civic, and psychological foundations for a protracted struggle and people's participation in direct forms of nonviolent collective action. The reliance on small acts of resistance is yet another illustration of activists' strategic and creative adjustment to the oppressive environment in which they operate.

The success of civil resistance movements can be immediately visible – a dictator leaving office, an occupying power forced to grant independence, or an ethnic group that wins its right to self-determination. The success of civil resistance can also take a more elusive form and have a long-term impact, such as common identity making, consciousness shaping, and institution building – the consequences of which are not immediately apparent. In the context of the investigation into the long-term effect of civil resistance, this chapter made small but important strides into the still little explored area of the enduring influence of civil resistance on democratization once a major political breakthrough has been achieved. In the final part, it showed the way future research could approach this subject: first, by looking at the propitious impact of nonviolent strategies and tactics to generate social capital during the civil resistance phase that, in turn, will be conducive to democratic transition after a dictator's fall; and, second, by considering the role of nonviolent mobilizations and actions once the transition process has begun.

Questions for discussion

1 What advantages does civil resistance have over violent resistance in challenging oppressive regimes?
2 How do you understand the concept of a two-level battlefield, and what examples of civil resistance struggles illustrate it?
3 How do you define success in a civil resistance movement? What outcomes of civil resistance struggle would you consider a success and why?
4 What are small acts of resistance and what are some examples? How are small acts important in broader movements?

Suggestions for further reading and research

Bartkowski, Maciej (2009) "Poland's Solidarity Movement (1980–1989)," International Center for Nonviolent Conflict, www.nonviolent-conflict.org/images/stories/pdfs/bartkowski_poland.pdf.

Hável, Vaclav (1990) *The Power of the Powerless*. New York: M. E. Sharpe.

Nepstad, Sharon Erickson (2011) *Nonviolent Revolutions: Civil Resistance in the Late 20th Century*. Oxford: Oxford University Press.

Roberts, Adam, and Ash, Timothy Garton (eds) (2009) *Civil Resistance and Power Politics: The Experience of Non-Violent Action from Gandhi to the Present*. Oxford: Oxford University Press.

CHAPTER 9

Rural Movements and Economic Policy

Kurt Schock

Civil resistance has been used throughout history by groups seeking social, political, and economic justice. In recent decades a wave of pro-democracy movements has contributed to democratic transitions throughout the world, including movements in the Philippines in 1986, Chile in 1988, Poland in 1989, East Germany in 1989, South Africa in 1994, Serbia in 2000, and Tunisia and Egypt in 2011. These manifestations of people power caught the popular imagination as well as the attention of scholars of civil resistance, who have overwhelmingly focused on urban-based pro-democracy movements (e.g., Chenoweth and Stephan 2011; Nepstad 2011a; Schock 2005). However, there also exists a long and deep tradition of rural-based nonviolent resistance against economic exploitation and inequality. Although the results are perhaps not as dramatic as toppling a dictator, these movements have successfully contributed to the attainment of rural workers' rights, the redistribution of land, and the adoption of sustainable development policies.

Compared to urban-based pro-democracy struggles aimed at regime change, where hundreds of thousands of people often occupy public spaces in major cities, rural-based campaigns of civil resistance typically do not have such a dramatic climax. Protests, demonstrations, marches, and occupations of public space in major cities do occur, of course, in order to raise the public's awareness about issues in the countryside and to generate pressure against the government, but typically these events occur within longer streams of contention rather than being the stunning endgame of a struggle. While pro-democracy campaigns challenge the political oppression of authoritarian regimes, rural social movements often challenge structural violence – i.e., diffuse or systemic injustices and inequalities imbedded in institutions or social relations that prevent people from meeting basic human needs (Galtung 1969, 1996).

The focus of the civil resistance literature on pro-democracy movements is understandable, as numerous democratic transitions have occurred since the early 1970s and civil resistance is almost always a component of democratic transitions. However, crosscutting the trend toward more democratic polities has been growing economic inequality, both within and between countries, in the era of neoliberal globalization from the 1980s onward (Wade 2004). Rural peoples are increasingly being displaced by the global food regime (as discussed in chapter 10) and global land grabbing (Borras and Franco 2012; McMichael 2007).

The overwhelming focus by scholars on pro-democracy struggles is somewhat paradoxical given Gandhi's emphasis on social and economic justice in addition to legal discrimination, democracy, and national liberation. Gandhi's campaigns to end British rule formed part of a broader struggle, and Gandhi maintained that, upon independence, India should avert the substitution of rule by the British elite for rule by an Indian elite. The greater part of Gandhi's work was to renew India's economy, and he envisioned the central government devolving much of its power and decision-making to local villages. Gandhi's larger struggle, in other words, was against structural violence.

Some critics suggest that, while civil resistance may be able to succeed where there is a clear dichotomy between oppressor and oppressed and most segments of society have been alienated by the regime or external occupier, as is the case in many struggles for democracy and national liberation, it is less effective for challenging exploitation and structured inequalities where multiplex ties connect people within a system legitimated by hegemonic ideologies. By contrast, some scholars of civil resistance have emphasized the potential of nonviolent struggle in combating structural violence and structural relations, such as militarism, capitalism, and imperialism (Burrowes 1996; de Ligt 1937; Martin 2001), but it seems we have barely scratched the surface in this regard – excepting, of course, the feminist literature that has laid the groundwork for challenges to patriarchal gender relations (e.g., Bennett 2006; Connell 1987).

Nevertheless, a variety of struggles have emerged across the globe in recent years to oppose neo-imperialism, accumulation through dispossession, and the dominant development paradigm. Movements prioritizing social and economic justice have been mobilized to oppose the construction of large dams, environmental degradation, land inequality, transnational agribusiness, privatization of public utilities, patenting nature and indigenous knowledge, and much more (Schock 2009). Many of these struggles are motivated by visions of participatory democracy, sustainable development, and a more equitable distribution of resources – visions that are Gandhian and anarchist whether or not they are recognized as such. Thus, while nonviolent resistance has been considered by some as a "bourgeois" method of struggle suitable only for extending liberal democracy and "free market" relations, the strategy is potentially much more radical and revolutionary.

In this chapter I examine three rural-based social movement organizations: the United Farm Workers (UFW)[1] in the United States; the Movimento dos Trabalhadores Rurais sem Terra (Movement of the Landless Rural Workers, or MST) in Brazil; and the Assembly of the Poor (Samatcha khon chon) in Thailand. Although issues of labor, land, and economic policy are interrelated, here I focus on the UFW's struggle for labor rights in the 1960s and 1970s, the MST's struggle for land since the mid-1980s, and the Assembly of the Poor's struggle to alter economic policy in the late 1990s.

Key challenges that rural social movements must overcome include mobilizing a constituency that is difficult to organize, forging networks across geographically dispersed areas, and cultivating the support of urban constituencies. First, organizing landless rural workers and small farmers is arduous given relatively high rates of illiteracy and the weight of traditional cultures of patronage, patriarchy, and acquiescence to authority. Adding to these organizational constraints in some cases is the status of rural workers and small farmers as minorities, itinerants or "guest workers."[2] Second, landless rural workers and small farmers tend to be geographically dispersed, therefore mobilizing structures and networking forms of organization that span dispersed constituencies must be utilized or forged. Third, in order to gain leverage in political systems that privilege large landowners and corporations, rural struggles must cultivate the support of influential allies outside of rural areas.

The three cases discussed in this chapter had some degree of success because they overcame these constraints through innovative tactics, organization, and vision. The United Farm Workers increased their leverage through consumer boycotts and transformed the struggle for higher wages and the right to organize into a more comprehensive struggle for social justice in the United States. The MST used land occupations in an organized, disciplined, and strategic manner, transforming the method into a potent weapon in the struggle for land reform. Moreover, once on the land, the MST organized *agrovilas*, or cooperative communities of producers, that further challenged the dominant industrial agriculture model in Brazil. In Thailand, the Assembly of the Poor forged networks among diverse rural communities and nongovernmental organizations as well as with urban constituents displaced from the countryside, brought their struggle to the seat of power in Bangkok, and impacted economic development policies and agendas.

Labor: The United Farm Workers movement

In the 1930s the US labor movement, through collective action and a favorable political context, succeeded in winning labor union recognition, higher wages, and better working conditions (Zeiger and Gall 2002). Farmworkers, however, were largely exempted from federal labor laws that protected industrial workers. Lacking these protections, farmworkers experienced low wages, poor working and living conditions, and a lack of job security. Some of the rural labor in California was supplied by "guest workers" from Mexico, who had none of the legal rights of citizenship, and many farmworkers were poor immigrants who faced barriers in all spheres of life. In effect, California farmworkers were largely powerless in comparison to the powerful agri-business and state agents, who regularly repressed, often with violence, collective attempts to challenge the status quo (Ganz 2009).

Labor organizations with greater resources, such as the AFL-CIO and the International Brotherhood of Teamsters, were unsuccessful in repeated attempts to organize California farmworkers. Thus, when Cesar Chavez founded the Farm Workers Association in 1962 in an effort to promote the labor rights of farm workers in California, the odds were high that it would be just one more in a series of failed attempts to organize farmworkers for better wages and working conditions (Ganz 2009).

Undeterred by previous failures to organize farmworkers, Chavez drew from his experience working with Fred Ross, an influential and skilled community organizer. Chavez became a disciple of Ross and an organizer for the Community Services Organization. He cut his teeth organizing Mexican Americans in California barrios in the 1950s and subsequently applied the principles of grassroots organizing to farm-workers. In what was referred to as the "most painstaking organizing campaign ever directed at Mexican immigrant workers, seeking supporters one on one and house to house" (Shaw 2008, p. 3), Chavez and his cadre engaged in assiduous and persistent grassroots organizing.

Grassroots mobilization of farmworkers was a necessary but not a sufficient condition for developing a successful farmworkers' movement. In order to gain leverage over the agricultural industry in California, Chavez expanded his campaign from the fields of California nationwide and transformed the struggle for workers' rights to a struggle for social justice. Alliances were forged with the Mexican-American com-munity, religious communities, civil rights groups, liberal Democrats, the labor movement, and college students (Ganz 2009, p. 159). Urban supporters participated through secondary actions, such as boycotts and refusing to load, transport, or sell boycotted products.

Chavez was deeply committed to working for social justice through principled nonviolence and drew inspiration from Mexican-American Catholic traditions as well as from the life of Mohandas Gandhi (Orosco 2008). This was evident in the first major struggle of the National Farm Workers Association, which commenced in September 1965 when Chavez supported farmworkers in Delano, California, who went on strike in an effort to attain higher wages. To generate broad-based support for the striking workers, Chavez, along with strikers and supporters, marched approximately 300 miles over twenty-eight days from Delano to the state capital in Sacramento. The march culmi-nated during Easter Week of 1966, when 10,000 supporters welcomed the marchers to Sacramento (Ganz 2009, pp. 146–61).

The march drew on the tradition of pilgrimage, rooted in Mexican culture, which included practices of petition, penance, and com-mitment, and it succeeded in generating media coverage across the country as well as demonstrating the dedication of the activists to the cause. By adeptly using Catholic religious symbolism, such as carrying pictures of Our Lady of Guadalupe, and framing the strike and march as a part of a Gandhian nonviolent struggle, Chavez was able to mobilize support from church groups (Ganz 2009, pp. 146–61; Orosco 2008).

The linchpin of the expansion of the farmworkers' struggle was the consumer boycott that was implemented in support of the Delano grape strike. Activists traveled to the San Francisco Bay area and convinced the International Longshoremen's and Warehousemen's Union, whose members were responsible for loading grape shipments, to cooperate with the protesters and refuse to load non-union grapes. This was followed by the launching of a formal nationwide boycott by the UFW of Schenley Industries and DiGiorgio Corporation, the two largest growers in the Delano grape industry. The boycott resulted in the first substantive union contract in California farmworker history, an increase in wages, and the formal recognition of the National Farm Workers Association (Ganz 2009).

These successes were followed by an industry-wide grape boycott launched in 1968. Perhaps the most successful consumer boycott in US history, the campaign turned the farmworkers' movement into a mass movement, as it brought in an influx of college student volunteers and mobilized conscience constituencies in urban areas. The UFW was innovative in using a consumer boycott to win a labor dispute, and, by expanding the struggle, the farmworkers were able successfully to challenge the dominance of agri-business (Ganz 2009).

Reframing the farmworkers' struggle as a mass movement for civil rights and social justice facilitated broad-based mobilization. By drawing on the collective identity of Mexican Americans, urban supporters could play a role in supporting the movement, and, by framing the struggle as one of an oppressed minority fighting for its freedom, it resonated with the public's understanding of the civil rights movement (Ganz 2009).

By 1972, the UFW had contracts with 150 growers and a membership of over 50,000 workers. For the first time in the history of California's agricultural labor, workers had decent wages, benefits, and working conditions. In 1975, ten years after the Delano grape strike, California enacted the Agricultural Labor Relations Act, which secured many of the rights and labor protections that industrial workers won in the 1930s, such as the right to organize and strike (Ganz 2009).

Marshall Ganz (2009) explains the success of the UFW in the 1960s and 1970s, as well as its subsequent decline in the 1980s, in terms of its strategic capacity.[3] Strategic capacity, according to Ganz, emerges from an interactive process of experimentation, learning, and adapting. When sufficiently developed, strategic capacity enables a movement to capitalize on opportunities by turning the resources they have into the power they need to attain their objectives. Strategic capacity is created by the skillful assembly of a leadership team and the careful structuring of its interactions among its members, constituents, and environment. If the leadership team is deeply motivated, has access to salient information, and is open to learning, then effective strategy is more likely to develop over the long run.

Compared to the leadership of the AFL-CIO and Teamsters, the leadership and volunteer activists of the UFW were highly motivated and committed to the cause and cultivated ties to farm worker communities and religious organizations. The participation of religious groups, civil rights activists, college students, and urban residents in the UFW struggle promoted access to salient information that was absent in the insular organizing drives of the more established labor unions. Compared to the AFL-CIO and Teamsters, the leadership team of the UFW was open to democratic deliberations, which promoted innovative strategies beyond the conventional practices of the traditional labor unions (Ganz 2009). The strategic capacity of the UFW enabled it to overcome crucial challenges facing rural social movements: mobilizing a constituency that is difficult to organize, forging networks across geographically dispersed areas, and cultivating the support of urban constituencies.

Land: The Landless Rural Workers Movement (MST)

The origins of land inequality in Brazil are traced back to Portuguese colonization when land was forcibly seized from indigenous peoples. Subsequently, a small number of families, with the consent of the Portuguese monarchy, governed vast tracts of land in the territory that is now Brazil. To this day a relatively small class of large land-owners owns much of the agricultural land and wields an inordinate influence in Brazilian politics. From the 1970s onward the number of landless and unemployed rural workers increased as a result of the building of giant hydroelectric dams and the expulsion of people from land to make way for large industrial farms as part of the green revolution. In the 1990s, neoliberal policies were implemented which contributed to the indebtedness of small farmers. Thus, growing numbers of landless people were aggrieved by increasing levels of land inequality and the failure of the government to address the issue through land reform (Branford and Rocha 2002; Wright and Wolford 2003).

In an effort to attain their own land to cultivate, in the late 1970s peasants began taking over unproductively used land through unarmed land occupations. Independent of each other and in different parts of the country, local activists planned and organized these occupations. Progressive members of the Catholic Church affiliated with the Comissão Pastoral da Terra (Pastoral Commission on Land) and activists concerned with rural violence and inequality subsequently began to coordinate land occupations. They recognized their potential power for redistributing land if action was implemented in an organized, disciplined, and strategic manner. They also recognized that a national social movement would be in a stronger position to resist repression and confront landowners and the state. Their efforts led to the founding in 1984 of the Movimento dos Trabalhadores Rurais sem Terra (Movement of the Landless Rural Workers, or MST) (Branford and Rocha 2002; Harnecker 2003; Wright and Wolford 2003).

The MST framed its struggle as a class conflict between exploited and dispossessed rural workers and large capitalist landowners, as well as, increasingly, international agri-business. Analyses informed by Marxism and liberation theology explained the connections between capitalism and landlessness and suggested the need for political struggle to achieve structural transformation. Moreover, the MST adapted liberation theology to the struggle of the landless through the development of *mística*, the representation of the struggle through words, art, symbolism, and music, to promote mobilization, empowerment, and solidarity (Issa 2007).

The MST draws inspiration from Che Guevara, the Cuban revolution, and the Nicaraguan Sandinistas. Nevertheless, while recognizing the struggles of Marxist revolutionaries, the MST rejected the Marxist strategy of taking over the state through violence and becoming a ruling party, realizing that such resistance would be counterproductive to land reform in the current context. Significantly the MST realized that its comparative advantage was with nonviolent resistance, given the monopoly on violence held by landowners and the state. Moreover, if they employed violence, they would lose support from the general public and from the more progressive segments of the Catholic Church, which was important for their success. The MST also acknowledged that substantial change could not occur by relying solely on institutional political channels. Requests for land reform through petitioning, lobbying, or negotiating were futile. Mass mobilization was necessary to gain political leverage (Branford and Rocha 2002; Stédile and Fernandes 1999; Wright and Wolford 2003).

Although not widely recognized as a "nonviolent" social movement, the MST used an imaginative array of methods of nonviolent action to promote land reform.[4] The movement generated pressure against the government through protest demonstrations, occupying government offices, and long marches that generated media coverage. Similar to Cesar Chavez's march from Delano to Sacramento, California, in 1966, approximately 12,000 landless people, activists, and supporters marched for seventeen days from Goiânia to Brasília in May 2005 to raise awareness about the plight of the landless and to keep pressure on the government to proceed with land reform. However, land occupation is the MST's defining method and the one that has proved most powerful in promoting land reform.

Activists realized the pragmatic fit of the tactic of land occupation to the Brazilian context. First, compared to other developing countries where the number of landless people is high relative to the amount of unused land, there is a highly favorable ratio of unused agricultural land to people; in other words, large tracts of land existed that were not being used productively by the owners. Second, the Brazilian constitution provides legal justification for redistributing land that is not in productive use.[5] Third, the government lacked the political will to implement reform in the absence of mass pressure that exposed the contradictions of inequitable land distributions. Through organized campaigns of land occupations, mass mobilization and political pressure were generated (Schock 2012).

From its origins in southern Brazil, the movement developed into a national movement as the MST sent activists throughout the country to organize the landless and carry out land occupations. Through grassroots organizing, MST activists locate communities with landless families interested in getting land. Ideally, mobilization is facilitated by an important figure in the community sympathetic to the MST, such as a priest or a union leader. If no such person exists, MST activists go door to door, recruiting people to participate in the movement. Meetings are held in churches or schoolrooms, where activists explain what the movement is about, why they struggle for land, and how land could be attained through land occupations. Each person attending the meeting is requested to invite additional people to subsequent meetings, thus increasing participation. Multiple meetings are carried out in a parallel way in different communities. When there is a critical mass of people interested in participating, a regional meeting is held and a date is set for a land occupation (Branford and Rocha 2002; Harnecker 2003; Wright and Wolford 2003).

After the land is occupied, the MST initiates legal proceedings to challenge any eviction notices from local authorities and to have the land officially expropriated by the government. If the legal battle is won, then the encampment is transformed into a settlement and the occupiers construct a more permanent community. If not, then planning and preparation for a new land occupation commences.

Since the mid-1980s, the MST has carried out hundreds of thousands of land occupations, thereby making land reform a national issue. Moreover, through land occupations and the subsequent attainment of land titles through this method, 20 million acres of agricultural land have been redistributed to over 350,000 families (Wright and Wolford 2003). The movement was successful not only in promoting land redistribution but also in transforming Brazil's agricultural sector. Traditionally, Brazilian agriculture has been geared toward growing cash crops for export, such as sugar, tobacco, and soybeans, rather than producing food for local markets. This has two negative consequences. First, it contributes to hunger in Brazil, since productive land is not being used to grow food staples. Second, industrial methods of monoculture farming contribute to environmental degradation through the use of chemical fertilizers, herbicides, and pesticides and the depletion of groundwater. In contrast, the MST encourages families to work the land cooperatively and to engage in organic farming to produce goods for local markets. The MST is also

Box 9.1 Land occupation

Land occupation is a highly organized and disciplined method of direct action involving substantial planning and preparation. Before an occupation occurs, the MST identifies land that fulfills two characteristics: first, it is not in productive use and is thus eligible for redistribution under the law; and, second, it is potentially productive and suitable for supporting an agricultural village, or *agrovila*. Typically the land that is occupied is privately owned, but sometimes occupations occur on unused government land as well.

While the date is announced in advance, the location of the land to be occupied is kept secret, known only to a few activists in order to prevent the authorities or landowners from taking actions to inhibit the occupation. Entire families participate and are transported to the site in a stealthy manner so as to not attract the attention of the authorities, leaving by busloads in the middle of the night from different places and at staggered times, then converging at the site of the occupation.

Basic necessities for living on the land are taken, such as material for constructing shelter, agricultural tools, cooking equipment, and a supply of nonperishable food staples. The occupiers cannot depend on outside help because police often set up roadblocks to prevent additional people or supplies from reaching the site (Branford and Rocha 2002; Harnecker 2003; Wright and Wolford 2003).

Occasionally armed agents of landowners or the state meet the occupiers to evict them from the land. Although reactive violence has sometimes occurred, especially in earlier years of the movement, the policy of the MST is to retreat and organize a new occupation rather than to respond with violence. Entire families rather than just men undertake land occupations, as this may reduce the likelihood that the action is met with violence.

committed to designating 20 percent of the land they obtain as an ecological reserve. Thus, the struggle to win land is viewed as part of a larger struggle to achieve a more democratic and ecologically sound society (Wright and Wolford 2003).

The MST overcame the key challenges of rural social movements: it mobilized a constituency that is difficult to organize, it forged networks across geographically dispersed areas, and it cultivated the support of urban constituencies. First, like the UFW, door-to-door organizing in rural communities was crucial for mobilization. Once land was attained, "imagined communities" (Wolford 2003) or "autonomous rural communities" developed by the MST promoted politicization of its membership and facilitated further mobilization (Vergara-Camus 2009). In each settlement some activists were freed from their agricultural responsibilities in order to work on organization and mobilization (Harnecker 2003).

Second, through the networks of the Comissão Pastoral da Terra and then through the networks forged by the MST itself, it was transformed from a regional to a national movement. Localized and isolated movements are much less likely to remain resilient in the face of repression than are movements that operate nationally. The power discrepancy between landowners and the landless diminished as the MST formed networks spanning a substantial part of the countryside (Fernandes 2005).

Third, the MST exerted leverage in the political sphere because of the support it cultivated from the Partido dos Trabalhadores (PT), a center-left political party, the Central Única dos Trabalhadores (CUT), the largest industrial trade federation in Brazil, and young activists from urban areas. Much as had been the case with the UFW in the US, the MST's fight was transformed from a landless rural workers' struggle to a broader struggle for social justice.

Economic policy: the Assembly of the Poor

The Assembly of the Poor (Samatcha khon chon) was founded in 1995 as a grassroots organization that grew out of preexisting small farmer and villagers' organizations in northeast Thailand. The assembly is not a centralized organization but, rather, a horizontal network of grassroots organizations and supporting NGOs. It was established to enable villagers' organizations from around the country to come together in a forum to exchange information and resources and to increase their bargaining power in their own campaigns by being part of a broad-based network.

The Assembly of the Poor is composed of various groups adversely affected by state policies implemented to promote industrialization, export-oriented agriculture, and commercial forestation. Its members come from the hundreds of thousands of people that have been adversely affected by the construction of large-scale dams over the past few decades, as well as urban slum dwellers, many of whom were forced off the land in the countryside. Dam construction resulted in the loss of fisheries and the flooding of land upon which people depended for their livelihood. The government failed to compensate people adequately for their losses. Thus a focus of the assembly is to suspend dam construction, compensate villagers for their losses, devolve decisions about land use to the local level, and push the state's economic policy in a more sustainable direction (Missingham 2003).

The Assembly of the Poor initially attempted to redress the grievances of its members through institutional political channels such as lobbying, but their efforts were ignored or stonewalled by the government. After exhausting conventional channels, the movement turned to methods of nonviolent action such as marches, rallies, protest demonstrations, and civil disobedience. Like the UFW and MST, it realized that mass protest was the most practical way to create the bargaining power needed to bring decision-makers to the negotiating table on a more equal footing. To broaden the movement, NGO activists framed the struggle in terms of the globalized discourse on environmentalism and sustainable development. Ties were forged with NGOs within Thailand as well as transnational ones, such as the International Rivers Network (Baker 2000; Missingham 2003).

A powerful method of protest developed by the Assembly of the Poor was the encampment. In an encampment, a makeshift 'rural village' is set up in the streets of Bangkok at the heart of the center of power, near the Government House, which accommodates the offices of the prime minister and other officials. During the course of the encampment, within which activists live for the duration of the protest campaign, political rallies and meetings are held on a daily basis, and marches through the streets are sometimes undertaken. Dramatic events are organized which receive considerable coverage in the mass media (Missingham 2003).

The first major encampment occurred in March and April of 1996, when up to 12,000 activists participated in the month-long campaign. As a result of the encampment, the Assembly of the Poor obtained agreements in principle from the government to compensate their members for the expropriation of land and the loss of livelihood. The assembly was vigilant in following up with committees and government agencies during the implementation stages, demanding that the agreements be honored. However, the government refused to adhere to its promises.

In response, the Assembly of the Poor organized a second, larger encampment (Missingham 2003), which took place from January 24 to May 2, 1997, outside the Government House in Bangkok. An estimated 25,000 people from thirty-five provinces demanded that the government adhere to its promises and take action on their grievances. The second encampment was the most sustained and well-organized mass protest ever mounted in Bangkok. By engaging in disciplined and nonviolent protest, it mobilized pressure against the government without raising the anxiety of the public beyond a critical threshold or justifying a violent response from the authorities. Because of the size and duration of the second encampment, along with the intense media coverage and the support of NGOs and segments of the middle class, the government was pressured to negotiate with the assembly and to implement the agreements it had made.[6]

The Assembly of the Poor won unprecedented concessions from the government, including compensation to almost 7,000 families for loss of land and livelihood as a result of dam construction, the cancellation of one dam project and the review of five others, three resolutions ending summary evictions of villagers from forest land, and the admission in principle that long-settled groups should be allowed to remain on forest land. Moreover, a bill was initiated in parliament that would recognize community rights to forest management (Missingham 2003).

The government of Prime Minister Chavalit Yongchaiyudh had given a guarantee to address all of the grievances in the assembly's petition. However, when the government of Prime Minister Chuan Leekpai took over from the Chavalit government in November 1997, the gains were lost, as the new government refused to honor previous agreements. During the more authoritarian rule of Chuan, rather than staging major political events in Bangkok, the assembly adopted the strategy of coordinated but geographically scattered protests at strategic locations of conflict throughout the country. The implementation of more diffuse protests sidestepped the possibility of concentrated repression of the movement. However, once Thaksin Shinawatra became prime minister in February 2001, the assembly again pressed the national government for reform through large-scale mobilizations, as he was seen as more sympathetic to the goals of the movement (Missingham 2003).

The Assembly of the Poor overcame key challenges that rural social movements face. First, it succeeded in mobilizing a constituency that is difficult to organize. Although activists did not engage in door-to-door mobilization, as did members of the UFW and MST, they were successful in aggregating diverse organizations already formed by villagers. The assembly's efforts to mobilize were "noteworthy in a society long argued to be inhabited by a passive and deferential people who relied on informal, largely patron–client, vertical bonds to reach the powerful when they needed redress or assistance" (Jumbala 1998, p. 266). Second, it forged broad horizontal networks across geographically dispersed areas connecting aggrieved rural villagers with each other and with slum dwellers displaced from the countryside. Third, it cultivated the support of influential urban allies, such as middle-class NGOs concerned with environmentalism and development and college students and academics (Baker 2000).

The Assembly of the Poor was significant because it represented the first major reassertion of the rural political voice in Thailand since the suppression of the Peasants' Federation in the 1980s. It differs from earlier rural political groups on account of its decentralized network style of organization, its diffuse leadership, and its ability to address local and national issues. While its success has varied depending on the political context, the assembly has successfully put the issue of sustainable development on the national agenda, and it works to transform social relations of power to enable local communities obtain the freedom to manage local resources and to compel the state to guarantee local community rights over the use of land and resources.

Conclusion

The campaigns of the UFW, the MST, and the Assembly of the Poor all led to unprecedented "firsts" in their respective contexts. The efforts of Cesar Chavez and the UFW resulted in the first successful organizing campaign of landless rural workers in the state of California, where industrial agricultural interests reigned supreme. The sustained campaigns of land occupations of the MST led to the first serious challenge to the power of the landowning elite and consequential redistribution of land in the history of Brazil. The occupations of public space in Bangkok by the Assembly of the Poor in 1996 and 1997 forced the Thai state, for the first time, to negotiate directly with marginalized populations over economic policy and land use.

How were these historic firsts attained? One contributory factor was the realization of the comparative advantage of nonviolent resistance. Activists recognized that the political interests that promoted agribusiness and large development projects had a decided advantage in the institutional political sphere. These interests could not be effectively challenged solely through conventional politics. However, activists also realized that violent resistance would not be effective because of the advantage that was held by large landowners and the state with regard to the means of violence. Violent resistance by challengers often justifies overwhelming repression by landowners and the state. Moreover, armed movements are less likely to mobilize broad-based support and the support of influential allies; the barriers to participation are higher in violent movements; and violence tends to promote social polarization (Chenoweth and Stephan 2011; Martin 2005).

The basis of power of nonviolent resistance is the sustained mobilization of large numbers of people, which generates pressure from outside the system in order to give challenges greater leverage within institutional political and legal channels. Mobilizing large numbers of committed people is typically necessary to win new collective benefits for those underrepresented in politics (Amenta et al. 2005). The UFW, the MST, and the Assembly of the Poor mobilized mass-based campaigns over an extended period of time that raised the public's awareness about problems in the countryside and forced the government to address entrenched systems of inequality and exploitation. Their campaigns provided the means for large numbers of people to actively pursue their interests while promoting solidarity and empowerment. Moreover, all these organizations cultivated the support of third parties and of the general public, which would not have been the case had they engaged in violent resistance.

The selection of specific methods of protest is shaped by contentious repertoires (the set of methods known and available in a given context) and by tactical considerations (projections about the effects of implementing actions and the responses of opponents or third parties) (Tilly 2006; Schock 2012). In each case activists thought strategically to figure out how certain methods could promote mass mobilization and promote leverage. The UFW did not invent the consumer boycott (which traces back to Ireland in the 1880s when townspeople refused to do business with Captain Boycott after he evicted tenants from his land) but rather adapted the method to the struggle for farmworkers' rights. The boycott led to a tremendous increase in the number of urban participants in the struggle, which was necessary for success. Throughout Latin America, isolated peasant communities dispossessed of their land have long engaged in land occupation to attain their rights. But the MST transformed the land occupation into a potent method for gaining land through mass mobilization, making it the defining method of their nationwide struggle. The Assembly of the Poor innovated by setting up village encampments at the seat of power, which made the government and the broader public aware of the conflicts over land use and development in the countryside and forced the government to act.

In conclusion, through the innovative and disciplined use of methods of nonviolent action, the UFW, the MST, and the Assembly of the Poor were able to mobilize constituencies that were difficult to organize, forge networks across geographically dispersed areas, and cultivate the support of urban constituencies. In doing so they demonstrated the possibility of civil resistance in combating structural violence as well as political oppression.

Questions for discussion

1 Why is it difficult to mobilize landless rural workers and small farmers?
2 How do rural social movements gain leverage over ostensibly more powerful opponents?
3 What is meant by the "comparative advantage" of nonviolent resistance?
4 Why is it important to examine issues of economic justice in the study of nonviolence?

Suggestions for further reading and research

Corr, Anders (1999) *No Tresspassing! Squatting, Rent Strikes and Land Struggles Worldwide*. Boston: South End Press.

Friends of the MST, www.mstbrazil.org.

Ganz, Marshall (2009) *Why David Sometimes Wins: Leadership, Organization, and Strategy in the California Farm Worker Movement*. Oxford: Oxford University Press.

McMichael, Philip (2012) *Development and Social Change: A Global Perspective*. 5th edn, Thousand Oaks, CA: Sage.

Missingham, Bruce D. (2003) *The Assembly of the Poor in Thailand: From Local Struggles to National Protest Movement*. Chiang Mai, Thailand: Silkworm Books.

CHAPTER 10

Transnational Movements and Global Civil Society

Peter (Jay) Smith

In the late twentieth century there was a remarkable increase in the number of social movement organizations working with one another for social and political change on the transnational level – that is, across the borders of two or more states (Smith 2008). These include transnational social movement organizations (TSMOs) engaged in such issues as human rights, the environment, peace, women's rights, development, and global economic justice. Increasingly, these diverse TSMOs were networking and working in concert against a common adversary, often identified as "transnational corporations," capitalism, or what is most commonly referred to as neoliberalism. According to Donatella della Porta and Sydney Tarrow, this transnational collective action is "the most dramatic change we see in the world of contentious politics" (quoted in Reitan 2007, p. 7). Contentious politics has exhibited itself in various forms and places, from parallel summits protesting meetings of such international bodies as the World Trade Organization (WTO) to creation by activists of their own organized events and spaces such as the World Social Forum (WSF).

The WSF embodies in many ways the culture of politics, activism, and contention that has arisen in the past thirty years in what has been described as the global justice movement (GJM), with its emphasis on decentralization, networking, participation, non-hierarchical organizing, diversity, and nonviolence.[1] The emphasis on diversity and pluralism is critical to attracting the myriad of social movements and NGOs to a global space. Importantly, the WSF's Charter of Principles, drafted by its governing International Council in the spring of 2001, makes it clear that it is a proponent of nonviolence (see World Social Forum 2001).

Nowhere, however, does the WSF or its charter define what it means by nonviolence, what nonviolent practices are, or what a nonviolent strategy would look like. Some, such as Stellan Vinthagen, argue that this is a lamentable absence in the GJM generally, stating there is a need to bring "the more than one century old nonviolent resistance tradition into the present global movement" (2006, p. 1). However, this chapter argues that, if one looks at nonviolence in a different way, not so much as a concern for conscious strategy but as incorporated into particular ways of life, then the result is different.

Indeed, these movements reflect Gandhi's belief that means and ends cannot be separated, that strategy cannot be separated from goals. Gandhi himself argued that:

> The belief that there is no connection between the means and the end is a great mistake . . . The means may be likened to a seed, the end to a tree; and there is just the same inviolable connection between the means and the end as there is between the seed and the tree . . . We reap exactly as we sow. (1999, pp. 286–7)

Violent means, Gandhi thought, would ultimately beget violent ends. This belief underscores the basis of prefigurative politics, the practice of living the means to the ends in politics, which is evident in many new transnational movements.

This chapter examines the role of nonviolence in the GJM, underlining the growing emphasis placed on prefigurative politics by transnational movements embodied in the creation of alternative forms of non-hierarchical and decentralized organizations and processes of horizontal decision-making. Here the WSF is of central importance in bringing together transnational movements in the GJM on a periodic basis. Yet, the WSF is not an actor, it is a political space, an incubator of further transnational action against neoliberal globalization. To show how transnational movements practice the prefigurative politics of nonviolence in both the GJM and the WSF, the chapter later examines the role of La Via Campesina (LVC), one of the largest transnational movements in the world.[2] Yet, as much as nonviolence is advocated and practiced in the GJM, it has been marked by streaks of violence as well.

The rise of transnational movements, digital technologies and the network organization

Historically, transnational social movements are nothing new. The first was the anti-slavery movement of the late eighteenth and early nineteenth centuries (Anti-Slavery International 2013). Others soon followed, including socialist, labor, pacifist, and women's movements. What is new is the rapid increase of transnational social movements beginning in the late twentieth century. What compelled and enabled social movements to become active beyond their borders?

We can point to two explanations: first, the changing relationships between the state, civil society, and the economy; second, the intro-

duction of new digital communications technologies which facilitated the ability to communicate and organize beyond borders. These
phenomena contributed to the creation of a new form of organization, the network organization, which, in turn, has its own cultural
logic, one distinct from that of more traditional hierarchical social
movement organizations operating on the state level.

In reference to the changing relationships, Voss and Williams (2009)
argue that the balance of power among the three domains of social
organization – state, civil society, and economy – is shifting. Over the
course of the nineteenth and twentieth centuries, all three expanded
in terms of organization and power, but eventually the balance of
power shifted in the direction of the state. This meant that what are
commonly referred to as political opportunity structures could be
found at the state level. As Van Der Heijden writes, "political opportunity structure refers to the specific features of a political system . . .
that can explain the different action repertoires, organizational forms
and impacts of social movements, and social movement organizations
in that specific country" (2006, p. 28). Social movements demanding
recognition and benefits therefore targeted political opportunity
structures at the state level.

However, by the late twentieth century, the balance of power among
the three domains shifted once again, this time more and more to the
economic arena with increasing globalization of the market, finance
and production. The state was progressively challenged by the economic domain and began retreating from its social welfare function.
Civil society once dominated by the state also became subordinated to
the market. As the economy penetrated decision-making of the state,
political opportunities at the state level began to close, and increasingly civil society organizations began to change scales in terms of
their activism. According to Voss and Williams, "the rapid growth in
transnational social movements corresponds with the retreat of the
state in granting social welfare concessions" (2009, p. 13).

What is being described above is the rise of neoliberalism and
its challenge to the state. Neoliberalism can be defined as a social,
political, and economic ideology that asserts that markets, not states,
should be the fundamental allocators of values in a society. According
to Manuel Castells, what made neoliberalism possible on a global
scale "was a technological revolution, centered around information
technologies" (2010, p. 1). Furthermore, globalization, facilitated by
the rise in computer-based technologies, is characterized by a network
structure, a new organizational logic forcing states and corporations
to work in a network pattern. Castells extends this argument to social

movements, arguing resistance to neoliberal globalization is also taking a network form (Castells, 2004).

According to Juris, activists in the new social movements employ a "cultural logic of networking" that orient them toward "(1) the building of horizontal ties and connections among diverse elements, (2) the free and open circulation of information, (3) collaboration through decentralized coordination and consensus-based decision making, and (4) self-directed networking" (2008, p. 11). Moreover, these computer-based networks provide a cultural model for emerging forms of direct democratic practices, practices which have their antecedents in the anarchist tradition. This logic is prefigurative in nature and is contrary to the form of bureaucratic organization that dominated society, politics, and government in the twentieth century. Bureaucracies are vertical, top-down, centralized command structures with a clearly defined division of labor based on expertise and rational rules established both as a means of control and in order to efficiently realize the organization's goals.

For new social networked movements, the traditional vertical left-based political organizations (whether they be authoritarian vanguard parties created to overthrow the state, social democratic parties and unions favoring the electoral route to state power, or professional top-down nongovernmental organizations) are remnants of another era and are a source of tension with the GJM. It is the new social networked organizations that have been particularly instrumental in challenging the dominating network logic of neoliberal global capitalism (globalization from above) by globalization from below. According to this perspective, as political opportunities at the state level closed, they opened up at meetings and summits of international organizations and through the building of alliances among social movements. The focus is clearly on civil society activism at the transnational level. As new social movements de-emphasized the state as an arena for activism, they simultaneously began to organize and network at both global and local levels, emphasizing participatory non-hierarchical decision-making. This phenomenon of networks permits many diverse movements and actors to work together in concert while maintaining their separate identities.

Nonviolence and prefigurative politics

With actors being able to act together in concert beyond the state, one sees the emergence of a global civil society with common core values, including consensus decision-making, direct democracy, and nonviolence. Pleyers emphasizes the centrality of nonviolent action among opponents of neoliberal globalization: "*Active non-violence* is a difficult form of action but it is adopted by a growing number of youth, self-proclaimed 'disobedients'" (2010, p. 78). Indeed, surveys of European activists protesting neoliberal globalization indicate that "there is a widespread belief that nonviolence is necessary," in particular to prevent negative publicity that would erode popular support and mobilization (della Porta et al. 2006, p. 143). This emphasis on nonviolence, stemming from the ultimate goals of transnational movements, is tied to "the notion of prefigurative politics – in which the means for attaining a nonviolent, noncapitalist and truly democratic society must be consistent with the goal" (quoted in Ribeiro 2009, p. 304). While della Porta and her colleagues do not use the expression "prefigurative politics," their survey reveals that activists emphasize the necessity of not separating means from ends. According to one of their survey respondents speaking in terms of nonviolent action:

> The only way to respond if we want to be different, we have to be coherent. The means must be the same as the end . . . that is, if we start saying the end justifies the means we won't get anywhere, it's old and it's been proved that it's not true and, in the end, the means becomes the end and you fall into the trap. (As quoted in della Porta et al. 2006, p. 143)

This emphasis on prefigurative politics and the linkage of means and ends so fundamental to transnational networked organizations and opponents of neoliberal globalization has, as noted in the introduction, remarkable parallels to perspectives on nonviolence suggested by Gandhi. It also reflects a radical disjuncture with visions of politics articulated by more traditional authoritarian socialist and left-wing movements in which ends are separated from means and the use of violence was an acceptable price to pay.

New social movements reject this notion. Pleyers suggests that how activists organize – their emphasis on subjectivity, their creativity, their emotions, their desire to construct their own world and identities – along with an emphasis on participation and direct action and opposition to hierarchy is very much a part of prefigurative activism. According to Pleyers, "Like Gandhi, activists of this way of subjectivity believe that 'We must be the change we want to see in the world.' Activists of the way of subjectivity have seized upon and developed this idea: 'It's not tomorrow that there will be changes; they are visible today in the movement'" (2010, p. 38). Thus in prefigurative politics one removes the distinction between what we do and act in the present and the goal that we are trying to achieve – for example, participatory democracy. Rather, our goal, the ideal, has to be embodied and enacted in the present.

The position that means and ends cannot be separated speaks to a classic debate about the role of means and ends in politics, one in which Gandhi was an active participant. According to Mantena (2012), contemporary normative political philosophy has been fixated on ends with less concern given to means. However, earlier in the twentieth century there was a vibrant philosophical debate concerning the relationship between means and ends. For Marxists such as Trotsky, what mattered was the justness of the end, while Gandhi rejected this notion. Mantena claims that it was "Gandhi who, more than any other thinker, took the problem of means and their consequences as the central and defining problem of political life" (ibid., p. 3). The use of violence to drive the British out of India would lead to a violent centralized state. Gandhi suggested an alternative, *swaraj* (self-rule), "based on the self-organizing capacity of the Indian village" (ibid., p. 7), an alternative that had to be constructed as part of the independence movement prefiguring what an independent India would look like.

Thus Gandhi presages key concerns of the contemporary GJM, namely, its recognition of the inseparability of means and ends, that violent means lead to violent ends, and that alternative organizations based on self-governance and participatory democracy have to be built during the course of struggle, not after. That is, the foundations of a new society with its alternative institutions have to be built while the old society is being dismantled. Today, this is evident in the tension between horizontally networked organizations and more traditional vertical left-wing movement organizations and parties comfortable with top-down decision-making.

Violence versus nonviolence: the early years of the GJM

In contesting neoliberal globalization, what means have activists employed? Here tension exists between the majority favoring nonviolent means and a minority favoring what many consider violent means. Indeed, violence did occur in protests, by participants and the police, in the early years of resistance to neoliberal globalization in the 1970s and 1980s, and it has continued as a minority element in transnational social movement organizing ever since. For example, as the International Monetary Fund (IMF) in the 1970s began forcing through neoliberal policies (primarily structural adjustment programs which imposed privatization, de-regulation and austerity on countries of the Global South as a result of their inability to pay back loans), waves of protests known as IMF riots occurred. In 1976 food riots took place in Egypt and Peru in which a plethora of tactics were employed, including strikes, mass street demonstrations, looting, and street violence (Walton and Seddon 1994). IMF riots have been episodic ever since, such as riots in Greece in 2011 when the IMF and the European Union imposed severe austerity measures upon the Greek government.

During the 1990s and the first years of the twenty-first century, discontent with neoliberal globalization continued to grow. Activists, involving environmentalists, unions, and indigenous groups, began organizing across borders to protest the creation of new international trade agreements, including the proposed North American Free Trade Agreement (NAFTA) and the Multilateral Agreement on Investment (MAI). United Nations conferences on women and the environment brought thousands of activists together and, with improvements to communications, transnational alliances of social movements began to emerge. Increasingly, corporate globalization became the master frame that served to unite diverse organizations and movements. Civil society activists found new political opportunities at the meetings (or summits) of the international governmental organizations serving as stewards of neoliberal globalization – for example, the World Bank, IMF, World Trade Organization and G8. They often met at the same time as these economic summits to network, discuss future campaigns, and protest against neoliberal policies.

Transnational activism opposing neoliberal globalization was inspired by two key events in the 1990s, the 1994 Zapatista (Mayan indigenous) uprising in Chiapas, a state in southern Mexico, against the NAFTA; and the 1999 "Battle of Seattle" protesting the ministerial meetings of the WTO. These events are also notable because they disrupted the progress of neoliberal globalization and helped create space for the later emergence of the WSF. Both stimulated debate about the role of violence versus nonviolence in transnational resistance.

Seattle as a transnational event

The question regarding the use of violence was particularly evident during organizing against the 1999 ministerial meetings in Seattle of the WTO, the *bête noir* (anathema) of globalization activists, as the WTO was the key international governmental organization responsible for liberalizing global trade and investment. The so-called Battle of Seattle, a result of local, national, and transnational organizing,

Box 10.1 The Zapatista movement and transnational organizing

The Zapatistas, who had skillfully used the emerging internet to reach and galvanize international support, were a great source of inspiration for transnational organizing, particularly the GJM and the activists who became engaged in the Seattle protests. The Zapatistas had taken a stand, declaring "*Ya Basta!*" ("Enough!") to the neoliberal policies of the NAFTA. These policies would have made communal ownership of land impossible, threatening their identity.

In taking a stand, the Zapatistas provided a master frame for transnational activists clearly identifying neoliberal globalization as their primary target. While most activists rejected the Zapatistas' use of force during the uprising (something they have not employed since 1994), they were attracted by their cultural politics, with its emphasis on diversity, direct democratic politics, horizontal decision-making, leaderless political action, and prefigurative politics of creating alternative institutions as they went along.

Transnational activists were also attracted by the internationalism of the Zapatistas. In January 1996 the Zapatistas called for intercontinental meetings to initiate the formation of global networks of resistance to neoliberal globalization. Their first meeting, or *encuentro*, attracted thousands of transnational activists from fifty countries to the Mexican jungle and proposed a global network to fight neoliberalism (Juris 2008).

became a formative event and a catalyst for anti-corporate globalization activists (Smith 2001). Much of the impetus for the organizing came from more formal entities with extensive transnational connections, such as Public Citizen, founded by Ralph Nader, the Council of Canadians, and the Third World Network of Malaysia, which were among seven groups coordinating the Seattle campaign, maintaining regular contact and holding conference calls every four weeks (Smith and Smythe 2004). Transnational organizations promoting the Seattle campaign included LVC, Greenpeace, the International Forum on Globalization, and Friends of the Earth. They were assisted by other organizations and networks such as the Direct Action Network (DAN) with more regional ties to Canada. DAN had been formed to coordinate the nonviolent direct action of the WTO protests. All these groups relied on the internet for circulating information about the ministerial meetings and mobilization efforts. On the ground, national unions, churches, and schools provided important logistical support and thousands of participants in the opening march.

Between 20,000 and 30,000 activists (Bornstein 2009) went to Seattle to protest the WTO ministerial meetings, among them environmental networks, women's organizations, farmers and indigenous peoples, economic justice and debt activists, organized labor, nonviolent direct action activists, the Black Bloc (a grouping of particularly militant anarchist anti-capitalist groups), and grassroots media activists (Juris 2008).[3] A key division of labor in Seattle was between those belonging to more formal organizations and those belonging to more horizontal prefigurative groupings. Leaders and experts in more formal organizations dominated in terms of numbers of speakers at the many seminars, workshops, and teach-ins as well as lobbying at the convention center itself. On the streets, engaging in nonviolent direct action attempting to stop the ministerial meetings, were masses of young people belonging to affinity groups associated with DAN, including the Rainforest Network and the Ruckus Society. Affinity groups represent prefiguration in action, with autonomous contingents of no more than five to fifteen activists democratically deciding by consensus how they will participate in direct actions – for example, blockading streets (Starhawk 2002). For months prior to Seattle, DAN (and the Ruckus Society) had been organizing courses in nonviolent resistance, in particular, what to do when confronted and arrested by police (della Porta et al. 2006). Groups affiliated with DAN had to agree not to use physical or verbal violence, drugs, or alcohol and not to destroy property (Conway 2003).

These groups engaged in a number of actions, most nonviolent, such as teach-ins, forums, a labor march and rally, and direct action, including blockades of streets. Among the tactics used by those blockading the streets was the "lockdown," whereby activists locked themselves together in a manner that was time-consuming for the police to separate. While locked down, protesters had tear gas sprayed directly into their eyes by the police. The tactics of the protesters prevented the ministerial meetings from opening on the first day. Once the meetings started, activists from one NGO who had been allowed into the opening ceremonies took over the speaker's podium and were subsequently arrested. Many of those arrested during the protests refused to cooperate and clogged up jails by not providing their names until all arrestees had their sentences reduced. Yet there was some violence as well, with property destruction by the Black Bloc, who, it is claimed, started to target corporate stores only after the police had begun a cycle of violent confrontation on those blockading streets (Smith 2001).

Overall, protesters in Seattle were peaceful and nonviolent in an event characterized by spectacle, creativity, and a festive atmosphere. Protesters demonstrated colorful ways of bringing their message to the public, including striking posters promoting the protests, street theater, and the hanging of banners symbolizing their cause. However, the actions of the Black Bloc created a schism among activists in Seattle, and its members were blamed for the intensification of police repression, already severe, against nonviolent protesters. This led to an ongoing debate over a diversity of tactics, dividing protest leaders from DAN and vertically organized NGOs such as the Sierra Club from more radical and militant activists. The latter insisted on respect for a diversity of tactics "as a non-negotiable basis of unity" (Conway 2003, p. 507), yet the demand for a pluralism of tactics precluded nonviolent agreements proposed by DAN. The diversity model was later visible in the transnational mobilizations in Quebec City in April 2001 over the proposed Free Trade Area of the Americas, in which the 60,000 protesters were overwhelmingly nonviolent. However, symbolic property destruction by a minority overshadowed the massive protests.

Similar tensions between nonviolent activists and the Black Bloc occurred at the G8 meeting in Genoa in July 2001. Elsewhere, global mobilizations, useful as they were for coalition building and action (Smith et al. 2008), were marred by a minority engaging in property destruction and the extensive use of police force. Increasingly, activists felt there was a necessity to go beyond meeting and protesting at the venues of intergovernmental organizations facilitating neoliberal globalization, to move from denouncing what they were against to articulating "a clear vision of what they were fighting *for*" (ibid., p. 23).

This perception that protest was not enough, that often it led to violence by some protesters and by the police, that alternatives needed to be articulated, led ultimately to the formation of the first ever World Social Forum in January 2001. The WSF was also positively stimulated by the practice of holding counter-summits at the summits of intergovernmental organizations in which networking and the building of alliances and the launching of campaigns occurred. In particular, however, the WSF was inspired by the Zapatista movement (see box 10.1), its cultural politics and internationalism serving as a catalyst for transnational mobilization and diffusion of prefigurative politics, though not by its use of violence. According to Smith and her colleagues, "the networks Zapatismo inspired . . . provided for an infrastructure of people, organizations, and ideas required for the WSF's emergence" (2008, p. 21). Moreover, the Zapatistas provided the WSF with its key slogan, "another world is possible." The irony, however, was that the Zapatistas were never allowed to attend the WSF, as they had engaged in violence.

The development of the WSF

The WSF represents a growing maturity of the GJM as it moved from condemnation of neoliberal globalization, to advocating for change, and, finally, to articulating the means to bring change about (Pinsky 2010). The first forum was held in January 2001 in Porto Alegre, Brazil, as a counterpoint to the World Economic Forum held in Davos, Switzerland, a meeting of those in positions of corporate and state power promoting neoliberal policies. Forums grew rapidly in size, with numbers reaching 150,000 in the 2004 Mumbai WSF, the last forum held on an annual basis. Forums, now held on a biannual basis, continue to record large numbers of activists, and regional, national and local forums have become common.

What attracts activists to the WSF? To a considerable extent, people are attracted to its prefigurative politics, including an emphasis on horizontality and participatory democracy with grassroots organizing. Second, it places high value on openness, diversity, inclusiveness, pluralism, the primacy of civil society actors, networking, and the necessity of creating alternatives. The disparate groups are united in their adherence to the principle of nonviolence and in terms of opposition to neoliberalism and corporate power. Yet, there are tensions in other areas. The WSF has been characterized by tension between more horizontal, autonomous groups and more professional top-down professional NGOs led by experts and academics, which prefer the approach of dialogue, reason, and education over direct activism (Pleyers 2010). However, over time, the more horizontally engaged groups have become more prominent. Of particular significance is that the WSF is not an actor but a space for the diffusion of ideas, strategies, and alternatives. In addition, the WSF Charter of Principles encourages its participants to think and act on a variety of scales, from the local to the global, all so necessary for transnational mobilizing.

Its diversity means that there are a wide variety of struggles that find expression at the WSF. According to Sousa Santos, these struggles have one point of agreement, "a consensus on non-violence." However, while the WSF endorses nonviolence, with the expectation that it will strengthen nonviolent transnational activism, "even non-violence is open to widely disparate interpretations" (Sousa Santos 2008, p. 247). The WSF makes it clear that those who have used or advocated violence or belong to military organizations may not attend the forum. This includes the Zapatistas because the latter define themselves as the Zapatista Army for National Liberation.[4]

> ### Box. 10.2 Liberation theology
>
> The role of liberation theology was central in the formation of the WSF. During the years of military dictatorship (1964–85), the Catholic Church in Brazil became "the most legitimate nation-wide, and useful organizational resource for the oppositional forces of civil society" (von Sinner 2007, p. 174). In so doing it also became theologically progressive, giving rise to liberation theology, which suffused the ideas of key individuals, organizations, and social movements associated with the creation of the WSF. Liberation theology as practiced in Brazil is a theology of the poor and the oppressed.
>
> Liberation theologians were clearly influenced by Gandhi and Martin Luther King, Jr., and disavowed all forms of violence – structural, repressive military, or revolutionary (Dear 2003, p. 6). Dom Hélder Câmara, late archbishop of Olinda and Recife, liberation theologian and advocate for the poor, considered the violence of poverty as the primary problem of his day. He saw Gandhi as a prophet and, like Gandhi, did not distinguish between means and ends, warning that "Violence is not the real answer to violence; that, if violence is met by violence, the world will fall into a spiral of violence; that the only true answer to violence is to have the courage to face the injustices which constitute violence" (1971, p. 55).
>
> Francisco (Chico) Whitaker, one of the founders of the WSF, took his theological inspiration from Archbishop Hélder Câmara, with whom he worked. Since 2001 Whitaker has served on the Brazilian Catholic Bishops' Justice and Peace Commission, one of the eight organizations credited with organizing the first WSF.

La Via Campesina: transnational participation in the GSM

One of the most active participants in the WSF and the GSM is La Via Campesina (LVC), an internationally networked social movement of peasants and small and medium farmers and indigenous groups. A strong advocate of nonviolent strategies, LVC "is considered by many to be the most important transnational social movement in the world" (Martínez-Torres and Rosset 2010, p. 150), with affiliated organizations in seventy countries representing 200 million people. LVC is important not just for its size but for its steadfast opposition to neoliberal globalization and its prefigurative politics emphasizing horizontality, democracy, the creation of alternatives, bottom-up organization, as well as an insistence on the inclusion of women. Importantly LVC was introduced to the world at large by means of its direct action participation in Seattle in 1999. Since then it has skillfully used the WSF to build and amplify its growing movement, focusing on its primary campaign of food sovereignty.

LVC was created in response to neoliberal agricultural policies that were being introduced in the 1980s. As a result of these policies many governments in the Global South started withdrawing the institutional support of local peasants and family agriculture, with its emphasis on production for local consumption. Neoliberal agricultural policies were seen as a threat for a variety of other reasons, including their insistence on free trade, the treatment of food as a commodity, the priority of export over local sustainable production, and the dumping of cheap food in their markets by subsidized farm production in the US and the European Union.

Since neoliberalism works on a global scale, peasant farmers all over the world faced a similar threat to their existence. In response, peasants, small farmers, indigenous peoples, and farmworkers from the Americas, Europe, Asia, and Africa met in Mons, Belgium, in April 1993 and created LVC, not just to combat neoliberalism but to produce an alternative model which since has become known as food sovereignty (Desmarais and Nicholson 2010).

Food sovereignty has been at the heart of the campaigns of LVC and represents the antithesis of the neoliberal model. Rather than food for export it favors food production for local markets, fair prices instead of low, food as a human right instead of a commodity, including access to affordable, nutritious food, organic farming methods, the right of rural peoples to produce, and genuine agrarian reform (Martínez-Torres and Rosset 2010).

In terms of strategies, LVC states that it should "seek to achieve its goals by using the most effective nonviolent strategies available, ranging from refusal to participate and direct action to full cooperation and negotiation" (as quoted in Borras 2004, p. 21). One of the reasons why nonviolence is preferred as a strategy may be because, in its initial years, peasant movements from Latin America were a driving force behind the creation of LVC. These movements (which included MST, discussed further in chapter 9) were influenced by liberation theology, with its belief in nonviolence (Martínez-Torres and Rosset 2010). The nonviolent strategies of LVC can be broken down into outside/ inside strategies; outside strategies represent outright opposition to neoliberalism and involve such tactics as "mass demonstrations, boycotts and direct action," while inside strategies include "cooperation and collaboration" (as quoted in Borras 2004, p. 21).

In political opportunity structures such as the WTO ministerial meetings, where their demands have been ignored, outside strategies have been employed. In the Battle of Seattle, LVC engaged in direct actions attempting to stop the delegates from meeting. One of the leading protesters from LVC in Seattle was José Bové, a French farmer and leader of Confédération paysanne, the second largest farmers' union in France and a member of LVC. In leading many other farmers in besieging a McDonald's restaurant in Seattle, a symbol of bad food according to LVC, lambasting Monsanto, a giant seed corporation, and passing out "healthy" Rocquefort cheese from France which was contraband (on account of a trade dispute with the US), Bové grabbed media attention and solidified his credentials as an icon of the GJM (Northcutt 2003). In France, his actions led to Bové being imprisoned for a brief period. Bové acknowledges the influence of King and envisages himself as a French Gandhi willing to use nonviolence, stressing that one could not distinguish means from ends, and stating "you can't change the world without making changes in your life" (Bové 2001, p. 1).

At other locations where it is welcome, such as the United Nations and the WSF, LVC emphasizes cooperation and collaboration. It has been at the WSF from the beginning, is a member of its governing International Council, and works to expand the movement, stressing the importance of food sovereignty and holding workshops whereby peasants share experiences and network to plan future actions and protests. For many peasant leaders, participation in the WSF is a formative experience. As one African peasant leader put it:

> In 2002 we went to the LVC peasant forum at the World Social Forum (WSF) in Porto Alegre. It was a revelation to us to participate in the nightly LVC meetings during the WSF, as all the LVC representatives there would discuss and debrief the day, and plan our collective strategy for the following day. What was at stake? What did we want to achieve? How would we do it? Who would do what? Wow! This is what it meant to be a movement, to be an international movement! (Quoted in Martínez-Torres and Rosset 2010, p. 161)

At the various forums, LVC has expanded its networking efforts to include the feminist and climate justice movements. Today, it can be said that LVC is very much at the heart of the GJM and enjoys increasing success.

Successes and challenges of the Global Justice Movement

Transnational resistance against neoliberal globalization and global corporate power began over thirty years ago and is ongoing. How successful has this resistance been? Measuring the success of a social movement is no easy task, particularly if one focuses on the extent to which it has accomplished its goal, and activism can go on for long periods of time before accomplishing its aims. However, if one starts with another measure of success, an internal measurement of growth and mobilization, then the metrics can be different.

What eventually became the GJM was initially rooted in the Global South and spread only later to Europe and later still to the US and Canada. The GJM took different shapes, with some aspects being more transnational than others, and some being more locally rooted but with transnational and global links. In an information age, strategies and methods of protest diffuse rapidly across borders. With improvements in communications technologies in the 1990s, activists could organize more easily, with the result that grassroots and transnational movements began to expand across the globe. Thus the GJM expanded and protests against neoliberalism spread. As this chapter indicates, strategies and methods of protest diffuse at counter-summits and meetings, whether at the *encuentro* of Chiapas, Mexico, or at the WSF.

Similarly, a core ideal and strategy of the GJM, nonviolence, had its major inspiration in the Global South, in the independence movement of India. As an ideal, nonviolence is principled and desires to create an alternative culture which emphasizes the use of just means to accomplish just ends, a world where violence is de-legitimated. As a strategy, it is a pragmatic means by which unjust dominant powers can be confronted. As an ideal and strategy, nonviolence spread north, with its notable success in the US civil rights movement, then diffused again to the Global South in terms of liberation theology, later becoming a key ideal of the GJM.

As the GJM has continued to grow and expand to more areas of the world, it spreads the ideas of prefigurative politics and nonviolence. The *Indignados* (Spain's 15-M Movement) and the Occupy movements of 2011 can be seen as protests against the growing inequalities and austerity resulting from neoliberal globalization. Like the WSF, both were concerned with creating public spaces and discussing alternatives to the current economic system. Both were characterized by prefigurative politics with an emphasis on nonviolence. In addition, the protests of the Arab Spring, which confronted harsh authoritarian rule, were networked and horizontally linked and emphasized nonviolence.

In sum, increasingly the preferred option of those opposing economic and political injustices is not to rely on vanguard leftist political parties but rather to emphasize bottom-up prefigurative nonviolent politics, as exemplified by LVC. The resilience and strength of grassroots prefigurative politics runs counter to most political theorists, who argue that models of democracy that require broad participation are not realistic given the abilities and inclinations of the population and the size and scale of the state and interstate systems. Yet, precisely the opposite is true, with participatory politics spreading (Menser 2008).

At a more intermediate level there have been successful results in the GJM. For example, the goal of the protesters in Seattle was to disrupt the ministerial meetings of the WTO, and that they did (Wallerstein 2011). Closer to the present, the Occupy movement, despite protestations of its purported failure (Roberts 2012), was successful in one very important respect: its highlighting of growing social and economic inequality in terms of "We are the 99 percent" created needed space in public discourse in the US, where the issue of inequality was recognized and debated.

Elsewhere, LVC has skillfully used its outside/inside nonviolent strategies to raise its profile and promote its campaign of food sovereignty. In this regard LVC has shifted the international terms of debate and discourse (Desmarais and Nicholson 2010). Food sovereignty is increasingly viewed as a sustainable option to the present method of large-scale industrial agricultural food production (Wittman 2009), with multiple countries – including Ecuador, Venezuela, Bolivia, Nepal, Mali, and Senegal – enshrining food sovereignty into their laws or national constitutions. Desmarais and Nicholson list other accomplishments of LVC, noting:

> It has put agrarian reform back on the agenda; achieved a temporary ban on GM crops in some countries and moratoriums in others while at the same time raised awareness on the importance of farmers' access to and control over seeds; [and] enhanced the participation and representation of women and youth in agriculture and food policy at the international level. (2010, p. 7)

Very importantly for LVC, the peasantry has survived when both liberal and Marxist political economists argued that in a modern age it was destined to disappear.

Measuring the success of the WSF is difficult given it is a public space, not an actor with specific goals and policies. One could argue that it has played a successful role in bringing together transnational movements believing in nonviolence. Moreover, it has helped to change the focus of debate with the GJM. That is, the WSF has assisted transnational movements which previously focused on single issues – human rights, women, the environment, indigenous peoples, farmers, poverty – in working together on multiple issues. For example, LVC is now involved with the climate justice, women's, indigenous peoples, and human rights movements.

Yet transnational movement activism faces many challenges,

including its great diversity – of languages, cultures, political ideologies, social backgrounds, and forms of organization (horizontal versus vertical). While the GJM favors participatory horizontal structures, many of these structures are short-lived and lack the historical memory that vertical organizations can provide for long-term political struggle. Together, these differences make it highly unlikely that the GJM will evolve into a coherent movement with the same goals, policies, and nonviolent strategies. Even LVC, which has created a transnational movement and organization, struggles with the issue of diversity.

These differences lead to tensions, notably the lingering issue between those advocating for a diversity of tactics, including violence, versus the vast majority favoring nonviolent strategies. This difference was evident in the Occupy movement; Occupy DC, for example, required members in its local encampment to adhere to nonviolent practices. Occupy Oakland, on the other hand, accepted the notion of a diversity of tactics and refused to expel activists who destroyed property or actively resisted the police (O'Brien et al. 2012).

Indeed, in the cases explored in this chapter, while nonviolence is the preferred option for most, a minority has engaged in violence, which, in turn, has been met with strong violence and repression by the police. And it is violence that has been the image captured by the corporate mass media. Indeed, this has particularly been a problem with many (but not all) meetings of international bodies presiding over the global economy. For example, in June 2010, Toronto, Canada, was host to the G20 (Group of Twenty) summit of heads of government to discuss the global financial system and the best means to revive the world economy, then in the grips of a severe recession. To ensure security from protesters, the Canadian government spent over a billion dollars in elaborate preparations, among them the deployment of 10,000 police officers – or about one police officer for every protester. Protesters included indigenous peoples, anti-poverty, and anti-corporate globalization groups, who marched and protested peacefully. Yet, peaceful protests were soon punctured by Black Bloc militants, who damaged windows of food chains, stores, and banks and set fire to police cruisers. At this point mass arrests began, with hundreds of protesters herded into massive fenced enclosures set up in the streets.

This, in fact, is just another example of a recurring pattern where protesters gather at summits of leaders of the global economy. It reflects a weakness of networked politics. While networking has its organizational advantages, its emphasis on horizontality and openness can be a disadvantage. Loosely, networked movements struggle with coherence and are not able to impose the internal discipline necessary to ensure all actions are nonviolent, as was the case of DAN in Seattle.

Here lessons could be learned from LVC. While LVC is a practitioner of nonviolent prefigurative politics (the horizontal), it does have sufficient organizational capacity to coordinate its actions across nine regions of the world (the vertical). It has leaders and spokespersons and is able to maintain solidarity and discipline within its ranks sufficient to engage in nonviolent direct actions. That is, LVC is able to maintain a consistency between practice and defended values.

Conclusion

This chapter has examined the rise of the Global Justice Movement, the World Social Forum, La Via Campesina, and the emphasis placed on prefigurative politics and nonviolence in each. The cases indicate how nonviolence is both intentionally and indirectly employed in new transnational social movements, as the majority of actors within these groups recognize the relation between means and ends and between short-term strategies and long-term goals. Thus, even when not articulated, the GJM, the WSF, and LVC all reflect the dictum attributed to Gandhi, "We must be the change we want to see in the world."

Questions for discussion

1 What are the strengths and weaknesses of prefigurative politics?
2 Does it matter if nonviolence is prefigured in transnational social movements or simply adopted pragmatically as a strategy without a deep cultural basis? Why?
3 It is a common view that progressive ideas spread from the Global North to the Global South. To what extent has this chapter challenged this perspective?
4 What are the challenges and opportunities for nonviolent activism presented by globally networked movements?

Suggestions for further reading and research

Juris, Jeff (2008) *Networking Futures*. Durham, NC: Duke University Press.
Pleyers, Geoffrey (2010) *Alter-Globalization: Becoming Actors in the Global Age*. Cambridge: Polity.
Reitan, Ruth (2007) *Global Activism*. New York: Routledge.
Smith, Jackie, et al. (2008) *Global Democracy and the World Social Forums*. Boulder, CO: Paradigm.

CHAPTER 11

Future Directions

Julie M. Norman and Maia Carter Hallward

In this book, we set out to explore the foundations of nonviolence as both a field of study and an applied strategy. We first examined the *contours* of nonviolence, looking at its varied but often overlapping approaches and challenging many assumed dichotomies between nonviolence/violence and strategic/principled approaches to the practice of civil resistance. We then discussed the diverse *contexts* in which nonviolence is utilized, analyzing how the trajectories of nonviolent movements differ according to their aim and scope. While we acknowledged the integral use of nonviolence in highly publicized political contestations at the national level, we also discussed how it is used in sustained movements at the local or regional levels to agitate for civil and economic rights or social justice or to advance issues of transnational concern.

The differing dynamics and trajectories of the movements discussed in the preceding chapters illustrate the importance of context, structure, and agency in employing and understanding nonviolence. Actor agency allowed movements to adapt to their unique situations and circumstances, demonstrating the significance of looking beyond structural factors to explain popular mobilization. Furthermore, the chapters emphasize how the tactical choices employed in many nonviolent movements directly influence the long-term outcomes of those campaigns, suggesting there is a link between nonviolent means and ends, even in strategic nonviolent campaigns.[1] Finally, the chapters reveal the dynamism of nonviolence, as nonviolent activists learn from the experiences of others and adapt their movements to incorporate new media, technology, and tools. Yet, even as ideas and tactics evolve, scholars and activists alike continue to engage with a familiar repertoire and to make reference to certain core foundations and historical examples, such as the American civil rights movement, South Africa's anti-apartheid movement, and Gandhi's campaign against British control in India.

Approaches, tactics, and trends

In the introduction to this book, we noted the difficulty in defining nonviolence, in part because of different terminology used to describe the phenomenon, and also because the adoption of different approaches and tactics means that no two nonviolent movements look exactly alike. The chapters in Part I illustrate the general contours of nonviolent movements, revealing strands of commonality amid diverse tactics and approaches.

One lesson that we learn from the chapters is that the majority of successful movements do not fit the assumed prototype for nonviolent revolutions. Even those that involve large-scale protests and civil disobedience rely largely on more subtle forms of resistance, including developing parallel institutions, engaging in small acts of defiance, and employing arts, humor, and creativity to attract attention to their cause and to shift public opinion. At the same time, however, movements continue to rely on many attention-grabbing tactics often associated with nonviolent struggle, such as marches, protests, and demonstrations, as illustrated in Smith's account of the 1999 WTO protests in Seattle (chapter 10), Popovic and Alvarez's recollection of the mass protests against Milošević's disputed election in 2000 (chapter 6), and Abu-Nimer's description of the Tahrir Square protests during Egypt's revolution in 2011 (chapter 3). Indeed, events such as these allow for the broad-based mobilization and participation that characterizes many movements, allowing them to increase their scope, breadth, and number of participants. Yet, in each of these cases (and most other case studies in the book), the dramatic events were made possible by less visible processes of organizing, such as the training of student activists in Nashville (chapter 7) and smaller-scale actions that contributed to the development of the movements' core foundations, provided organizers with experience, and built momentum.

Sustained nonviolent movements, which extend beyond a few protests or demonstrations, often utilize or develop institutions that serve as parallel alternatives to the state or oppressive power. In other cases, movements work at least partially through existing institutions such as religious networks, as reflected in the cooperation with some progressive churches in the American South during the civil rights movement (Clark and Coy, chapter 7), in Chile during the struggle against Pinochet in the 1980s (Clark, chapter 4), and in Brazil in the early years of the MST (Schock, chapter 9). Likewise, as Abu-Nimer (chapter 3) notes, many activists in Egypt and other Arab states that experienced uprisings in 2011 used mosques as key sites for organization. This use of existing institutions affirms the findings of other scholars of nonviolence that having space in which to organize is a necessary element for success (Nepstad 2011a).

However, perhaps more notably, nonviolent movements tend to be strongest when they develop their own alternative institutions. For example, Egypt experienced massive protests, and activists cooperated with existing networks, but they also established alternative "citizens' committees" with elements such as a clinic, a kindergarten, media hubs, food stalls, and water stations; there were citizens' departments of customs (to stop the flow of weapons into the square), the interior (to check IDs to prevent infiltration), defense (to assemble barricades and protect protesters), and infrastructure (to provide fuel and electricity to the square). Other movements have developed institutions more gradually over time, such as the establishment of workers' unions and human rights councils that preceded the large-scale strikes in Poland in the 1980s, as described by Bartkowski in chapter 9, and the development of municipal governments, court systems, and social services by residents of South Africa's black townships, as explained by Zunes in chapter 5. More recently, as Smith discusses in chapter 10, transnational movements such as the World Social Forum and La Via Campesina have worked to develop alternative economic institutions. Still other movements have leveraged high rates of political arrests to use prisons as sites for organizing, with prisoners in Northern Ireland, Palestine, and Burma, for example, developing counter-order institutions and coordinating political education inside the jails.

In all of these examples, what might have been isolated episodes of protest have grown into sustained movements largely because of the development of such frameworks to provide alternatives to dominant structures. Accordingly, these movements not only express dissatisfaction with dominant realities but also offer an alternative vision, thus being movements *for* something visible and feasible rather just a movement *against* the status quo.

The development of alternative institutions also parallels the use of small-scale or submerged resistance. In chapter 4, for example, Clark explains how Chilean women in sewing circles started documenting their experiences in *arpilleras*, which were then smuggled out and distributed and sold, thus providing a source of income while also raising political consciousness. In Western Sahara, as documented by Zunes in chapter 5, activists have unfurled the Sahrawi flag in public plazas, used graffiti, or celebrated cultural or religious holidays with political references. In chapter 8, Bartkowski discusses other forms of small-scale resistance, such as when activists in China and Russia have

engaged in "strolls" in public places to challenge the authorities' pro-
hibitions on public gatherings.

Small-scale acts of resistance can use humor to creative effect
in order to attract public attention while making a more serious,
political point. In chapter 6, Popovic and Alvarez recount how Otpor!
activists readily employed humor through tactics such as painting
Milošević's face on a barrel and inviting passersby to hit the barrel
with a baseball bat. Likewise, in chapter 8, Bartkowski explains how
activists can use humorous tactics to get around the system, or at least
to expose its absurdity, as when activists in Siberia assembled Lego
people and other cartoon toys holding signs protesting rigged elections, thus avoiding personal arrest and inviting local police to come
and "arrest" or remove the toys.

The use of humor attracts media attention as well. While the use of
media is discussed most thoroughly by Popovic and Alvarez in chapter
6, it is evident that nearly all successful nonviolent movements are
increasingly utilizing media both to organize internally and to export
news about the movement to the outside world. While Popovic and
Alvarez caution us to avoid over-emphasizing the role of media in
determining the success of nonviolent movements, it is evident that
media and technology tools have been used through the history of
nonviolent campaigns, from the publication of photographs of harsh
police crackdowns during the American civil rights movement (Clark
and Coy, chapter 7) to the use of Twitter to export news from states
during the Arab uprisings when there were blackouts of traditional
media sources. Popovic and Alvarez also discuss how technology such
as cell phones can support the decentralized, horizontal nature of
many current nonviolent movements, making it more difficult for
authorities to identify and arrest movement leaders in more vertical
structures. Social media is further enabling greater communication
and organization in transnational movements (Smith, chapter 10).

The use of both traditional and social media links to movements'
appeals to the international community for support. While some
movements may seek solidarity through horizontal networks and
citizens' actions, others may look for the assistance of other states in
pressuring the regime through diplomatic incentives or sanctions. As
Zunes notes in chapter 5, advanced industrialized states often support dictatorial regimes and occupation armies, and activist pressure
on governments to withdraw that support, as evident in the Boycott,
Divestment, and Sanctions (BDS) movement in South Africa, can
significantly weaken those regimes. In other cases BDS can be influential in drawing global attention to an issue, as evident in current

Palestinian solidarity campaigns that call for divestment from companies or institutions seen as sustaining the Israeli occupation of the West Bank and Gaza Strip. According to Zunes, however, international pressure from global civil society should not be seen as undermining the agency of internal activists, but rather recognized as a complementary, parallel avenue for seeking change. Smith (chapter 10) looks more deeply at the relationship between local activists and global civil society, examining how some transnational movements work horizontally to target industrialized states on international issues including economic equality, climate change, and labor rights.

International leverage is just one of many factors that contribute to the extent of movements' adherence to nonviolence. As Smith (chapter 10) notes, some movements do not explicitly define themselves as nonviolent, yet, by adopting tactics that seek to maximize popular participation and minimize injury, operate as such. In contrast, the civil rights movement, as described by Clark and Coy in chapter 7, intentionally defined itself as nonviolent, with activists trained to endure humiliation, abuse, and arrest without responding with violence. Still other movements, such as the anti-apartheid movement and the ongoing Western Sahara independence movement, illustrate how campaigns may shift from relying primarily on armed struggle to embracing unarmed tactics for strategic purposes, while not directly renouncing violence. As Zunes discusses, movements of this sort illustrate the need to challenge the assumption of a clear dichotomy between "nonviolence" and "violence." Indeed, many authors in this book, and many activists in the case studies they discuss, prefer to use terms such as "popular struggle" or "civil resistance" to refer to those who rely primarily on unarmed means. Such terminology also seeks to frame nonviolence through a positive description of what it *is* rather than to rely on a descriptor based on what it is *not*.

Just as it may be difficult to classify a movement as purely "nonviolent" or "violent," the preceding chapters also indicate the difficulty in attempting to differentiate between solely principled and entirely strategic approaches to nonviolence. Principled approaches are often associated with religious or spiritual beliefs, yet religious leaders, institutions, and networks often play key roles in mostly secular movements that call on nonviolence as a strategy. Indeed, in chapter 3, Abu-Nimer explores the role of religion in the Egyptian revolution, noting, for example, how mosques were used as sites for mobilization, even though the movement was not religious in nature. Likewise, liberation theology has undergirded many non-religious social movements emerging in Latin America, such as the MST (Schock, chapter 9) and La

Via Campesina (Smith, chapter 10). Even Gandhi, often held up as the exemplar of principled or spiritually based nonviolence, recognized the strategic importance of the approach, engaging in nonviolent actions for political rather than solely spiritual objectives.

The chapters in this book thus challenge us to rethink traditional either/or distinctions and recognize instead how movements create contentious pressure for change. Movements are dynamic, adapting to changing assessments of power and using varied tactics and language to challenge dominant systems and develop more equitable societies and just relationships.

Applications, issues, and trajectories

The strategy and tactics of nonviolence have been used in a wide range of contexts spanning time and place. Nonviolent movements often differ in character based on the levels at which they operate (local, national, regional, and/or global) and their goals and objectives (reform, revolution, and/or transformation). In order to be successful, movements must utilize and/or respond to specific local contexts. Strategies that work in one campaign may not be effective in another, whether for cultural, political, or organizational reasons; consequently, nonviolent movements take on many different forms.

Activists and organizers must be aware of the context in which they are working, not only to gauge potential obstacles but also to identify potential opportunities. In chapter 7, for example, Clark and Coy avail themselves of the pillars of support model to illustrate how activists in Nashville were able to gain leverage through local institutions such as churches, the press, a moderate mayor's office, and black representation on the city council and in the police and fire departments. While this model is often used by nonviolent activists to identify which pillars of the regime they need to strike down, Clark and Coy employ it here to discuss how movements can identify sources of strength and support in their given context.

In chapter 8, however, Bartkoswki cautions us to avoid overemphasizing an external "opportunity structures" approach to organizing, suggesting a more agent-oriented approach that explores how activists create opportunities, even in highly restrictive political contexts. The case studies in chapters 7 and 8 illustrate the difference between nonviolent struggles to push for reform and change within a domestic political system, on the one hand, and those that seek to completely change the government or the governing system through revolution, on the other. In this particular set of examples, the presence of existing (albeit flawed) democratic institutions allowed the Nashville students to push for reform, whereas activists in Poland, like those in Egypt (chapter 3) and Serbia (chapter 6), ultimately sought to replace their authoritarian system of government. Because of these differing goals, activists deployed varying mobilization structures and crafted their messages with different audiences and goals in mind.

Chapters 9 and 10 show how nonviolent movements relate not only to political issues but to economic grievances as well. As Schock explains in chapter 9, while much of the literature on civil resistance focuses on pro-democracy movements, the use of nonviolence also extends to movements that challenge structural violence; Schock reminds us that Gandhi emphasized social and economic rights alongside civil and political rights, as did US civil rights leaders such as Martin Luther King, Jr. Movements that challenge economic inequality and exploitation often emerge in rural settings rather than in urban areas, tend to have longer temporal trajectories than most political revolutions on account of the nature of the change desired, and often lack definable dramatic climaxes that are often characteristic of political revolutions. Instead, these movements focus on the gradual attainment of workers' rights and the long-term implementation of sustainable development practices.

While some rural resistance movements are grounded at the local level, focused on securing rights or reforms within a state or states, other economic movements operate at the transnational level, seeking to transform broader institutionalized systems. As Smith illustrates in chapter 10, transnational movements reflect a synergy between local struggles and global organizing, with issues (often) from rural areas of the Global South being articulated in large-scale protests in the urban centers of industrialized states, such as the "Battle in Seattle" in 1999 and the G20 protests in Toronto in 2010. As Smith notes, however, despite the horizontal nature of most transnationally networked movements, it is often challenging to maintain coherent strategies across groups operating in different countries and contexts, including the extent to which the movement as a whole commits to nonviolence. Smith explains how some movements may not explicitly define themselves as nonviolent but, in the spirit of prefigurative politics (linking means to ends), still rely primarily on nonviolent tactics. His chapter thus echoes some of the themes raised by Abu-Nimer and Clark in terms of thinking about the overlap between principled and pragmatic approaches to nonviolence while also reflecting Zunes's discussion of activists' struggles to negotiate between nonviolence and violence. The history of colonialism and neo-imperialism, as well as the power differential between activists (and countries) in the Global North and Global South, complicates the terms of debate and the framing strategies used by movement organizers in various contexts.[2]

Insights

As indicated above, the ideas and examples in the Contours and Contexts sections of this book complement one another, providing a nuanced overview of nonviolence and several important insights.

First, all the chapters push us to challenge assumed dichotomies in the study and practice of nonviolence, including perceived distinctions between violence/nonviolence, strategic/principled approaches, reformist/revolutionary aims, political/economic grievances, and local/global levels of organizing. The book illustrates through various case studies that the lines between these categories are in reality quite blurred, with most movements functioning in between the apparent poles, sometimes leaning more one way or more another as they adapt to different circumstances. Given the horizontal nature of much nonviolent organizing, individuals and groups also come to a movement with different ideas, opinions, and objectives, which can result in notable diversity of emphasis or perspective even within a single movement.

Second, nearly all the chapters emphasize both the individual and collective agency of activists. While many of the authors note the structural circumstances that provided opportunities (or constraints) for movements, they emphasize that structural conditions alone do not create a movement or establish a trajectory. Rather, activists seize and indeed create opportunities for struggle and are responsible for determining the shape of the movement, especially the extent to which it exhibits nonviolent discipline. At the same time, because most of the movements discussed here operate through horizontal networks rather than through vertical hierarchies with a clear figurehead or leaders, it may be more difficult to articulate or sustain a clear strategy and enforce adherence to nonviolence.

Third, as noted in many of the chapters, activists see a clear link between using nonviolent means and achieving peaceful and just outcomes, and they assert that the horizontal organizing structures typical of nonviolent campaigns help prefigure democratic institutions. From Gandhi's early campaigns to recent global justice movements, activists utilize nonviolence not only for reasons of short-term strategy, religious belief, or gaining solidarity, but also because they believe the movement itself should reflect the sort of society they hope to build. This notion is not just activist idealism, since historical precedent illustrates that nonviolent movements are more likely to result in peaceful transitions, more stable governments, and sustainable reforms.

Looking ahead

The field of nonviolence will continue to develop and expand as the use of civil resistance continues to be recognized and documented. In this book, we have identified innovative tactics that will no doubt inform the future study and practice of nonviolence, especially those involving new media and technologies. These tools are not necessarily changing the core foundations of nonviolent struggle, but they are influencing its dynamics. As the book indicates, we are also witnessing an increased documentation of "creative actions" that incorporate humor and/or arts to communicate a political message; this use of humor in protest, especially when communicated or disseminated via new media, will form one area of potential interest for scholars and activists in future years.

This book also shows how the range of issues addressed by nonviolent movements is expanding. While much of the literature to date understandably focuses on democratic transitions, including recent scholarship following the Arab uprisings, we expect to see more studies in the future examining movements for economic, social, and cultural rights, as well as those relating to international issues such as climate change, public health, and economic equality.

Finally, we are seeing new developments in how we study nonviolent movements. While case study approaches are still common, researchers in this book and elsewhere are employing more comparative methodologies, quantitative analyses, and "big-data" studies to better understand the emergence, dynamics, trajectories, and outcomes of nonviolent movements.

This is an exciting time to be studying nonviolence, as the field emerges as an area distinct from peace studies or social movement studies while also drawing from and complementing those fields. We encourage scholars, students, and activists alike to think critically and creatively about nonviolence in theory and practice as they pursue future study and research on the topic, and we look forward to the development of further diversity and debate in the field.

Notes

CHAPTER 1 INTRODUCTION

1 To browse cases and search methods of hundreds of cases where nonviolent action was used, see http://nvdatabase.swarthmore.edu/ (accessed June 27, 2013).
2 To see the complete listing of the principles, as well as their definition, see http://www.thekingcenter.org/king-philosophy#sub2 (accessed August 1, 2013).

CHAPTER 2 UNDERSTANDING NONVIOLENCE

1 Gandhi arrived at this after sponsoring a contest for a term that would better capture the spirit of nonviolent action than the misleading "passive resistance."
2 While Dr King is typically remembered as the icon of the civil rights movement, it should be noted that his efforts were in concert with other African-American community leaders and educators, including Ella Baker, Bayard Ruskin, A. Philip Randolph, and Bob Moses.
3 Although there were Egyptian and Tunisian activists who had been involved in pro-democracy organizing prior to the uprisings, the activists had not engaged in the same type of strategic planning carried out by students in the Serbian Otpor! movement, for example.
4 The consent theory of power was elaborated on by Etienne de la Boétie in the sixteenth century (de la Boétie, 2008). Political theorists such as Antonio Gramsci, Hannah Arendt, and Michel Foucault have contributed to this relational view of power, which holds that power is not held as a commodity but, rather, ebbs and flows as a result of relationships; citizens can elect to grant or withhold their consent, thereby changing the nature of power in their relationship with the regime (Atack 2006; Nepstad 2011b).
5 The uprisings first labeled with the "people power" moniker were often examples of spontaneous nonviolent action, and not strategically planned campaigns in which activists analyzed power relations ahead of time.
6 For example, at the annual International Studies Association annual convention, the number of panels on nonviolent resistance has increased dramatically in recent years, and such panels are well attended, with more than just the same small handful of scholars in attendance.

7 For example, Pope John Paul II remarked, "Peacemaking is not an optional commitment. It is a requirement of our faith" (cited in Cortwright 2006, p. 51), and Rabbi Abraham Joshua Heschel noted that a commitment to social justice is an act of worship (ibid., p. 63). In the United States in particular, historic peace churches, including the Mennonite Church, the Church of the Brethren, and the Religious Society of Friends (Quakers), have played a central role in movements for peace and justice.

8 For a more extensive discussion of the debates surrounding the tactics of boycott as a nonviolent tool, see Hallward (2013).

9 Even those equated with the principled school, such as the Dalai Lama, Gandhi, and King, recognized that there were exceptional circumstances in which violence (but not killing) was permissible – for example, to protect one's child or if the capacity for nonviolent self-defense was lacking (Raab 2006; Merton 1965).

CHAPTER 3   SPIRITUAL AND RELIGIOUS APPROACHES TO NONVIOLENCE

1 The author extends much appreciation to Timothy Seidel for his editorial assistance and valuable comments during the production of this chapter.

2 While these features were suggested in part by Reinhold Niebuhr (1960, pp. 244–54), it is Gandhi and King who are the classical sources for these definitions of nonviolence (King 1998).

3 It bears mentioning here that not only is nonviolence not exclusive to a single faith group, it is not exclusive to a faith orientation. There are also instances of secular pacifists – non-religious people committed to nonviolence. For example, though war resisters in the United States during World War II were largely religious conscientious objectors (COs), there were also secular COs who were imprisoned for refusing military service based on philosophical, ethical, or humanitarian principles.

4 Primary faith language is when religious actors use their own unique and exclusive terms to describe their faith, such as the Trinity for Christians, the holy Quran for Muslims, etc. Secondary faith language is when the religious actors use terms and values that are common with other groups, such as peace, harmony, justice, love, etc.

5 This speaks to the argument that religion has the potential to inspire both nonviolence and violence (Appleby 2000; Kimball 2002), an argument whose premise has also been challenged in conversations interrogating categories such as "religious violence" (Cavanaugh 2009).

6 There are a number of organizations, such as Gene Sharp's Albert Einstein Institution, that promote strategic nonviolence and offer training to build capacity and develop skills for trainees establishing and leading nonviolent movements. Other organizations that promote principled nonviolence approaches are the Metta Center and the Martin Luther King Center in Atlanta, Georgia.

7 Gandhi's call for individuals to "reduce yourself to zero" is indicative of the

spiritual depth and change that he expected from his followers, to ensure success not only on the level of the system but on the personal level too.

8 These two terms refer to the perceptions among parties of any conflict of their power basis. The strong have more access to economic, political, or military resources. However, perceptions of weakness and strength are also influenced by individual and collective framing of reality. For example, youth in a nonviolent political uprising might confront soldiers and still feel powerful and strong.

9 The principle of suffering is not without criticism. In particular, a feminist critique might reject the acceptance of suffering because it represents a continuation of patriarchal oppression.

10 Gandhi's teaching about the nonviolent individual's suffering is central: "*ahemsa* in its dynamic condition means conscious suffering. It does not mean meek submission to the will of the evil-doer, but it means pitting of one's whole soul against the will of the tyrant. Working under this law of our being, it is possible for a single individual to defy the whole might of an unjust empire to save his honor, his religion, his soul, and lay the foundation for that empire's fall or its regeneration" (see Easwaran 1978; cited in Barash and Webel 2009, p. 460).

11 Personal testimony of a Buddhist monk released from a Chinese prison in 2004 (lecture on Reconciliation and Justice at American University, Washington, DC, September 2004).

12 Emad Siyam sat in Cairo's Tahrir Square from January 25, 2011, to the end of the protest. He had been jailed eighteen times by the then regime and the previous one, spending a total of nine years in Egyptian prisons (interview with the author, Cairo, 27 January 2011).

13 For example, in Egypt, three major groups that led many of the peaceful mobilization activities were Kefaya ("Enough"), the Egyptian Movement for Change, which is made up of socialists, Marxists, secularists, and even Islamists; Mahalla/April 6, a large group of unionists/socialists and their youth supporters; and the January 25 group, the youth leaders who used all sorts of multimedia and internet resources to mobilize many protesters.

14 See the *Washington Post* photo gallery feature "Yemeni Women Struggle for Liberties" (2011). In slide number five, the caption reads: "Anti-government protesters, with men and women separated, take part in a rally in Sanaa, Yemen, to celebrate the anniversary of South Yemen's independence from British colonial rule (Mohamed al-Sayaghi / Reuters)" (www.washingtonpost.com/world/yemeni-women-struggle-for-liberties/2011/12/23/gIQAFgujHP_gallery.html).

15 Some peace and conflict resolution analysts have argued that the Egyptian revolution erupted in part because protesters had been trained in Gene Sharp's methodology of nonviolent action. However, some Egyptian activists became agitated and objected to the fact that even their own homegrown revolution was being attributed to outside agencies or sources (see Horgan 2011; Wyman 2011).

16 Many international donors (both governments and NGOs) tend to impose their

models and frameworks of political change on local civil society groups and activists (see Abu-Nimer 2003).

17 The realist paradigm rests on many assumptions, among them (a) that the use of violence is a necessary instrument in resolving conflicts; (b) that states and even human beings are motivated only by their own self-interest; (c) that states are the main actors in the international context; and (d) that state actors are guided mainly by rational cost–benefit analysis (see chapter 4, "Tactical and Strategic Approaches to Nonviolence").

CHAPTER 4   TACTICAL AND STRATEGIC APPROACHES TO NONVIOLENCE

1 The author gratefully acknowledges helpful comments from the editors, April Carter, Brian Martin, and Michael Randle.

2 *Arpilleras* are three-dimensional appliqué textiles that depict the impact of political violence on everyday life and how local people responded. *Arpilleristas* are women who sew *arpilleras*. The information here is taken from Agosin (2008), Bacic (2010), and Sepulveda (1996).

3 The account in this section is based largely on Clark (2000, 2009b, and 2013).

CHAPTER 5   QUESTIONS OF STRATEGY

1 South Africa was colonized by European settlers from the Netherlands in the seventeenth century (who became known as "Afrikaaners"), eventually followed by colonists from Great Britain and other European countries, who subjugated and marginalized the indigenous black Africans. The British Empire later took control of the country, defeating both the blacks and the Afrikaaners, eventually granting South Africa independence under white minority rule in 1910. While there had always been segregation and discrimination against the indigenous Africans – as well as the smaller populations of South Asians and mixed-race peoples (known as "coloreds") – an Afrikaaner movement known as Christian Nationalism took control of South Africa in 1948 and imposed the system of apartheid, which brought the segregation and discrimination to an unprecedented level. In addition to the kind of segregation in public facilities common in the American South until the 1960s, blacks in South Africa were forced to live in separate townships outside of all-white cities, and their opportunities for employment were restricted largely to menial labor serving the white minority, which comprised less than 20 percent of the population. In addition, the families of many black laborers were forced to live in tribal homelands, known as Bantustans, in remote and often marginal lands far from the white cities. Only whites were allowed to vote or have any say in the political process, and dissent against the apartheid system was considered treasonous and ruthlessly suppressed. Democracy and majority rule did not come to the country until 1994.

2 Western Sahara is a former Spanish colony about the size of the state of

Colorado on the Atlantic coast of northwest Africa, just south of Morocco. The inhabitants are Arab Muslims with a distinct culture and dialect who historically lived a nomadic lifestyle and have traditionally resisted foreign domination. On the verge of scheduled independence from Spain in 1975, Morocco – supported by France and the United States – seized the territory in defiance of a series of United Nations resolutions and a landmark decision by the International Court of Justice, prompting a sixteen-year war with the nationalist Polisario Front, supported by Algeria. Morocco ended up taking control of 85 percent of the territory, forcing nearly half the population into refugee camps in neighboring Algeria and moving Moroccan settlers into the occupied territory to the point of greatly outnumbering the indigenous Western Saharans, known as Sahrawis. In 1991, a ceasefire was arranged in return for Morocco allowing an internationally supervised referendum of the territory to provide the indigenous population with the choice of independence or incorporation with Morocco. While UN peacekeeping forces moved in to oversee the plebiscite, Morocco never allowed the vote to take place. Negotiations between the Western Saharan government-in-exile (which has been recognized by more than eighty countries) and the Moroccan government continue under UN auspices, with Morocco pushing for an "autonomy" plan for the territory, which most observers note would fall well short of granting Western Sahara its legal right of self-determination.

CHAPTER 6   NEW MEDIA AND ADVOCACY

1 Special thanks to CANVAS analytical researcher Elliott Memmi, as well as to Jordan Maze and Tori Porell.
2 See Indiegogo (2013).
3 It should be noted, however, that Libya had shifted into civil war by the time of Gaddafi's death.
4 See https://www.gnu.org/gnu/manifesto.html.

CHAPTER 7   CIVIL RIGHTS AND DOMESTIC POLICY

1 The authors contributed equally to the research and writing of this chapter.
2 Gene Sharp calls instances when the powerful are negatively impacted by the actions of the apparently less powerful masses "political jiu-jitsu" (Sharp 1973).
3 One could also use Gene Sharp's (1973) six-stage model of the dynamics of nonviolent action – laying the groundwork; challenge brings repression; maintaining nonviolent discipline; political jiu-jitsu; three roads to success; and redistribution of power – to analyze the Nashville case. However, for clarity of focus, this chapter focuses on applying a single model.

CHAPTER 8   REVOLUTIONS AND DEMOCRATIC TRANSITIONS

1 In this chapter, I define civil resistance as an *organized nonviolent contestation* undertaken by ordinary people, either individually or en masse, in order to challenge the status quo that deprives them of their rights and freedoms and/ or to oppose political or violent oppression. In the contestation, people deploy various categories of methods of nonviolent actions that can be either disruptive to the ruling system or constructive for organizing, sustaining the movement and resistance, or both.

2 Despite the vastness of the writings on revolutions, the dominant view of these uprisings is shaped by the literature on revolutionary wars. Nonviolent revolutions are either not recognized or are seen more as anomalies than as the norm or as strategic occurrences. See, for example, Goldstone (1980, 2008); Goldstone et al. (1991); Goodwin (2001); Van Inwegen (2011); and Halliday (1999).

3 Author's own estimates combined with NAVCO 1.0 & 2.0 datasets. The figures are: 1801–1900: 6; 1901–50: 9; 1951–2000: 65; and 2001–11: 50. This last figure includes the 2011 nonviolent uprisings in the Arab world.

4 Bartkowski (2013d).

5 For an excellent documentary on the emergence of the Free South Africa campaign and the involvement of former American civil rights activists, see *Have You Heard from Johannesburg?*.

6 Author's conversation with an Iranian political dissident, June 24, 2013.

7 See Beyerle and Hassan (2009).

8 A number of these nations and their nonviolent resistance are discussed in greater details in Bartkowski (2013c).

9 See https://www.facebook.com/KSovetOppoziciiRF (accessed July 30, 2013).

10 See www.orangealternativemuseum.pl/#homepage (accessed May 26, 2013).

11 Keynote address at the Fletcher Summer Institute for the Advanced Study of Nonviolent Conflict, June 27, 2012.

12 Although nonviolent popular risings that brought down oppressive rulers and led to the establishment of liberal democracies might not have brought about the radical social change which many left-wing, anti-capitalist thinkers hoped for, they still were able to initiate important progress – from closed to open societies, with more political space and freedoms that would allow for much easier and more effective organization, enabling people to push forward with further more radical changes (author's conversation with Jeff Goodwin, American Sociological Association conference, Denver, August 19, 2012).

13 For more, see Bartkowski (2009).

CHAPTER 9   RURAL MOVEMENTS AND ECONOMIC POLICY

1 The Farm Workers Association was founded in 1962, then changed its name to the National Farm Workers Association, in 1965, and to the United Farm Workers Organizing Committee when it merged with the Agricultural

Workers Organizing Committee in 1966. When referring to its history as a whole, I use the United Farm Workers (UFW) moniker.

2 Guest worker programs allow foreign workers to reside and work temporarily in a host country. Workers are required to return home once their contract has expired, are not considered permanent immigrants, and do not have the rights of citizens. The Bracero program, for example, allowed Mexicans to work on a temporary basis as agricultural laborers in the United States.

3 Ganz (2009) explains the decline of the UFW as a result of the increasing insularity of the leadership team leading to a decrease in strategic capacity.

4 See Chabot and Vinthagen (2007) and Carter (2010), who argue persuasively that the MST, despite being labeled as "violent," is best understood as a nonviolent social movement.

5 The 1964 Land Statute Act and the 1988 Brazilian Constitution specify that the government has the power to redistribute land that is not being productively used.

6 In addition to his *The Assembly of the Poor in Thailand: From Local Struggles to National Protest Movement* (2003), see Missingham (2002) for a detailed account of the 1997 "Village of the Poor" encampment in Bangkok.

CHAPTER 10   TRANSNATIONAL MOVEMENTS AND GLOBAL CIVIL SOCIETY

1 The global justice movement has been defined by one analyst as "the loose network of organizations . . . and other actors engaged in collective action of various kinds, on the basis of the shared goal of advancing the cause of justice (economic, social, political, and environmental) among and between peoples across the globe" (della Porta 2006, p. 6). There are a number of equivalents used. "Anti-globalization movement" is one but, since the movement is not against globalization but a variant of it, I do not use the expression. Others refer to the anti-corporate globalization movement or alter-globalization movement, terms which are sometimes used in the chapter.

2 See http://viacampesina.org/en/index.php/organisation-mainmenu-44.

3 Protests, however, were not held just in Seattle. Solidarity protests occurred all around the world. In India, thousands of farmers marched to Bangalore in solidarity. In France, 75,000 people protested, and marches were held across the US, Canada, Turkey, South Korea, and other countries. In Geneva, activists besieged the WTO headquarters (Olson 2009).

4 According to Teivainen, the reasons for the emphasis on nonviolence and the barring of military organizations were pragmatic. Members of Fuerzas Armadas Revolucionarias de Colombia (FARC) had attended the first WSF, before the creation of the Charter of Principles. Among many participants at the forum there was unease over the presence of an organization that had committed atrocities. In June 2001 the Charter of Principles thus excluded the participation of armed organizations and emphasized the importance of nonviolence (Teivainen 2003).

CHAPTER 11   FUTURE DIRECTIONS

1 Often, the equation of means and ends is attributed to Gandhian forms of non-violent resistance, but the cases here suggest that the means used in struggles, even if not selected for reasons of principle, impact the eventual outcomes.

2 As discussed in chapter 2, some scholars, such as Gelderloos, have expressed significant criticism of "nonviolence" on account of its failure to challenge systems of racism and patriarchy.

References and Bibliography

Abedin, Mahan (2011) "Tunisia: The Advent of Liberal Islamism – An Interview with Rashid Al-Ghannouchi," *Religioscope*, January 30, http://religion.info/english/interviews/article_516.shtml (accessed September 9, 2013).

Abu-Nimer, Mohammed (2003) *Nonviolence and Peace Building in Islam: Theory and Practice.* Gainesville: University Press of Florida.

—— (2004) "Nonviolence in the Islamic Context," *Fellowship*, September/October, http://forusa.org/fellowship/2004/september-october/nonviolence-islamic-conte xt/12208 (accessed June 4, 2014).

—— (2011) "Non-violent Resistance in the Arab World: The Demythologizing of Essentialist Myths about Arab Societies," *Arab World Geographer* 14(2): 153–9.

—— (2012) "Support Nonviolent Direct Action: Muslim Reflection," in Susan B. Thistlethwaite (ed.), *Interfaith Just Peacemaking: Jewish, Christian, and Muslim Perspectives on the New Paradigm of Peace and War.* New York: Palgrave Macmillan: 19–31.

Ackerman, Peter, and DuVall, Jack (2000) *A Force More Powerful: A Century of Nonviolent Conflict.* New York: Palgrave.

—— (2005) "People Power Primed: Civilian Resistance and Democratization," *Harvard International Review* (summer): 42–7.

Ackerman, Peter, and Kruegler, Christopher (1994) *Strategic Nonviolent Conflict: The Dynamics of People Power in the Twentieth Century.* Westport, CT: Praeger.

Agosin, Marjorie (2008) *Tapestries of Hope, Threads of Love: The Arpillera Movement in Chile.* 2nd edn, Lanham, MD: Rowman & Littlefield.

Aliaga Rojas, Fernando (2012) *La No Violencia durante la dictadura.* Santiago de Chile: Serpaj.

Alinsky, Saul (1971) *Rules for Radicals: A Pragmatic Primer for Realistic Radicals.* New York: Random House.

Almeida, Paul D. (2010) "Globalization and Collective Action," in Kevin T. Leicht and J. Craig Jenkins (eds), *Handbook of Politics: State and Society in Global Perspective.* New York: Springer: 305–26.

Amenta, Edwin, Caren, Neal, and Olasky, Sheera J. (2005) "Age for Leisure? Political Mediation and the Impact of the Pension Movement on US Old-Age Policy," *American Sociological Review* 70: 516–38.

Anti-Slavery International (2013) "Frequently Asked Questions," www.antislavery.org/english/what_we_do/antislavery_international_today/frequently_asked_que stions.aspx (accessed October 23, 2013).

Appleby, R. Scott (2000) *The Ambivalence of the Sacred: Religion, Violence, and Reconciliation.* Lanham, MD: Rowman & Littlefield.

Arriagada, Genaro (1988) *Pinochet: The Politics of Power.* London: Unwin Hyman.

Arsenault, Raymond (2006) *Freedom Riders: 1961 and the Struggle for Racial Justice.* New York: Oxford University Press.

Ash, Timothy Garton (2009) "A Century of Civil Resistance: Some Lessons and Questions," in Adam Roberts and Timothy Garton Ash (eds), *Civil Resistance and Power Politics: The Experience of Non-Violent Action from Gandhi to the Present.* Oxford: Oxford University Press: 371–90.

Associated Press (2013) "Egypt Post-Revolution Timeline: Key Events since Fall of Mubarak," *Huffington Post*, July 1, www.huffingtonpost.com/2013/07/01/egypt-post-revolution-timeline_n_3528293.html (accessed September 15, 2013).

Atack, Iain (2006) "Nonviolent Political Action and the Limits of Consent," *Theoria* 53: 87–107.

Bacic, Roberta (2010) "Saying 'No' to Pinochet's Dictatorship through Nonviolence," *OpenDemocracy*, March 1, www.opendemocracy.net/5050/roberta-bacic/saying-no-to-pinochet%E2%80%99s-dictatorship-through-non-violence (accessed October 18, 2013).

Baiasu, Kira (2011) "Social Media: A Force for Political Change in Egypt," *New Middle East* April 13, http://new-middle-east.blogspot.com/2011/04/social-media-force-for-political-change.html (accessed May 14, 2014).

Baker, Chris (2000) "Thailand's Assembly of the Poor: Background, Drama, Reaction," *South East Asia Research* 8: 5–29.

Barakat, Halim (1993) *The Arab World: Society, Culture, and State.* Berkeley: University of California Press.

Barash, David P., and Webel, Charles P. (2009) *Peace and Conflict Studies.* London: Sage.

Barrell, Howard, and Bartkowski, Maciej (n.d.) "Snowball Effects and Political Space in Civil Resistance: How Nonviolent Movements Multiply Leverage against the Regimes They Oppose," unpublished paper, Washington, DC: International Center on Nonviolent Conflict.

Barry, Ellen (2012) "A Dozen Writers Put Down Their Pens to Prove the Might of a March," *New York Times*, May 13, www.nytimes.com/2012/05/14/world/europe/russian-writers-demonstrate-the-might-of-a-march.html?_r=0 (accessed May 13, 2012).

Bartkowski, Maciej J. (2009) "Poland's Solidarity Movement (1980–1989)," International Center for Nonviolent Conflict, www.nonviolent-conflict.org/images/stories/pdfs/bartkowski_poland.pdf (accessed August 1, 2013).

—— (2010) Presentation on Civil Resistance and Democratization, Fletcher Summer Institute on the Advanced Study of Nonviolent Conflict.

—— (2013a) "Insights into Nonviolent Liberation Struggles," in Maciej J. Bartkowski (ed.), *Recovering Nonviolent History: Civil Resistance in Liberation Struggles.* Boulder, CO: Lynne Rienner: 339–54.

—— (2013b) "Recovering Nonviolent History," in Maciej J. Bartkowski (ed.), *Recovering Nonviolent History: Civil Resistance in Liberation Struggles.* Boulder, CO: Lynne Rienner: 1–30.

— (ed.) (2013c) *Recovering Nonviolent History: Civil Resistance in Liberation Struggles*. Boulder CO: Lynne Rienner.

— (2013d) *Does Civil Resistance Reduce Civilian Deaths?*, October 31, http://maciejbartkowski.com/2013/10/31/does-civil-resistance-reduce-civilian-deaths/ (accessed November 1, 2013).

Bartkowski, Maciej J., and Kahf, Mohja (2013) "The Syrian Resistance: A Tale of Two Struggles," *Popular Resistance*, September 24, www.popularresistance.org/the-syrian-resistance-a-tale-of-two-struggles/ (accessed October 16, 2013).

BBC (2013) "Egypt: Return to a Generals' Republic?" *BBC*, August 21, www.bbc.co.uk/news/world-middle-east-23780839 (accessed September 15, 2013).

Bennett, Judith (2006) *History Matters: Patriarchy and the Challenge of Feminism*. Philadelphia: University of Pennsylvania Press.

Beyerle, Shaazka, and Hassan, Arwa (2009) "Popular Resistance against Corruption in Turkey and Egypt," in Maria Stephan (ed.), *Civilian Jihad: Nonviolent Struggle, Democratization, and Governance in the Middle East*. New York: Palgrave Macmillan.

Bharadwaj, Lakshmi K. (1998) "Principled versus Pragmatic Nonviolence," *Peace Review* 10: 79–81.

Birnbaum, Michael (2013) "In Turkey, Protesters Try a New Approach: Standing Still," *Washington Post*, June 18, http://articles.washingtonpost.com/2013-06-18/world/40044425_1_security-forces-taksim-square-late-monday (accessed September 15, 2013).

Black, Ian (2011) "Egypt Protest Leaflets Distributed in Cairo give Blueprint for Mass Action," *The Guardian*, January 27, www.guardian.co.uk/world/2011/jan/27/egypt-protest-leaflets-mass-action (accessed August 18, 2013).

de la Boétie, Etienne (2008) *The Politics of Obedience: The Discourse of Voluntary Servitude*. Auburn, AL: Ludwig von Mises Institute, https://mises.org/rothbard/boetie.pdf (accessed July 25, 2013).

Bondurant, Joan (1965) *Conquest of Violence: The Gandhian Philosophy of Conflict*. 2nd edn, Berkeley: University of California Press.

Bornstein, Avram (2009) "N0 + 10: Global Civil Society, a Decade after the Battle of Seattle," *Dialectical Anthropology* 33: 97–108.

Borras, Saturnino M., Jr. (2004) *La Vía Campesina: An Evolving Transnational Social Movement*. Amsterdam: Transnational Institute, www.tni.org/sites/www.tni.org/archives/reports/newpol/campesina.pdf (accessed October 22, 2013).

Borras, Saturnino M., Jr., and Franco, Jennifer C. (2012) "Global Land Grabbing and Trajectories of Agrarian Change: A Preliminary Analysis," *Journal of Agrarian Change* 12: 34–59.

Bose, Nirmal K. (ed.) (1957) *Selections from Gandhi*. Ahmedabad: Navajivan.

Boserup, Anders, and Mack, Andrew (1974) *War without Weapons: Nonviolence in National Defence*. London: Frances Pinter.

Bové, José (2001) "A Farmers' International?," *New Left Review* 12 (November–December): 89–102, http://newleftreview.org/II/12/jose-bove-a-farmers-international (accessed October 23, 2013).

Boyd, Andrew (2012) *Beautiful Trouble: A Toolbox for Revolution*. London: OR Books.

Branagan, Marty (2003) "The Art of Nonviolence," *Social Alternatives* 22: 50–5.

Branch, Taylor (1988) *Parting the Waters: Martin Luther King and the Civil rights movement, 1954–63.* New York: Touchstone.

Branford, Sue, and Rocha, Jan (2002) *Cutting the Wire: The Story of the Landless Movement in Brazil.* London: Latin American Bureau.

Brewster, Tom (2013) "From Bahrain to Belarus: Attack of the Fake Activists," *TechWeek Europe*, July 31, www.techweekeurope.co.uk/news/cyber-repression-attack-of-the-fake-activists-123239 (accessed May 14, 2014).

Bunce, Valerie, and Wolchik, Sharon (2011) *Defeating Authoritarian Leaders in Post-Communist Countries.* New York: Cambridge University Press.

Burrowes, Robert (1996) *The Strategy of Nonviolent Defense: A Gandhian Approach.* Albany: State University of New York Press.

Câmara, Dom Hélder (1971) *Spiral of Violence.* London: Sheed & Ward.

Carson, Clayborne (1981) *In Struggle: SNCC and the Black Awakening of the 1960s.* Cambridge, MA: Harvard University Press.

Carter, April (2009) "People Power and Protest: The Literature on Civil Resistance in Historical Context," in Adam Roberts and Timothy Garton Ash (eds), *Civil Resistance and Power Politics: The Experience of Non-Violent Action from Gandhi to the Present.* Oxford: Oxford University Press: 25–42.

Carter, Miguel (2010) "The Landless Rural Workers Movement and Democracy in Brazil," *Latin American Research Review* 45: 186–217.

Castells, Manuel (2004) *The Information Age: Economy, Society, and Culture*, Vol. 3: *The Power of Identity.* 2nd edn, Malden, MA: Wiley-Blackwell.

—— (2010) *The Information Age: Economy, Society, and Culture*, Vol. 1: *The Rise of the Network Society*, 2nd edn, Malden, MA: Wiley-Blackwell.

Cavanaugh, William T. (2009) *The Myth of Religious Violence: Secular Ideology and the Roots of Modern Conflict.* Oxford: Oxford University Press.

CBS (2009) "Transcript: Obama's Press Conference," *CBS News*, June 23, www.cbsnews.com/stories/2009/06/23/politics/main5107407.shtml (accessed May 13, 2014).

Celestino, Mauricio Rivera, and Gleditsch, Kristian Skrede (2013) "Fresh Carnations or All Thorn, No Rose? Non-Violent Campaigns and Transitions in Autocracies," *Journal of Peace Research* 50: 385–400.

Chabot, Sean, and Vinthagen, Stellan (2007) "Rethinking Nonviolent Action and Contentious Politics: Political Cultures of Nonviolent Opposition in the Indian Independence Movement and Brazil's Landless Workers Movement," *Research in Social Movements, Conflicts and Change* 27: 91–121.

Chenoweth, Erica (2013) Presentation at the Peace Research Institute, Oslo, Norway, May 14.

Chenoweth, Erica, and Stephan, Maria (2011) *Why Civil Resistance Works.* New York: Columbia University Press.

Chernus, Ira (n.d.) *Reinhold Neibuhr's Critique of Nonviolence*, www.colorado.edu/ReligiousStudies/chernus/Niebuhr.htm (accessed March 16, 2013).

Childress, James F. (1982) *Moral Responsibility in Conflicts: Essays on Nonviolence, War, and Conscience.* Baton Rouge: Louisiana State University Press.

Chowdhury, Mridul (2008) *The Role of the Internet in Burma's Saffron Revolution.* Cambridge, MA: Berkman Center for Internet and Society.

Christensen, Caitlin (2008) "Seeds of the New Society," *Peace Review* 20(2): 200–8.

Clark, Howard (2000) *Civil Resistance in Kosovo.* London: Pluto Press.

—— (2002) *Kosovo Work in Progress: Closing the Cycle of Violence.* Coventry: Coventry University Centre for the Study of Forgiveness and Reconciliation.

—— (ed.) (2009a) *People Power: Unarmed Resistance and Global Solidarity.* London: Pluto Press.

—— (2009b) "The Limits of Prudence: Civil Resistance in Kosovo, 1990–98," in Adam Roberts and Timothy Garton Ash (eds), *Civil Resistance and Power Politics: The Experience of Non-Violent Action from Gandhi to the Present.* Oxford: Oxford University Press: 277–94.

—— (2013) "Kosovo: Civil Resistance in Defense of the Nation, 1990s," in Maciej J. Bartkowski (ed.), *Recovering Nonviolent History: Civil Resistance in Liberation Struggles.* Boulder, CO: Lynne Rienner: 279–96.

Columbia Encyclopedia (2009) 6th edn, New York: Columbia University Press.

Connell, Robert W. (1987) *Gender and Power: Society, the Person and Sexual Politics.* Stanford, CA: Stanford University Press.

Conser, W. H., Jr. (2013) "The United States: Reconsidering the Struggle for Independence, 1765–1775," in Maciej J. Bartkowski (ed.), *Recovering Nonviolent History: Civil Resistance in Liberation Struggles.* Boulder, CO: Lynne Rienner.

Conway, Janet (2003) "Civil Resistance and the 'Diversity of Tactics' in the Anti-Globalization Movement: Problems of Violence, Silence, and Solidarity in Activist Politics," *Osgoode Hall Law Journal* 41(2–3): 505–29.

Cortwright, David (2006) *Gandhi and Beyond: Nonviolence for an Age of Terrorism.* Boulder, CO: Paradigm.

Coy, Patrick. G. (2013) "Whither Nonviolent Studies?," *Peace Review* 25: 257–65.

Coy, Patrick G., and Hedeen, Timothy (2005) "A Stage Model of Social Movement Co-optation: Community Mediation in the United States," *Sociological Quarterly* 46: 405–35.

Cozzens, Lisa (1998) "The Civil Rights Movement 1955–1965," *African American History,* http://fledge.watson.org/~lisa/blackhistory/civilrights-55-65 (accessed April 16, 2013).

Crawshaw, Steve, and Jackson, John (2010) *Small Acts of Resistance: How Courage, Tenacity and Ingenuity Can Change the World.* New York: Union Square Press.

Crow, Ralph E., Grant, Philip, and Ibrahim, Saad E. (1990) *Arab Nonviolent Political Struggle in the Middle East.* Boulder, CO: Lynne Rienner.

Curle, Adam (1971) *Making Peace.* London: Tavistock.

Dainotti, Alberto, Squarcella, Claudio, Aben, Emile, Claffy, Kimberly C., Chiesa, Marco, Russo, Michele, and Pescapé, Antonio (2011) *Analysis of Country-Wide Internet Outages Caused by Censorship,* November 4, www.caida.org/publications/papers/2011/outages_censorship/outages_censorship.pdf (accessed May 14, 2014).

Dajani, Souad (1995) *Eyes without Country: Searching for a Palestinian Strategy of Liberation.* Philadelphia: Temple University Press.

Dear, John (2003) *Liberating Nonviolence and Institutionalized Violence: Making Peace with Liberation Theology*, www.fatherjohndear.org/pdfs/LiberatingNonviolence_and_ Institutionalized_Violence.pdf (accessed September 14, 2013).

Deasy, Kristin (2012) "Syria's Nonviolent Resistance Movement Ignored by Media," *World Affairs*, Millenial Letters, December 12, www.worldaffairsjournal.org/blog/ kristin-deasy/syrias-nonviolent-resistance-ignored-media (accessed October 16, 2013).

Debray, Regis (1967) *Revolution in the Revolution? Armed Struggle and Political Struggle in Latin America.* Westport, CT: Greenwood Press.

Della Porta, Donatella, Andretta, Massimiliano, Mosca, Lorenzo, and Reiter, Herbert (2006) *Globalization from Below.* Minneapolis: University of Minnesota Press.

Demick, Barbara, and Pierson, David (2011) "Calls for Subtle Protests have China Security Forces in Tizzy," *Los Angeles Times*, March 5, http://articles.latimes. com/2011/mar/05/world/la-fg-china-jasmine-revolution-20110305 (accessed March 8, 2011).

Deming, Barbara (1971) *Revolution & Equilibrium.* New York: Grossman.

Democracy Now (2011) "'The Arab People Have Woken Up': Yemeni Activist Tawakkul Karman Accepts Nobel Peace Prize," *Democracy Now*, December 14, www.democracynow.org/2011/12/13/the_arab_people_have_woken_up (September 13, 2013).

Desmarais, Annette, A., and Nicholson, Paul (2010) *La Via Campesina: An Historical and Political Analysis*, www.viacampesina.org/downloads/pdf/openbooks/EN-10. pdf (accessed October 25, 2013).

Dobson, William J. (2012) *The Dictator's Learning Curve: Inside the Global Battle for Democracy.* New York: Anchor Books.

Doyle, Don Harrison (1985) *Nashville since the 1920s.* Knoxville: University of Tennessee Press.

Dudouet, Véronique (2012) "Intra-Party Dynamics and the Political Transformation of Non-State Armed Groups," *International Journal of Conflict and Violence* 6(1): 96–108.

DuVall, Jack (2013) "The Dynamics of Civil Resistance," Fletcher Summer Institute, June 17.

Easwaran, Eknath (1978) *Gandhi, the Man.* Petaluma, CA: Nilgiri Press.

The Economist (2011) "Tunisia's Troubles: Sour Young Men," *The Economist*, January 6.

Ekiert, Grzegorz, and Kubik, Jan (2001) *Rebellious Civil Society: Popular Protest and Democratic Consolidation in Poland, 1989–1993.* Ann Arbor: University of Michigan Press.

Esfandiari, Golnaz (2010) "The Myths and Realities of New Media in Iran's Green Movement," *Radio Free Europe*, June 11, www.rferl.org / content / Irans _ Green _ Movement _ And _ New _ Media / 2068714.html (accessed May 14, 2014).

Fathi, Nazila (2009) "In a Death Seen Around the World, a Symbol of Iranian Protests," *New York Times*, June 22, www.nytimes.com/2009/06/23/world/ middleeast/23neda.html?ref=middleeast&_r=0 (accessed May 14, 2014).

Fernandes, Bernardo Mançano (2005) "The Occupation as a Form of Access to Land in Brazil: A Theoretical and Methodological Contribution," in Sam Moyo and

Paris Yeros (eds), *Reclaiming the Land: The Resurgence of Rural Movements in Africa, Asia, and Latin America*. London: Zed Books: 317–40.

Fink, Christina (2009) *Living Silence in Burma: Surviving Under Military Rule*. London: Zed Books.

Fox, Zoe (2013) *"Kony 2012" One Year Later: Success or Failure?* March 5, http://mashable.com/2013/03/05/kony-2012-retrospective/ (accessed May 14, 2014).

Frederikse, Julie (1986) *South Africa: A Different Kind of War*. Boston: Beacon Press.

Fruhling, Hugo (1992) "Resistance to Fear in Chile: The Experience of the Vicaría de la Solidaridad," in Juan E. Corradi, Patricia Weiss Fagen, and Manuel Antonio Garretón (eds), *Fear at the Edge: State Terror and Resistance in Latin America*. Berkeley: University of California Press: 121–41.

Fry, Douglas P., and Björkqvist, Kaj (1997) *Cultural Variation in Conflict Resolution: Alternatives to Violence*. Mahwah, NJ: Lawrence Erlbaum Associates.

Galtung, Johan (1965) "On the Meaning of Nonviolence," *Journal of Peace Research* 2: 228–57.

—— (1969) "Violence, Peace, and Peace Research," *Journal of Peace Research* 6: 167–91.

—— (1996) *Peace by Peaceful Means: Peace and Conflict, Development and Civilization*. Thousand Oaks, CA: Sage.

Gandhi, Mohandas (1999) *The Collected Works of Mahatma Gandhi Online*, www.gandhiserve.org/e/cwmg/cwmg.htm (accessed September 8, 2013).

Ganz, Marshall (2009) *Why David Sometimes Wins: Leadership, Organization, and Strategy in the California Farm Worker Movement*. Oxford: Oxford University Press.

Gause, F. G., III (2011) "Why Middle East Studies Missed the Arab Spring: The Myth of Authoritarian Stability," *Foreign Affairs*, 90(4): 81–90.

Gaydazhleva, Stanislava (2013) "Turkey's 'Standing Man' Awarded German Rights Prize," *New Europe*, September 6, www.neurope.eu/article/turkeys-standing-man-awarded-german-rights-prize (accessed May 14, 2014).

Gelderloos, Peter (2007) *How Nonviolence Protects the State*, http://theanarchistlibrary.org/library/peter-gelderloos-how-nonviolence-protects-the-state (accessed June 6, 2014).

Gerhart, Gail (1978) *Black Power in South Africa: The Evolution of an Ideology*. Berkeley: University of California Press.

Gladwell, Malcolm (2010) "Small Change: Why the Revolution Will Not be Tweeted," *New Yorker*, October 4, www.newyorker.com/reporting/2010/10/04/101004fa_fact_gladwell?currentPage=1 (accessed May 14, 2014).

Global Nonviolent Action Database, http://nvdatabase.swarthmore.edu/.

Goldstone, Jack A. (1980) "Theories of Revolution: The Third Generation," *World Politics* 32(2): 425–53.

—— (2008) *Revolutions: Theoretical, Comparative, and Historical Studies*. Belmont, CA: Wadsworth.

Goldstone, Jack A., Gurr, Ted Robert, and Moshiri, Farrokh (eds) (1991) *Revolutions of the Late Twentieth Century*. Boulder, CO: Westview Press.

González-Bailón, Sandra, Borge-Holthoefer, Javier, Rivero, Alejandro, and Moreno, Yamir (2011) "The Dynamics of Protest Recruitment through an Online Network," *Scientific Reports*, December 15.

Goodwin, Jeff (2001) *No Other Way Out: States and Revolutionary Movements, 1945–1991*. Cambridge: Cambridge University Press.

Gottlieb, Rabbi Lynn (2011) "Tikkun Olam: The Art of Nonviolent Civil Resistance," *Tikkun*, 26: 42–3.

Gow, James (2003) *The Serbian Project and its Adversaries: A Strategy of War Crimes*. London: Hurst.

Guevara, Ernesto Che (1967) "Create Two, Three, Many Vietnams," Message to the Tricontinental, Havana, April 16, www.marxists.org/archive/guevara/1967/04/16.htm (accessed May 14, 2014).

Halberstam, David (1998) *The Children*. New York: Random House.

Halliday, Fred (1999) *Revolution and World Politics: The Rise and Fall of the Sixth Great Power*. Durham, NC: Duke University Press.

Hallward, Maia C. (2013) *Transnational Activism and the Israeli–Palestinian Conflict*. New York: Palgrave Macmillan.

Hallward, Maia C., and Norman, Julie M. (eds) (2011) *Nonviolent Resistance in the Second Intifada: Activism and Advocacy*. New York: Palgrave Macmillan.

Hampton, Henry, Fayer, Steve, and Flynn, Sarah (1990) *Voices of Freedom: An Oral History of the Civil Rights Movement from the 1950s through the 1980s*. New York: Bantam Books.

Harnecker, Marta (2003) *Landless People: Building a Social Movement*. São Paulo: Editora Espressão Popular.

Hashemi, Nader (2013) "Syria, Savagery, and Self-Determination: What Those against Military Intervention Are Missing," in Nader Hashemi and Danny Postel (eds), *The Syria Dilemma*. Cambridge, MA: MIT Press: 221–36.

Hashim-Waris, Sarah (2013) "Demonstrators in Los Angeles Raise Awareness about Turkish Protests," *Los Angeles Times*, August 19, www.latimes.com/visuals/video/la-demonstrators-in-los-angeles-turkish-protests-20130613-premiumvideo.html (accessed May 14, 2014).

Hauslohner, Abigail (2011) "After Tunisia: Why Egypt Isn't Ready to Have its Own Revolution," *Time*, January 20.

Hável, Vaclav (1990) *New Year's Address to the Nation*. [Online] available from http://old.hrad.cz/president/Havel/speeches/1990/0101_uk.html (accessed May 14, 2014).

Helvey, Robert L. (2004) *On Strategic Nonviolent Conflict: Thinking about the Fundamentals*. Boston: Albert Einstein Foundation.

Hobsbawm, E. J. (1974) "Peasant Land Occupations," *Past and Present* 62: 120–52.

Horgan, John (2011) "Egypt's Revolution Vindicates Gene Sharp's Theory of Nonviolent Activism," *Scientific American*, Cross-Check Blog, February 11, http://blogs.scientificamerican.com/cross-check/2011/02/11/egypts-revolution-vindicates-gene-sharps-theory-of-nonviolent-activism/ (accessed September 9, 2013).

Houston, Benjamin (2007) "An Interview with Will D. Campbell," *Journal of Southern Religion* 10, http://jsr.fsu.edu/Volume10/Front10.htm (accessed April 17, 2013).

Howes, Dustin Ells (2014) "Defending Freedom with Civil Resistance," in Kurt Schock (ed.), *Comparative Perspectives on Civil Resistance*. Minneapolis: University of Minnesota Press: 282–311.

Human Rights Watch (1995) *Keeping it Secret: The United Nations Operations in the Western Sahara*. New York: Human Rights Watch.

—— (2008) *Human Rights in Western Sahara and in Tindouf Refugee Camps*. New York: Human Rights Watch.

Huneeus, Carlos (2009) "Political Mass Mobilization Against Authoritarian Rule: Pinochet's Chile, 1983–88," in Adam Roberts and Timothy Garton Ash (eds), *Civil Resistance and Power Politics: The Experience of Nonviolent Action from Gandhi to the Present*. Oxford: Oxford University Press: 197–212.

Huntington, Samuel (1984) "Will More Countries Become Democratic?" *Political Science Quarterly* 99 (summer): 193–218.

Huzier, Gerrit (1972) "Land Invasion as a Non-Violent Strategy of Peasant Rebellion: Some Cases from Latin America," *Journal of Peace Research* 9: 121–32.

Indiegogo (2013) "Full Page Ad for Turkish Democracy in Action," *Indiegogo*, June 2, http://www.indiegogo.com/projects/full-page-ad-for-turkish-democracy-in-action (accessed May 14, 2014).

International Crisis Group (2007) *Western Sahara: Out of the Impasse*. Brussels: International Crisis Group.

Isaac, Larry W., Cornfield, Daniel B., Dickerson, Dennis C., Lawson, James M., and Coley, Jonathan S. (2012) "'Movement Schools' and Dialogical Diffusion of Nonviolent Praxis: Nashville Workshops in the Southern Civil Rights Movement," *Research in Social Movements, Conflicts and Change* 34: 155–84.

Issa, Daniela (2007) "Praxis of Empowerment: Mística and Mobilization in Brazil's Landless Rural Workers' Movement," *Latin American Perspectives* 34: 124–38.

Jasper, James, and Poulsen, Jane (1995) "Recruiting Strangers and Friends: Moral Shocks and Social Networks in Animal Rights and Anti-Nuclear Protests," *Social Problems* 42(4): 493–512.

Johnstad, Petter G. (2010) "Nonviolent Democratization: A Sensitivity Analysis of How Transition Mode and Violence Impact the Durability of Democracy," *Peace & Change* 35(3): 464–82.

Johnston, Hank (2011) *States and Social Movements*. Cambridge: Polity.

Judah, Tim (1997) *The Serbs: History, Myth, and the Destruction of Yugoslavia*. New Haven, CT: Yale University Press.

Jumbala, Prudishan (1998) "Thailand: Constitutional Reform amidst Economic Crisis," *Southeast Asian Affairs*: 265–92.

Juris, Jeffrey (2008) *Networking Futures*. Durham, NC: Duke University Press.

Kanalley, Craig (2011) "Egypt Revolution 2011: A Complete Guide to the Unrest," *Huffington Post*, May 25, www.huffingtonpost.com/2011/01/30/egypt-revolution-2011_n_816026.html (accessed September 21, 2013).

Karatnycky, Adrian, and Ackerman, Peter (2005) *How Freedom is Won: From Civic Resistance to Durable Democracy*. Washington, DC: Freedom House.

Karis, Thomas (1983–4) "Revolution in the Making: Black Politics in South Africa," *Foreign Affairs* (winter).

—— (1986) "Black Politics: The Road to Revolution," in Mark A. Uhlig (ed.), *Apartheid in Crisis*. New York: Vintage Books.

Kasmir, Sharryn (1996) *The Myth of Mondragón: Cooperatives, Politics, and Working-Class Life in a Basque Town*. Albany, NY: State University of New York Press.

Kaufman, Edy (1992) "Limited Violence and the Palestinian Struggle," in Graeme MacQueen (ed.), *Unarmed Forces: Nonviolent Action in Central America and the Middle East*. Toronto: Science for Peace: 95–103.

Kenney, Padraic (2002) *A Carnival of Revolution: Central Europe 1989*. Princeton, NJ: Princeton University Press.

Khalek, Rania (2013) "Syria's Nonviolent Resistance is Dying to be Heard," *Aljazeera America*, September 9, http://america.aljazeera.com/articles/2013/9/9/syria-s-non-violentresistanceisdyingtobeheard.html (accessed October 16, 2013).

Khalidi, Rashid (1988) "The Uprising and the Palestine Question," *World Policy Journal* 5(3): 497–517.

Kimball, Charles (2002) *When Religion Becomes Evil*. San Francisco: Harper.

King, Martin L. (1957) "Nonviolence and Racial Justice," *Christian Century* 74 (February): 165–7.

—— (1967) *Where Do We Go from Here: Chaos or Community?* New York: Harper & Row.

—— (1998) *The Autobiography of Martin Luther King, Jr.*, ed. Clayborne Carson. New York: Intellectual Properties Management in association with Warner Books.

King, Mary E. (1999) *Mahatma Gandhi and Martin Luther King Jr.: The Power of Nonviolent Action*. Paris: UNESCO.

—— (2007) *A Quiet Revolution: The First Palestinian Intifada and Nonviolent Resistance*. New York: Nation Books.

Kriesberg, Louis (2007) *Constructive Conflicts: From Escalation to Resolution*. Lanham, MD: Rowman & Littlefield.

Kurtz, Lester R. (2009) *Chile: Struggle against a Military Dictator (1985–1988)*, International Center on Nonviolent Conflict, www.nonviolent-conflict.org/images/stories/pdfs/kurtz_chile.pdf (accessed August 22, 2013).

Kurzman, Charles (2010) "Cultural Jiu-Jitsu and the Iranian Greens," in Nader Hashemi and Danny Postel (eds), *The People Reloaded: The Green Movement and the Struggle for Iran's Future*. New York: Melville House.

Lakey, George (1969) "Strategies for Non-violent Revolution," *Peace News* (December 12).

Lee, Barry E. (2010) *The Nashville Civil Rights Movement: A Study of the Phenomenon of Intentional Leadership Development and its Consequences for Local Movements and the National Civil Rights Movement*, Georgia State University, History Dissertations, Paper 16, http://scholarworks.gsu.edu/cgi/viewcontent.cgi?article=1015&context=history_diss (accessed May 14, 2014).

Lerner, Michael (2012) *Embracing Israel/Palestine: A Strategy to Heal and Transform the Middle East*. Berkeley, CA: Tikkun Books.

Lewis, John, and D'Orso, Mike (1998) *Walking with the Wind: A Memoir of the Movement*. San Diego: Harcourt Brace.

Leyne, Jon (2011) "No sign Egypt Will Take the Tunisian Road," BBC News, January 17, http://www.bbc.co.uk/news/world-middle-east-12202937 (accessed May 14, 2014).

de Ligt, Bart (1937) *The Conquest of Violence: An Essay on War and Revolution*. London: Routledge. NB: London: Pluto Press, 1989.

Limbo, Ernest M. (2006) "James Lawson: The Nashville Civil Rights Movement," in Susan M. Glisson (ed.), *The Human Tradition in the Civil Rights Movement*. Lanham, MD: Rowman & Littlefield.

Losurdo, Domenico (2010) "Moral Dilemmas and Broken Promises: A Historical-Philosophical Overview of the Nonviolent Movement," *Historical Materialism* 18: 85–134.

Maeckelbergh, Marianne (2011) "Doing is Believing: Prefiguration as Strategic Practice in the Alterglobalization Movement," *Social Movement Studies* 10(1): 1–20.

Magid, Shaul (2005) "A Monk, a Rabbi, and the 'Meaning of this Hour': War and Nonviolence in Abraham Joshua Heschel and Thomas Merton," *Cross Currents* 55(2): 184–213.

Mahoney, Liam, and Eguren, Luis Enrique (1997) *Unarmed Bodyguards: International Accompaniment for the Protection of Human Rights*. West Hartford, CT: Kumarian Press.

Maliqi, Shkëlzen (1998) *Kosova: Separate Worlds: Reflections and Analyses*. Prishtina: MM Society and Dukagjini.

Mantena, Karuna (2012) *Gandhi and the Means–Ends Question in Politics*, www.sss.ias. edu/files/papers/paper46.pdf (accessed September 8, 2013).

Mao Zedong (1961) *On Guerrilla Warfare*. New York: Praeger.

Marchant, Eleanor (ed.) (2007) *Enabling Environments for Civic Movements and the Dynamics of Democratic Transition*. Washington, DC: Freedom House.

Martin, Brian (1989) "Gene Sharp's Theory of Power," *Journal of Peace Research*, 26(2): 213–22.

—— (2001) *Nonviolence versus Capitalism*. London: War Resisters' International.

—— (2002) "Nonviolence versus Terrorism," *Social Alternatives* 21(2): 6–9.

—— (2005) "Researching Nonviolent Action: Past Themes and Future Possibilities," *Peace & Change* 30: 247–70.

—— (2007) *Justice Ignited: The Dynamics of Backfire*. Lanham, MD: Rowman & Littlefield.

—— (2009a) "Dilemmas in Promoting Nonviolence," *Gandhi Marg* 31: 429–53.

—— (2009b) "Paths to Social Change: Conventional Politics, Violence and Nonviolence," in Ralph V. Summy (ed.), *Nonviolent Alternatives for Social Change*. UNESCO-EOLSS: 156–82.

Martin, Brian, and Varney, Wendy (2003) "Nonviolence and Communication," *Journal of Peace Research* 40(2): 213–32.

Martinez, Javier (1992) "Fear of the State, Fear of Society: On the Opposition Protests in Chile," in Juan E. Corradi, Patricia Weiss Fagen, and Manuel Antonio Garretón (eds), *Fear at the Edge: State Terror and Resistance in Latin America*. Berkeley: University of California Press: 142–60.

Martínez-Torres, Maria E., and Rosset, Peter M. (2010) "La Vía Campesina: The Birth and Evolution of a Transnational Social Movement," *Journal of Peasant Studies* 37(1): 149–75.

Mattaini, Mark A. (2003) "Constructing Nonviolent Alternatives to Collective Violence: A Scientific Strategy," *Behavior and Social Issues* 12: 148–63.

Mayton, Daniel M., III (2001) "Nonviolence within Cultures of Peace: A Means and an Ends," *Peace and Conflict: Journal of Peace Psychology* 7: 143–55.

McAdam, Doug (1983) "Tactical Innovation and the Pace of Insurgency," *American Sociological Review* 48: 735–54; repr. in Doug McAdam and David A. Snow (eds), *Readings on Social Movements: Origins, Dynamics and Outcomes.* 2nd edn, Oxford: Oxford University Press: 478–98.

McCarthy, Ronald M., and Kruegler, Christopher (1993) *Toward Research and Theory Building in the Study of Nonviolent Action.* Cambridge, MA: Albert Einstein Institution.

McClintock, Michael (1984) *The American Connection: State Terror and Popular Resistance in El Salvador.* London: Zed Books.

McElroy, Damien (2013) "Angela Merkel Hits Out at 'Harsh' Response to Turkey Protests," *Daily Telegraph*, June 17, www.telegraph.co.uk/news/worldnews/europe/turkey/10125814/Angela-Merkel-hits-out-at-harsh-response-to-Turkey-protests.html (accessed September 21, 2013).

McMichael, Philip (2007) "Globalization and the Agrarian World," in George Ritzer (ed.), *The Blackwell Companion to Globalization.* Oxford: Blackwell.

Measuring the Information Society (2013) International Telecommunication Union, www.itu.int/en/ITU-D/Statistics/Documents/publications/mis2013/MIS2013_without_Annex_4.pdf (accessed 19 May 2014).

Menser, Michael (2008) "Transnational Participatory Democracy in Action: The Case of La Via Campesina," *Journal of Social Philosophy* 39(1): 20–41.

Merton, Thomas (ed.) (1965) *Gandhi on Non-Violence: A Selection from the Writings of Mahatma Gandhi.* New York: New Directions.

Metta Center for Nonviolence (n.d.) "Strategic Nonviolence," http://mettacenter.org/definitions/gloss-concepts/strategic-nonviolence/ (accessed September 9, 2013).

Missingham, Bruce (2002) "The Village of the Poor Confronts the State: A Geography of Protest in the Assembly of the Poor," *Urban Studies* 39: 1647–63.

Missingham, Bruce D. (2003) *The Assembly of the Poor in Thailand: From Local Struggles to National Protest Movement.* Chiang Mai, Thailand: Silkworm Books.

Moeller, Susan D. (1999) *Compassion Fatigue: How the Media Sell Disease, Famine, War, and Death.* London: Routledge.

Momba, Jotham C., and Gadsden, Fay (2013) "Zambia: Nonviolent Strategies against Colonialism, 1900s–1960s," in Maciej J. Bartkowski (ed.), *Recovering Nonviolent History: Civil Resistance in Liberation Struggles.* Boulder, CO: Lynne Rienner: 71–88.

Morris, Aldon D. (1981) "Black Southern Student Sit-In Movement: An Analysis of Internal Organization," in Doug McAdam and David A. Snow (eds), *Social Movements: Readings on Their Emergence, Mobilization, and Dynamics.* Los Angeles: Roxbury.

—— (1984) *The Origins of the Civil Rights Movement: Black Communities Organizing for Change.* New York: Free Press.

Mundy, Jacob (2011a) "The Dynamics of Repression and Resistance: Sahrawi Nationalist Activism in the Moroccan Occupied Western Sahara," *Pambazuka News* 17(551): 1–17.

—— (2011b) "Western Sahara's 48 Hours of Rage," *Middle East Report* 257: 2–5.

Munson, Ziad (2008) *The Making of Pro-Life Activists: How Social Movement Mobilization Works*. Chicago: University of Chicago Press.

Nagler, Michael (2011) "Non-Violence: Key for Change in Egypt," *Common Ground News Service*, February 15, www.commongroundnews.org/article. php?id=29299&lan=en&sp=0 (accessed September 9, 2013).

Neier, Aryeh, and Omang, Joanne (1985) *Psychological Operations in Guerrilla Warfare: The CIA's Nicaragua Manual*. New York: Vintage Books.

Nepstad, Sharon E. (2011a) "Nonviolent Resistance in the Arab Spring: The Critical Role of Military-Opposition Alliances," *Swiss Political Science Review* 17: 485–91.

—— (2011b) *Nonviolent Revolutions: Civil Resistance in the Late 20th Century*. Oxford: Oxford University Press.

Nepstad, Sharon E., and Kurtz, Lester R. (eds) (2012) *Nonviolent Conflict and Civil Resistance*. Bradford: Emerald.

Niebuhr, Reinhold (1960) *Moral Man and Immoral Society: A Study in Ethics and Politics*. New York: Scribner.

Nikolayenko, Olga (2014) "Youth Mobilization Before and During the Orange Revolution: Learning from Losses," in Kurt Schock (ed.), *Comparative Perspectives on Civil Resistance*. Minneapolis: University of Minnesota Press.

Nojeim, Michael J. (2004) *Gandhi and King: The Power of Nonviolent Resistance*. Westport, CT: Praeger.

Nolutshungu, Sam (1982) *Changing South Africa: Political Considerations*. Manchester: Manchester University Press.

Noman, Helmi (2011) *The Emergence of Open and Organized Pro-Government Cyber Attacks in the Middle East: The Case of the Syrian Electronic Army*, Open Net Initiative, https:// opennet.net/emergence-open-and-organized-pro-government-cyber-attacks-mid-dle-east-case-syrian-electronic-army (accessed October 24, 2013).

Norman, Julie M. (2010) *The Second Palestinian Intifada: Civil Resistance*. London: Routledge.

Northcutt, Wayne (2003) "José Bové vs. McDonald's: The Making of a National Hero in the French Anti-Globalization Movement," *Proceedings of the Western Society for French History* 31, http://hdl.handle.net/2027/spo.0642292.0031.020 (accessed June 5, 2014).

O'Brien, Sean, Lawson, Phil, Edwards, Matthew, Haga, Kazu, Merin, Melissa, Shepherd, Josh, Paolo, and Starhawk (2012) "Nonviolence vs. 'Diversity of Tactics' in the Occupy Movement," *Tikkun*, March 29, www.tikkun.org/nextgen/ nonviolence-vs-diversity-of-tactics-in-the-occupy-movement (accessed October 23, 2013).

O'Flynn, Kevin (2012) "Toys Cannot Hold Protest Because They Are Not Citizens of Russia, Officials Rule," *The Guardian*, February 15, www.theguardian.com/ world/2012/feb/15/toys-protest-not-citizens-russia?newsfeed=true   (accessed February 16, 2012).

Olson, Geoff (2009) "The Battle of Seattle – Looking back 10 Years," *Common Ground*, http://commonground.ca/2009/11/the-battle-of-seattle-looking-back-10-years/ (accessed October 22, 2013).

Oppenheimer, Martin (1965) "Towards a Sociological Understanding of Nonviolence," *Sociological Inquiry* 35: 123–31.

Orosco, José-Antonio (2008) *Cesar Chavez and the Common Sense of Nonviolence*. Albuquerque: University of New Mexico Press.

Overy, Bob (2002) "Gandhi as a Political Organiser," in Michael Randle (ed.), *Challenge to Nonviolence*. Bradford: University of Bradford Department of Peace Studies: 135–56, www.civilresistance.info/challenge [final chapter of Overy's PhD dissertation, 1982, "Gandhi as a Political Organiser: An Analysis of Local and National Campaigns in India, 1915–1922"].

Palmer, Mark (2009) *A Diplomat's Handbook for Democracy Development Support*. 2nd edn, Washington, DC: Community of Democracies, www.diplomatshandbook. org/pdf/Diplomats_Handbook.pdf (accessed May 14, 2014).

Parkman, Patricia (1990) *Insurrectionary Civic Strikes in Latin America 1931–1961*. Cambridge, MA: Albert Einstein Institution.

Passy, Florence, and Marco Giugni (2001) *Social Networks and Individual Preferences: Explaining Differential Participation in Social Movements*. University of Geneva, Department of Political Science, www.nd.edu/~dmyers/cbsm/vol2/passy.pdf (accessed May 14, 2014).

PBS (2013) "Timeline: What's Happened Since Egypt's Revolution?," *PBS Frontline*, September 17, www.pbs.org/wgbh/pages/frontline/foreign-affairs-defense/egypt-in-crisis/timeline-whats-happened-since-egypts-revolution/ (accessed September 21, 2013).

Pearlman, Wendy (2011) *Violence, Nonviolence, and the Palestinian National Movement*. Cambridge: Cambridge University Press.

—— (2012) "Precluding Nonviolence, Propelling Violence: The Effect of Internal Fragmentation on Movement Protest," *Studies in Comparative International Development* 47: 23–46.

Pinker, Steven (2011) *The Better Angels of our Nature*. New York: Viking.

Pinsky, Marian (2010) "From Reactive to Proactive: The World Social Forum and the Anti-/Alter-Globalization Movement," *McGill Sociological Review* (January): 3–28, www.mcgill.ca/msr/volume1/article1 (accessed September 4, 2013).

Pleyers, Geoffrey (2010) *Alter-Globalization: Becoming Actors in the Global Age*. Cambridge: Polity.

Powers, Roger S., and Vogele, William B. (eds) (1997) *Protest, Power, and Change: An Encyclopedia of Nonviolent Action from ACT-UP to Women's Suffrage*. New York: Routledge.

Price, Robert M. (1991) *The Apartheid State in Crisis: Political Transformation in South Africa, 1975–1990*. New York: Oxford University Press.

Raab, Joseph Q. (2006) "Comrades for Peace: Thomas Merton, the Dalai Lama and the Preferential Option for Nonviolence," *Merton Annual* 19: 255–66.

Ramet, Sabrina Petra (1995) *Social Currents in Eastern Europe: The Sources and Consequences of the Great Transformation*. 2nd edn, Durham, NC: Duke University Press.

Randle, Michael (1991) *People Power: The Building of a New European Home*. Stroud: Hawthorn Press.

—— (1994) *Civil Resistance*. London: Fontana; http://civilresistance.info/randle1994 (accessed May 14, 2014).

Reitan, Ruth (2007) *Global Activism*. New York: Routledge.

Ribeiro, Gustavo L. (2009) "Non-Hegemonic Globalizations: Alter-Native Transnational Processes and Agency," *Anthropological Theory* 9(3): 297–329.

Rigby, Andrew (1991) *Living the Intifada*. London, Zed Books; http://civilresistance.info/rigby1991 (accessed October 18, 2013).

Roberts, Adam (2009) "Introduction," in Adam Roberts and Timothy Garton Ash (eds), *Civil Resistance and Power Politics: The Experience of Non-Violent Action from Gandhi to the Present*. Oxford: Oxford University Press: 1–24.

Roberts, Adam, and Ash, Timothy Garton (eds) (2009) *Civil Resistance and Power Politics: The Experience of Non-Violent Action from Gandhi to the Present*. Oxford: Oxford University Press.

Roberts, Alasdair (2012) "Why Occupy Failed," *Prospect Magazine*, June 21, www.prospectmagazine.co.uk/blog/occupy-failed-adbusters-on-year-anniversary/#.Uk tmMD8aW9M (accessed September 30, 2013).

Rosenberg, Tina (2011) "Revolution U: What Egypt Learned from the Students Who Overthrew Milosevic," *Foreign Policy* (February 16).

Said, Jawdat (1997) "Peace or Nonviolence in History and with the Prophets," paper presented at the Forum on Islam and Peace in the Twenty-First Century, American University, Washington, DC.

Satha-Anand, Chaiwat (2002) "Overcoming Illusory Division: Between Nonviolence as a Pragmatic Strategy and a Way of Life," paper given at the conference of the International Peace Research Association's Nonviolence Commission, Kyung Hee University, Seoul, South Korea.

Schell, Jonathan (2003) *The Unconquerable World: Power, Nonviolence, and the Will of the People*. New York: Metropolitan Books.

Schock, Kurt (2003) "Nonviolent Action and its Misconceptions: Insights for Social Scientists," *Political Science and Politics* 36: 705–12.

—— (2005) *Unarmed Insurrections: People Power Movements in Nondemocracies*. Minneapolis: University of Minnesota Press.

—— (2009) "Defending and Reclaiming the Commons through Nonviolent Struggle," in Ralph V. Summy (ed.), *Nonviolent Alternatives for Social Change*. UNESCO-EOLSS: 183–201.

—— (2012) "Land Struggles in the Global South: Strategic Innovations in Brazil and India," in Gregory M. Maney, Rachel V. Kutz-Flamenbaum, Deana A. Rohlinger, and Jeff Goodwin (eds), *Strategies for Social Change*. Minneapolis: University of Minnesota Press.

—— (2014) *Comparative Perspectives on Civil Resistance*. Minneapolis: University of Minnesota Press.

Scott, James C. (1985) *Weapons of the Weak: Everyday Forms of Peasant Resistance*. New Haven, CT: Yale University Press.

—— (1986) "Everyday Forms of Peasant Resistance," in J. C. Scott and J. T. Kerkvliet (eds), *Everyday Forms of Peasant Resistance in South-East Asia*. Totowa, NJ: Frank Cass: 5–35.

—— (1990) *Domination and the Arts of Resistance: Hidden Transcripts*. New Haven, CT: Yale University Press.

Sepúlveda-Pulvirenti, Emma (ed.) (1996) *We, Chile: Personal Testimonies of the Chilean Arpilleristas*. Falls Church, VA: Azul.

Sharp, Gene (1959) "The Meanings of Nonviolence: A Typology," *Journal of Conflict Resolution* 3(1): 41–66.

—— (1973) *The Politics of Nonviolent Action*, 3 vols. Boston: Porter Sargent.

—— (1990a) *Civilian-Based Defense: A Post-Military Weapons System*. Princeton, NJ: Princeton University Press.

—— (1990b) *The Role of Power in Nonviolent Struggle*. Boston: Albert Einstein Institution, www.informedcynic.com/resist/documents/The%20role%20of%20power%20in%20non-violent%20struggle.pdf (accessed May 14, 2014).

—— (2005) *Waging Nonviolent Struggle: 20th Century Practice and 21st Century Potential*. Boston: Extending Horizons Books.

Shaw, Randy (2008) *Beyond the Fields: Cesar Chavez, the UFW, and the Struggle for Justice in the 21st Century*. Berkeley: University of California Press.

Shirkey, Clay (2008) *Here Comes Everybody*. London: Penguin.

Sibley, Mulford Q. (1944) *The Political Theories of Modern Pacifism: An Analysis and Criticism*. Philadelphia: Pacifist Research Bureau.

Smith, Clagett G. (1976) "Nonviolence in International Conflict: A Programmatic Research Statement," *Sociological Inquiry* 46: 117–25.

Smith, Jackie (2001) "Globalizing Resistance: The Battle of Seattle and the Future of Social Movements," *Mobilization* 6: 1–20.

—— (2008) *Social Movements for Global Democracy*. Baltimore: Johns Hopkins University Press.

Smith, Jackie, Karides, Marina, Becker, Marc, Brunelle, Dorval, Chase-Dunn, Christopher, della Porta, Donatella, Garza, Rosalba I., Juris, Jeffrey S., Mosca, Lorenzo, Reese, Ellen, Smith, Peter (Jay), and Vasquez, Rolando (2008) *Global Democracy and the World Social Forums*. Boulder, CO: Paradigm.

Smith, Peter J., and Smythe, Elizabeth (2004) "Globalization, Citizenship and New Information Technologies: From the MAI to Seattle," in Mattie Malkia, Ari-Veikko Anttiroiko, and Reijo Savolainen (eds), *eTransformation in Governance: New Directions in Government and Politics*. Philadelphia: Idea Group: 272–307.

Smithey, Lee (2013) "Identity Formation in Nonviolent Struggles," in Maciej J. Bartkowski (ed.), *Recovering Nonviolent History: Civil Resistance in Liberation Struggles*. Boulder, CO: Lynne Rienner.

Smolar, Aleksander (2009) "Towards 'Self-Limiting Revolution': Poland, 1970–89," in Adam Roberts and Timothy Garton Ash (eds), *Civil Resistance and Power Politics: The Experience of Non-Violent Action from Gandhi to the Present*. Oxford: Oxford University Press: 127–43.

Sørensen, Majken Jul, and Martin, Brian (2014) "The Dilemma Action: Analysis of an Activist Technique," *Peace & Change* 39(1): 73–100.

Sousa Santos, Boaventura de (2008) "The World Social Forum and the Global Left," *Politics & Society* 41(3): 247–70.

Spence, Rebecca, and McLeod, Jason (2002) "Building the Road as We Walk it: Peacebuilding as Principled and Revolutionary Nonviolent Praxis," *Social Alternatives* 21: 61–4.

Starhawk (2002) *Webs of Power: Notes from the Global Uprising*. Gabriola, BC: New Society.

Stédile, João Pedro, and Fernandes, Bernardo Mançano (1999) *Brava gente: a trajetória do MST pela terra no Brasil*. São Paulo: Editora Fundação Perseu Abramo.

Stephan, Maria J. (ed.) (2009) *Civilian Jihad: Nonviolent Struggle, Democratization, and Governance in the Middle East*. New York: Palgrave Macmillan.

Stephan, Maria J., and Mundy, Jacob A. (2006) "A Battlefield Transformed: From Guerrilla Resistance to Mass Nonviolent Struggle in the Western Sahara," *Journal of Military and Strategic Studies* 8(3): 1–32.

Stiehm, Judith (1968) "Nonviolence is Two," *Sociological Inquiry* 38: 23–30.

Stokes, Gale (1993) *The Walls Came Tumbling Down: The Collapse of Communism in Eastern Europe*. Oxford: Oxford University Press.

Stollman, Jennifer A. (2006) "Diane Nash: 'Courage Displaces Fear, Love Transforms Hate': Civil Rights Activism and the Commitment to Nonviolence," in Susan M. Glisson (ed.), *The Human Tradition in the Civil Rights Movement*. Lanham, MD: Rowman & Littlefield.

Summy, Ralph (1993) "Democracy and Nonviolence," *Social Alternatives* 12: 15–19.

—— (1996) "Nonviolence and the Extremely Ruthless Opponent," in Mahendra Kumar and Peter Low (eds), *Legacy and Future of Nonviolence*. New Delhi: Gandhi Peace Foundation.

Tarrow, Sidney (1995) "Mass Mobilization and Elite Exchange: Democratization Episodes in Italy and Spain," *Democratization* 2: 221–45.

Tarrow, Sidney, and della Porta, Donatella (2005) "Conclusion: 'Globalization,' Complex Internationalism, and Transnational Contention," in Donatella della Porta and Sidney Tarrow (eds), *Transnational Protest and Global Activism*. Lanham, MD: Rowman & Littlefield: 227–46.

Teivainen, Teivo (2003) "World Social Forum: What Should it be When it Grows Up?," *OpenDemocracy*, July 10, www.opendemocracy.net/democracy-protest/article_1342.jsp (accessed September 28, 2013).

Teorell, Jan (2010) *Determinants of Democratization: Explaining Regime Change in the World, 1972–2006*. Cambridge: Cambridge University Press.

Tilly, Charles (2006) *Regimes and Repertoires*. Chicago: University of Chicago Press.

Tocqueville Alex de (1980) *On Democracy, Revolution, and Society*, ed. John Stone and Stephen Mennell. Chicago: University of Chicago Press.

Uhlig, Mark A. (1986) "The African National Congress," in Mark A. Uhlig (ed.), *Apartheid in Crisis*. New York: Vintage Books.

University of Oxford (2011) "Social Media in Protests: Study finds 'Recruiters' and 'Spreaders,'" December 16, www.ox.ac.uk/media/news_releases_for_journalists/111216.html (accessed May 14, 2014).

Van Der Heijden, Hein-Anton (2006) "Globalization, Environmental Movements, and International Political Opportunity Structures," *Organization and Environment* 19(1): 28–45.

Van Inwegen, Patrick (2011) *Understanding Revolution*. London: Lynne Rienner.

Vergara-Camus, Leandro (2009) "The Politics of the MST: Autonomous Rural Communities, the State and Electoral Politics," *Latin American Perspectives* 36(4): 178–91.

Vidal, Hernan (2002) *El movimiento contra la tortura "Sebastian Acevedo": derechos humanos y la producción de simbolos nacionales bajo el fascism chileno*. 2nd edn, Santiago de Chile: Mosquito.

Vinthagen, Stellan (2006) *A Call for a Nonviolent Strategy of the Global Peace & Justice Movement*, www.resistancestudies.org/files/SVGlobalisingNV.pdf (accessed May 14, 2014).

—— (2011) "The Operational and Transformative Force of Nonviolent Action," Central European University, Budapest, September 12.

von Sinner, Rudolf (2007) "The Churches' Contribution to Citizenship in Brazil," *Journal of International Affairs* 61(1): 171–84.

Voss, Kim, and Williams, Michelle (2009) *The Local in the Global: Rethinking Social Movements in the New Millennium*. University of California, Institute for Research on Labor and Employment, www.irle.berkeley.edu/workingpapers/177-09.pdf (accessed May 14, 2014).

Waddle, Ray (2002) "Days of Thunder: The Lawson Affair," *Vanderbilt Magazine* (fall): 35–43.

Wade, Robert Hunter (2004) "Is Globalization Reducing Poverty and Inequality?," *World Development* 32: 567–89.

Wallerstein, Immanuel (2011) "Structural Crisis in the World-System: Where Do We Go From Here?" *Monthly Review* 62(10): 31–9.

Walton, John, K., and Seddon, David (1994) *Free Markets & Food Riots: The Politics of Global Adjustment*. Malden, MA: Blackwell.

Weinberg, Bill (2004) "Zapatistas and the Globalization of Resistance," *Yes!*, May 20, www.yesmagazine.org/issues/a-conspiracy-of-hope/zapatistas-and-the-globalization-of-resistance (accessed October 26, 2013).

Weber, Thomas (2000) *On the Salt March: Historiography of Gandhi's March to Dandi*. New Delhi: HarperCollins India.

—— (2003) "Nonviolence is Who? Gene Sharp and Gandhi," *Peace & Change* 28: 250–70.

Wehr, Paul (1995) "Commentary: Toward a History of Nonviolence," *Peace & Change* 20: 82–93.

Weschler, Lawrence (1982) *Solidarity: Poland in the Season of its Passion*. New York: Simon & Schuster.

Wink, Walter (1987) *Violence and Nonviolence in South Africa: Jesus' Third Way*. Philadelphia: New Society.

Wirmark, Bo (1974) "Nonviolent Methods and the American Civil Rights Movement 1955–1965," *Journal of Peace Research* 11: 115–32.

Wittman, Hannah (2009) "Reworking the Metabolic Rift: La Vía Campesina, Agrarian Citizenship, and Food Sovereignty," *Journal of Peasant Studies* 36(4): 805–26.

Wolford, Wendy (2003) "Producing Community: The MST and Land Reform Settlements in Brazil," *Journal of Agrarian Change* 3: 500–20.

World Social Forum (2001) *Charter of Principles*, http://www.forumsocialmundial. org.br/main.php?id_menu=4&cd_language=2 (accessed June 6, 2014).

Wright, Angus, and Wolford, Wendy (2003) *To Inherit the Earth: The Landless Movement and the Struggle for a New Brazil*. Oakland, CA: Food First Books.

Wright, Robin (2009) "In Iran, One Woman's Death May have Many Consequences," *Time*, June 21, www.time.com/time/world/article/0,8599,1906049,00.html (accessed May 14, 2014).

Wyman, Jason (2011) "International Connections: Gene Sharp and Egypt," *Fellowship of Reconciliation*, March 2, http://forusa.org/blogs/jason-wyman/international-con nections-gene-sharp-egypt/8580 (accessed September 9, 2013).

Wynn, Linda T. (2005) "Economic Withdrawal During the Nashville Sit-Ins," www. tnstate.edu/library/documents/sit-ins.pdf (accessed May 14, 2014).

Yoder, John H. (1992) *Nevertheless: The Varieties and Shortcomings of Religious Pacifism*. Scottdale, PA: Herald Press.

Zaru, Jean (2008) *Occupied with Nonviolence: A Palestinian Woman Speaks*. Minneapolis: Fortress Press.

Zeiger, Robert H., and Gall, Gilbert J. (2002) *American Workers, American Unions: The Twentieth Century*. Baltimore: Johns Hopkins University Press.

Zouhour, Line (2013) "Whither the Peaceful Movement in Syria?" *Jadaliyya*, March 18, www.jadaliyya.com/pages/index/10616/whither-the-peaceful-movement-in- syria (accessed October 16, 2013).

Zunes, Stephen (2001) "Indigestible Lands? Comparing the Fates of the Western Sahara and East Timor," in Brendan O'Leary, Ian Lustick, and Thomas Callaghy (eds), *Rightsizing the State: The Politics of Moving Borders*. New York: Oxford University Press.

—— (2010) "Upsurge in Repression Challenges Nonviolent Resistance in Western Sahara," *OpenDemocracy*, November 17, http://www.opendemocracy.net/stephen- zunes/upsurge-in-repression-challenges-nonviolent-resistance-in-western-sahara (accessed May 14, 2014).

—— (2011) "Tunisia's Democratic Revolution," *Huffington Post*, January 20, www. huffingtonpost.com/stephen-zunes/tunisias-decmocratic-revo_b_811342.html (accessed May 14, 2014).

—— (2012) "Mali's Struggle: Not Simply of their Own Making," *OpenDemocracy*, May 11, www.opendemocracy.net/stephen-zunes/mali%E2%80%99s-struggle-not-sim ply-of-their-own-making-0 (accessed May 14, 2014).

Zunes, Stephen, and Kurtz, Lester. R. (1999) "Conclusion," in Stephen Zunes, Lester R. Kurtz, and Sara B. Asher (eds), *Nonviolent Social Movements: A Geographical Perspective*. Malden, MA: Blackwell.

Zunes, Stephen, Kurtz, Lester R., and Asher, Sara B. (eds.) (1999) *Nonviolent Social Movements: A Geographical Perspective*. Oxford: Blackwell.

Index